Praise for *Wonder*

"You don't need a seminary degree to talk to your kids about scripture. You need *Wonder* by Meredith Miller. With clarity and practicality, Meredith sets you free from the panic of answering your child's faith questions on the spot and ushers you into the joy of engaging with the Bible. I'm so grateful to parent in a world where we have access to a gift like *Wonder*."

—Erin Hicks Moon, cohost of the *Faith Adjacent* and *Shelf Respect* podcasts, *Publisher's Weekly* bestselling author of *I've Got Questions: The Spiritual Practice of Having It Out with God*

"Meredith Miller has written the resource every parent and pastor needs. *Wonder* is a book that equips us to move from teaching kids about the Bible to exploring it alongside them. If you've ever frozen when your kid asked a tough question about God, this book is for you."

—Zach Lambert, author of *Better Ways to Read the Bible*

"In *Wonder*, Miller offers adults a compelling guide for reparenting ourselves in the faith and passing it on. Generous, captivating, and clear—*Wonder* will help liberate generations into the untamable presence of God, who delights in our curiosity and loves us endlessly."

—Shannan Martin, author of *Counterweights* and *The Ministry of Ordinary Places*

"As a parent who has had to unravel and rebuild my faith from the ground up, one of the hardest parts was walking that road with kids who had big questions of their own. I certainly didn't have the answers. How was I supposed to respond to theirs? None of us want to pass down harm or confusion, so we often feel caught between saying nothing at all or repeating the patterns we're trying to unlearn. It just feels like a lot, you know?

Wonder is the reset for our physical and spiritual nervous systems. Meredith gently dissolves the pressure to be an expert and shows us how to be companions who are curious, honest, and excited to explore Scripture together. *Wonder* turns 'I don't know' into an invitation. This book is wise, compassionate, and genuinely fun. It's the book I wish had formed the scaffolding of my faith, and I'm grateful that my kids (and yours!) will have that gift."

—Kristen LaValley, author of *Growing Up Saved: When Loving God Feels Like Losing Yourself*

WONDER

52 Conversations to Help Kids
Fall in Love With Scripture

MEREDITH MILLER

Nashville   New York

Copyright © 2026 by Meredith Miller

Cover design by Whitney J. Hicks

Cover copyright © 2026 by Hachette Book Group, Inc.

Hachette Book Group supports the right to free expression and the value of copyright. The purpose of copyright is to encourage writers and artists to produce the creative works that enrich our culture.

The scanning, uploading, and distribution of this book without permission is a theft of the author's intellectual property. If you would like permission to use material from the book (other than for review purposes), please contact permissions@hbgusa.com. Thank you for your support of the author's rights.

Worthy
Hachette Book Group
1290 Avenue of the Americas, New York, NY 10104
worthypublishing.com
X.com/WorthyPub

First Edition: March 2026

Worthy is a division of Hachette Book Group, Inc. The Worthy name and logo are trademarks of Hachette Book Group, Inc.

The publisher is not responsible for websites (or their content) that are not owned by the publisher.

Worthy Books may be purchased in bulk for business, educational, or promotional use. For information, please contact your local bookseller or the Hachette Book Group Special Markets Department at special.markets@hbgusa.com.

Unless otherwise indicated, all Scripture quotations are taken from the Holy Bible, New Living Translation, copyright © 1996, 2004, 2015 by Tyndale House Foundation. Used by permission of Tyndale House Publishers, Carol Stream, Illinois 60188. All rights reserved.

Scripture quotations marked NRSV are taken from the New Revised Standard Version Bible, copyright © 1989 National Council of the Churches of Christ in the United States of America. Used by permission. All rights reserved worldwide.

Scripture quotations marked NRSVUE are taken from the New Revised Standard Version Updated Edition. Copyright © 2021 National Council of Churches of Christ in the United States of America. Used by permission. All rights reserved worldwide.

Print book interior design by Bart Dawson

Library of Congress Control Number: 2025044002

ISBNs: 978-1-5460-0943-6 (paper over board); 978-1-5460-0945-0 (ebook)

Printed in the United States of America

LSC-C

Printing 1, 2025

To Curtis, my coauthor in so many ways

CONTENTS

Introduction — xi

PART I
Pentateuch Pack

You Ask: How does the Bible work if it's not all about morality and memory verses? — 3

Creation: Genesis 1 — 11
The Dream Is Disrupted: Genesis 3 — 17
A Plan for a Tower of Protection: Genesis 11 — 23
Waiting for Baby Isaac: Genesis 17; 18; 21:1–7 — 29
God Is with Joseph: Genesis 37–45 — 35
A Conversation with a Burning Bush: Exodus 3 — 43

You Ask: I know it's in the Bible, but do I need to tell it to my kid? — 49

God Splits the Red Sea: Exodus 5–15 — 53
God Provides Manna and Water in the Wilderness: Exodus 16 — 59
The Law—Love God, Love Your Neighbor: Deuteronomy 6:5 — 65

You Ask: Why are we devoting two whole "stories"—because c'mon, these aren't full stories—to the chapters where "Walk Through the Bible in a Year" plans go to die? — 71

The Law—Festivals and Jubilee: Exodus 20; 23; 31; Leviticus 23 — 75

PART II
Life in the Land

Rahab: Joshua 2 — 83
The No-Fight Battle: Judges 6 — 89
God Speaks to Young Samuel: 1 Samuel 3 — 95
The People Want a King: 1 Samuel 8–13 — 101

Anointing David to Become King: 1 Samuel 16 — 107
Elijah, the Widow, and the Last Cup of Flour: 1 Kings 17 — 113
God's Still, Small Voice: 1 Kings 19 — 119
Josiah and the Law: 2 Kings 22–23 — 125

> **Your Kid Asks:** Where'd they go? I thought they were in the Promised Land. — 131

Daniel Eats His Veggies: Daniel 1 — 137
The Prophets: Yep, All of 'Em — 143

PART III
Christmas Stories

An Angel Visits Mary: Luke 1:26–56 — 151
An Angel Visits Joseph: Matthew 1:18–25 — 157
Jesus Is Born!: Matthew 1:18–25; Luke 2:1–7 — 161
Angels and Shepherds: Luke 2:8–20 — 167
Wise Men Visit Jesus: Matthew 2 — 173

> **Your Kid Asks:** Are miracles really real? Because that isn't how things happen. — 179

PART IV
Jesus Stories

Jesus Extends a Wedding Party: John 2:1–12 — 185
Jesus Calls the Twelve: Matthew 4:18–25; Mark 1:16–20; Luke 5:27–30; John 1:35–51 — 191
Jesus Feeds a Crowd: Matthew 14:13–21; Mark 6:31–44; Luke 9:12–17; John 6:1–14 — 195
Jesus Meets Zacchaeus: Luke 19:1–10 — 201

> **Your Kid Says:** "I know this one already!" — 207

Jesus Walks on Water: Matthew 14:23–33; Mark 6:45–51; John 6:16–21 — 211

Jesus Welcomes the Children: Matthew 19:13–15; Mark 10:13–16;
  Luke 18:15–17 — 217
Four Friends Bring a Fifth Friend Through the Roof: Mark 2:1–12;
  Luke 5:17–26 — 221
Jesus Raises Lazarus: John 11:1–46 — 227
Jesus Heals a Woman and a Girl: Mark 5:21–43; Luke 8:40–56 — 233
The Samaritan Woman at the Well: John 4:1–42 — 239

PART V
Easter Stories

Jesus Enters Jerusalem as King: Matthew 21:1–11; Mark 11:1–11;
  Luke 19:29–44; John 12:9–19 — 247

   Your Kid Asks: If Jesus already won, then why doesn't
     it seem like it? — 251

Jesus Anointed by Mary and the Last Supper: Matthew 26:26–29;
  Mark 14:3–25; Luke 22:14–20 — 253
Jesus Washes the Disciples' Feet: John 13:1–20 — 259
Jesus' Arrest, Trial, and Peter's Denial: Matthew 26:47–75;
  Mark 14:43–72; Luke 22:54–62 — 263
The Women Visit Jesus' Tomb: Matthew 28:1–10; Mark 16:1–8;
  Luke 24:1–12 — 269

   Your Kid Asks: Um, did this story actually happen? — 275

Breakfast on the Beach: John 21 — 279
On the Road to Emmaus: Luke 24:13–35 — 285

PART VI
The Church Carries On

The Holy Spirit Comes at Pentecost: Acts 2 — 293

   Your Kid Asks: Is eternal life just living up in heaven? — 299

Peter Heals, Then Preaches, Then Gets in Trouble: Acts 3–4   303
Persecution Comes: Acts 6–12   309

> **Your Kid Asks:** If there's a good and powerful God, why do bad things happen, especially to people who are trying to follow God?   315

Philip and the Ethiopian Eunuch: Acts 8:26–40   319
Paul Meets Jesus: Acts 9:1–19   325
Peter's Vision and Cornelius's Invitation: Acts 10   331
Paul Knows the Unknown God: Acts 17:16–34   337
Communion Gone Wrong: 1 Corinthians 11:17–34   343
Philemon   349
Revelation   355

Works Consulted   361
Spiral the Stories in Wonder   365
Acknowledgments   373
About the Author   375

INTRODUCTION

"WHY DOES BLOOD HAVE TO BE THE PAYMENT FOR SIN? THAT'S SO GROSS AND MEAN AND STUPID."

Welcome to the world of your kid's faith questions.
Now it's your turn, so do you:

A. Freeze up — "Uhhhhhhh..."
B. Attempt distraction — "Oh look, a bird!"
C. Parrot an answer you're not even sure you believe. — "Because God said so."
D. Pass the buck — "You should totally ask that at church next time."

Faced with the challenge of a real, curious child in front of you asking about a complicated topic, each of these possible responses makes sense.
But what if there was a secret option E?

E for excitement. Your kid has brought up faith and that means you get to talk about it together. E for exploration because there are lots of different ways talk about this question. (Because "blood as payment" is debatable, after all.)

And not, by the way, E for expert, as if a person can only look forward to these kinds of conversations once they've mastered enough biblical and theological information.

No, it's more like E for equipped, knowing how to have great conversations with the kids in your life about God and the Bible even without all the answers.

Secret option E is available for you and for me. I'm sure of it, and I wrote *Wonder* to help you be sure of it, too.

After twenty-five years in ministry with kids, and parenting two sharp kids who never let a detail slide, I know the Bible can be a doozy of a book. It's full of little details we read and think, "Why is that there?" and "Do I need to remember that?" and, for our purposes, "Would this be helpful in conversations about God and the Bible with my kid?" (Or, perhaps more honestly, "I hope to goodness my kid never asks me about that.")

One reason I wrote this book for you is to help you know why a detail is there and how it might be helpful as you talk with kids about the Bible. But even more importantly, I wrote it to help your conversations with kids about the Bible to become just that—conversations. Not lessons or lectures.

I want to help kids fall in love with Scripture and the God whose story it tells. And you're here, I imagine, because you do, too.

These two questions speak to the heart of that desire:

1. How can we help kids come to know the Bible on its terms—ancient, stylistic, containing multiple genres and writers' points of view; and
2. how can we help kids come to the Bible *as kids*?

Kids ask questions. So many questions.

So we, as adults, welcome their wonderings.

For many years my kids and I made a Bible story podcast for kids. Every episode began with us saying, "The Bible is amazing because it helps us get to know who God is. It's also confusing, old, from a very different community and culture than our own. So we want you to know, when it comes to God; when it comes to the Bible—"

"Every question is okay!"

"And you can ask away!" Then there's twinkle music.

This book will help with modeling for kids that every question really is okay, and that you, the grown-up, aren't a Bible expert, and that's okay, too. You can ask together, learn together, wonder together. Sometimes you might find an answer, and sometimes you won't, which is also just fine.

Because what if kids fall in love with the Bible *not* because it contains every answer but because it's fun to explore questions—wherever they lead? Not because they can figure the Bible out but because they learn how to get to know God bit by bit as they hear its stories?

No matter how old we are, if we're reading the Bible well, one thing it should do for us is activate our curiosity. Why did a person say what they did? Or go where they went? Or act in that way? Sadly, too often we hold back on our curiosity, biting our tongue about what we wonder. Sometimes that happens because we feel like a Bible dummy. Or perhaps we tamp down our curiosity because the *real* task of Bible reading is serious study.

When I first started regularly talking with kids about the Bible—at the "extremely ready for that" age of sixteen—the general assumption was that the goals of those conversations were:

- To pass on information, aka biblical literacy in the narrowest sense. What book, chapter, and verse did this come from? What were the exact details of a story? Have you memorized the verse word for word? (And if so, here's a prize!) This often meant the stories were

overloaded with factoids or skipped altogether in favor of verses that could be pulled out and taught in isolation.
- Application, aka behavior modification, but for Jesus. What should a child do, specifically, because of what the Bible says? This often meant the stories were told as if the humans were the most important characters because they offered examples for us to learn from.

But over time, as I talked about the Bible with more kids in more ways—as a teacher and small group leader, a camp counselor and parent—and after completing seminary, my thinking shifted about these goals.

When it comes to faith overall, I regularly advocate for the goal of being with our kids as they get to know God, so they can discover God can be trusted. We offer the kids in our lives presence. We can be a companion in their spiritual journeys, and we can offer processes, space, time, and experiences that help them get to know God and evaluate the claim that the Bible and our faith make: Our God is trustworthy.

With the Bible specifically, then, I've begun to believe that the goal of our conversations should be exploration, aka looking for what the writer wants to say about who God is and what God is like. Put another way, it's to help kids fall in love with the Bible on its own beautiful, bold, and sometimes baffling terms, as it helps us get to know God and helps us see that God is and always will be greater and more mysterious than we can pin down.

Even for people who agree with the goals of presence and process for kids in faith, and with the goal of exploration as our posture toward conversation about the Bible, the conversations we have with the kids in our lives following those guidelines can be a challenge.

One of the most common things I hear from adults about why they don't talk about the Bible more with their kids is that they simply think they don't know enough. The Bible is a complex book, and parents believe they are supposed to be experts with all the answers, so they feel stuck.

But I want to help break down these myths. Let's start with the myth just mentioned: that in order to talk about the Bible with your kids, you need to be an expert with all the answers.

You don't. That's impossible to do and a silly thing to expect. The feeling is real, though, and I'm sorry you've carried an unrealistic and unnecessary burden. And kids don't need that from you anyway.

Kids need the opportunity to explore the stories.

This happens when adults keep the whole story open and follow the lead of their child, picking up on what is interesting or strange to them, rather than steering everything toward a predetermined lesson.

Kids need to hear God-centered storytelling. This is when adults tell the stories in ways that make God a primary character, rather than assuming the humans should be the heroes we learn from most of all. The humans matter; it's just that they get to be fully and imperfectly human. And as we listen to how those humans practiced trusting and not trusting God along the way, we are also listening for who God is, what God is like, and what God does.

Kids need to be invited to interrupt. As humans, we remember far more of what we say than what we hear. When we invite kids to interrupt right in the middle of the story, so that they can talk about what they notice, wonder about, or think is weird, they are far more likely to remember the story. We also can pivot the conversation as needed based on their input.

So these days, I like to approach conversations about the Bible as an exploration of the stories. When we read the stories, we're looking for who God is and what God is like. I want to know what the kid I'm with has to say about all of it. Because that is what they need from us. They don't need an answer wizard. They need an exploration partner. Not a guru, but a guide.

Now, back to that other sticking point, the one where we know the Bible is complex, *Wonder* is written with two key features to help you with that complexity and adjust your approach for kids.

First, it's a collection of paraphrased Bible stories, using God-centered storytelling in a style that is written especially for kids. Whenever we talk about the Bible with children, we are doing interpretive work. We have to. It's an essential part of the process to help take these ancient, deeply cultural, sometimes confusing stories for and by adults and make them accessible to kids while staying faithful to what the authors intended to say through the stories.

Second, each of these paraphrased Bible stories comes with a variety of commentary notes that help shed light on the details, meaning, context, and culture. The notes for *Wonder* are going to be the most handy-dandy resource for you to dive deeper into the why and what and who of the stories. They'll offer insights to help you answer questions. They'll add details that make a kid say, "Oh, cool! I didn't know that." They'll help you work out some bits of information that you know are in the real Bible but of course aren't right for a kid just yet.

Yes, the Bible is complex, so let's help kids fall in love with it both by telling stories accessibly and adding in details when they're ready to make that complexity fascinating rather than intimidating.

What This Book Is and Is Not

While *Wonder* is a collection of fifty-two Bible stories, paraphrased in a style you can read to kids, it is not a kid's Bible, for several reasons.

A kid's Bible can't say too much about Potiphar's wife or the debate about who or what the talking snake in Genesis 3 is, for instance. Those pieces are either inappropriate (at least until a kid is ready—and that depends on the kid) or too niche for good storytelling (one kid's fascination is another's snooze-fest, after all, and a kid's Bible often tries to reach as broadly as it can).

A kid's Bible has to make one set of interpretive choices once and for all; then it goes to print. Even so, the writer knows that there were likely a dozen very cool ways to tell a kid that story. With *Wonder*, the commentary you have here will help you talk about the stories again and again, because you can camp out on one cool thing one time and something new the next.

Mainly, though, it's not a kid's Bible because those are often given to a kid, which is great. But a kid's Bible is given directly to a kid who goes off and reads it on their own. This book is written for grown-ups. I want to help you have conversations about the Bible with kids. I want to give you something you can turn to that does the following:

1. Offers possible language for how to tell a story to a kid.
2. Offers background and insights for the questions a kid might ask or the ways a kid might need to take a story deeper or have a fresh insight.

In other words, *Wonder* is a grown-up's guide for exploring the Bible with kids in God-centered, kid-appropriate ways.

What You'll Find:

The fifty-two stories in *Wonder* are organized into six sections:

1. Part 1: Pentateuch Pack. Ten stories from the first five books of the Bible that set up the larger arc of Scripture but also help tell the story of the beginning of God's world and family.
2. Part 2: Life in the Land. Ten stories from the remainder of the Old Testament that focus on Israel's move into the Promised Land, and the patterns and predictable cycles the people lived out generation after generation.

3. Part 3: Christmas Stories. Five stories telling how God came in the form of baby Jesus.
4. Part 4: Jesus Stories. Ten stories from Jesus' life that highlight what he did and why those actions were meaningful.
5. Part 5: Easter Stories. Seven stories spanning Jesus' final week before being crucified, to his resurrection, and his early post-resurrection appearances.
6. Part 6: The Church Carries On. Ten stories from Acts to Revelation that focus on the role the community of Jesus' followers played in continuing to live together in ways that aligned with God's character and work.

The selection of stories I chose to include tell the larger story of Scripture, helping kids see God's dream for the world at work. I also intentionally omitted some stories that are common in other children's Bible resources because they do not align with my "skip and save" principle. If a story cannot be told in a kid-accessible way that is also faithful to its meaning, but instead would have to be "kidified"—changed in meaning so a kid can handle it—it gets saved until they're older. This honors both children and the Bible.

The paraphrases themselves practice God-centered storytelling, focusing on God as a main character rather than on the humans as the heroes.* I've also included an index (see "Spiral the Stories in Wonder" at the end of this book) of a variety of God's attributes (not all of them, but a lot) and which of these

---

* When I'm speaking of God, I tend to use the singular *They* and *Them*, which I'll note by capitalizing it. If I'm speaking of Jesus, I use *he* and *him*. I find the singular *They* can be one helpful way to (a) use language that reflects the fact that God is not male; and (b) remind me that God is more expansive than and distinct from human beings. Additionally, when God is named in English as I Am or Lord, I often use the Hebrew of God's name, "Yahweh." Hearing God's specific name can be a helpful way to remember that the story is trying to talk about this specific God. Of course, feel free to change these things as you read aloud if you have different preferences.

fifty-two stories could help a child see that attribute on display. So I might have told about manna in the wilderness as *God caring for us*, but you'll see it as *God listening* and *God providing* as well, so you can revisit that story with those lenses another time.

From time to time, you'll also come across a mini-essay that goes deeper into a topic related to the Bible, one that needs more space than the notes.

Within each story you'll find a main idea to help steer you and commentary notes in the margins along the way. There are nine basic categories for these notes, but not all nine are relevant to every story. You'll see which ones will help pull back the curtain for you, but you won't see every category every time. These are:

Key Image—These are images like mountains, fire, or trees that often serve a symbolic, metaphorical, or otherwise significant purpose in the story.

Key Word—Wordplay sometimes escapes us if we are rusty on our Greek or Hebrew, so we point out important or interesting ones. We also highlight words that have taken on certain contemporary meanings that would not be shared by the original community to help us more easily enter their world.

Key Number—Numbers in the Bible are rarely literal and often repeat throughout various stories to make connections or serve another important function in narrative.

Historical Context—These are details about the customs, values, and cultural norms that the original communities shared (and this may go without saying) but we don't.

 **Genre**—Certain Bible stories fit a literary category, and they may share certain features accordingly. When that genre shapes the storytelling, we dive deeper into what to expect from that type of story.

 **Literary Feature**—Just like the writers of today, biblical writers use a variety of literary tools to convey their meaning to their readers. Whether it be parallelism, irony, humor, or archetype, literary features play a role in reading Scripture well.

 **Fun Detail**—Sometimes the Bible is funny on purpose. Sometimes Jesus is too. When that happens, we highlight it, because at every age it helps to know this book can be both very important and not always serious.

 Connections—Bible stories become more interesting and take on deeper meaning as we hear how one echoes another, how this setting is like that setting, how this event feels reminiscent of that other one. So when two or more stories connect, we name them.

 Your Kid Asks—These are paraphrased stories that adhere to the guiding principle of "skip and save." As such, major details may be intentionally omitted. However, we also know those details matter and at some point your kid may wonder about them. Challenging, confusing, and unclear passages get a little more time to help you feel more prepared to talk about them whenever the time is right.

Getting Started

While *Wonder* is aimed at helping you talk with kids about the Bible, it is not a strict program to follow.

If you have a predetermined time or space when you talk about faith things—bedtime, for instance—you could use this book then, certainly.

Or this book could be a reference guide that you as the adult read through, banking the ideas that will connect most with the kid in your life. You could explore one story a week; there are fifty-two here. Even then, whether you go in order or jump around is totally up to you. You might:

1. Start from the beginning.
2. Start with a story that's always tripped you or your kid up (hello, Revelation!).
3. Start with Jesus stories.
4. Line up with the stories your church or faith community is talking about.

Once you've picked a starting point, read the story out loud, inviting interruption and leaning into what makes you all curious. Use the notes to help with questions that may come up, and if you're asked something not included here, write it down to follow up with later. Remember, saying, "I don't know" is helpful, not harmful, in a kid's faith experience. It shows that we do not have to be certain and yet can still find God trustworthy, and also gives you the chance to model how we carry questions—learning new things, listening to experts, and even sometimes sitting with the unknown indefinitely.

You're at the trailhead, and there are lots of good ways to go exploring. Whichever way you head, my prayer is that *Wonder* will be a helpful guide along the way, keeping you and the kids in your life curious about God and the Bible, together.

Kids do not primarily need Bible information, where they memorize minutiae from the stories.

They do not need Bible application, where they are told by an adult what to do because of the stories.

They need exploration.

They need conversation.

They need the chance to bring their curiosity and critical thinking to the Bible and its stories.

They need to be invited to wonder.

PART I

PENTATEUCH PACK

YOU ASK

HOW DOES THE BIBLE WORK IF IT'S NOT ALL ABOUT MORALITY AND MEMORY VERSES?

One of the best ways to help kids understand the Bible is to highlight for them who God is and what God is up to. In other words, to **name God's purposes**. As you do, it makes **the overarching plot** come together in ways that make more sense. That's my hope for you and for the kids in your life as you explore the Bible.

As you go through these stories, you'll notice God's purposes in four major recurring themes:

Theme #1:
God dreams of a world that works in ways that match who God is.

God's dream is that the world would be in harmony with and reflective of God's own character. We see this in the creation story, where God makes a good world, intended to be full of life, creativity, and diversity. We see it in the Law, which is about how Israel can live in ways that reflect God's character to their world. We see it in the critiques the prophets bring that center around how Israel's life together has failed to reflect God's character. We see it in Jesus, and how life and joy and abundance followed him around. We see it in the vision of what the Church might be in the New Testament letters. We see it in the picture of the new heaven and the new earth that concludes Revelation.

Theme #2:
God partners with humans to make the dream come true because God is both creative and a collaborator by character.

God will not *force* the dream into being, and God will not do it alone. Both of these would actually be in opposition to the dream itself, because they would be in opposition to who God is. In other words, God doesn't just choose to share power with humanity, God *is* a power-sharing God at a character level. God doesn't just like the idea of human creativity echoing God's character, God *is* a creates-with-humans God at a character level.

So God invites Adam and Eve, then Noah, then Abraham. In each case, the invitation is to be God's representatives on earth, embodying God's character in the way they live and fill the earth.

God frees the Hebrews from slavery in Egypt and then gives them the job of being a holy people, different from all the other nations in ways that show how much more beautiful a family anchored in God's character can be from the ways the world usually works.

Jesus comes not to start some new project, but to re-form the people of God. The Church is not a replacement for Israel, but a continuation of the family of God, with the same dream of a life together that reflects God's character to the world. Crucially, this partnership is *always* open, with no restrictions, to whoever wants to join in.

Theme #3:
Humans have the (God-given) power to really mess things up. And they do...repeatedly.

Usually, God lets humans wander as far as they want down paths that lead away from God and the dream. The result for the world is that it is badly damaged and doesn't work at all like God intended. Injustice and violence and exploitation grow instead of abundance and peace and mutual flourishing.

Often we bump up against this, wondering how a good God could allow such terrible things to happen in this world. But as far as these things are from the dream God has for the world, God forcing things to be better would actually take the dream further away. Partnering with humans who freely choose to trust God and reflect God's character is an essential part of the dream.

Humans are free to follow the idols of violence and greed and power, and the path leads where it leads. Sometimes, when things threaten to get too far off track, God allows the natural consequences of human actions to take effect. When Israel chooses to put their trust in the Canaanite storm god Baal, they discover he is unable to save them from the natural cycles of rain and drought. When they bow down to the promises of military might despite the warnings of the prophets, they find themselves overrun by stronger empires. When Jesus came warning that the path of violent resistance to Rome would only end in disaster but he was there offering a path to peace, most refused to listen. Sure enough, fewer than fifty years later, Roman legions invaded Jerusalem and destroyed the temple. These events, as difficult as they are, happen as part of the freedom God grants us.

Theme #4:
The way to life is through trusting God, not idols.

God is always at work trying to get humans to return to a place of trust, showing them the ways that lead to life, accepting them back. As much as humans mess things up, God is always faithful to the dream, inviting them to come back to God, who is the only one who offers life.

Again and again through the Old Testament, the character of God is held up in contrast to the character of the idols of the surrounding nations. God is holy, not in the sense of being perfect (although that is surely true, too), but in the sense that our God is different from the gods of war and sex and power. Our God is gracious and compassionate, slow to anger and rich in faithful love. Our God cares for the vulnerable and the oppressed, bringing freedom and life to all. Our God offers real life, not the false promises of the idols who demand our service.

The New Testament continues this work, with Jesus living out the character of God in ways that oppose the powers of his world—the Jewish leaders and Romans officials. Jesus offers a yoke that is easy, and a burden that is light.

These four themes aren't comprehensive, by any means, but together they do offer one helpful way to think about the *purpose* for many of the stories of Scripture. They are often included because the community found them helpful in representing the truth of one or more of these things:

- Why did God pick Israel? For no special reason at all, and also because God hopes the whole world will come to live in joyful, beautiful, loving ways if we, Israel, live well together.
- Why are we in exile? We trusted idols, not God, and we followed that path where it led, which included a lot of oppression and suffering.

- Why are our kings so crummy? Because we really did use our power to put a king in place and trusted him like an idol, and that path didn't lead to the life it promised.

And so on...

Now, let's talk *plot*, with a quick sketch of the narrative arc of the Bible, as well as some notes on how these stories fit together. We're especially going to focus on the Old Testament, because we're about to explore twenty stories that are often poorly explained, seen as at best a prelude to the real stuff that starts happening when Jesus arrives, or at worst irrelevant stories about an angry God.

Creation

God created a good world and invited humans to help make it even better. All humans, male and female, rich and poor, are made in God's image and invited to help fill the earth and rule well over it. In order to represent God well, humans need to trust and stay connected to God. This isn't some arbitrary or ego-driven thing on God's part; rather, it is essential in the way that a hose staying connected to the spigot is essential to carry water.

Sin

Humans walked away not by doing bad things, but by putting their trust in things other than God. The story of Adam and Eve is the first instance in a recurring theme throughout the Bible of humans putting their trust in not-gods—idols—with the results being oppressive and violent and death-bringing instead of life-giving like those idols promised.

Israel

God promised Abraham and Sarah that their family would get things back on track, blessing the whole world in the process. Their story calls back to creation, a reaffirmation of God's dream. It also points forward to Jesus, as the representative of Abraham's family who would bring fully to life the blessing of the whole world.

Egypt and the Exodus

The family ended up enslaved in Egypt. But God's people couldn't do the work of partnering with God to bless the whole world in slavery, so God set the people free by overpowering the gods of Egypt, showing the world that this God, named Yahweh, I Am, is a God who can be trusted. Whoever wanted to join this newly formed family of God was welcomed.

The Land and the Law

God gave Israel a good and abundant land, and asked in return that they would be a people who showed the world what God is like in the way they lived together. The Law is an example of some of what this would have looked like in their time and place, and within the limitations of their culture.

Judges and Cycles

The dream was that Israel would be a fundamentally different sort of people, trusting Yahweh alone and living in ways that reflected God's character. They did…sometimes. And then they would forget what God had done for them, or they would get lured away by the false promises of the gods of war, fertility, power, and rain. Over and over a cycle would occur, where the life those gods promised wouldn't materialize and the people would call out for help. Each time, God would faithfully welcome them back, often using the leadership of a temporary judge. Each time, God hoped the people would keep on trusting Yahweh, not idols, offering them another chance to be the people they were meant to be.

Kings (and more cycles)

One of the key ways Israel was supposed to be different was that their King was Yahweh, not a human hoarding power for himself. But the temptation of having a leader like all the other nations was too great. The result was that Israel became like the other nations, dependent on the character of that king. Some kings put their trust in God and thus led the people toward more justice and life. But most did what people with power do—tried to hoard more and more for themselves, with disastrous consequences.

Prophets and Exile

God sent prophets to warn the kings (and the people) that the path they were on wouldn't lead to life, but usually they refused to listen. Eventually, the prophets warned that God would not keep on protecting a nation that claimed to represent Yahweh while not living in ways that reflected Yahweh. The empires of Assyria and Babylon did what empires do and conquered Israel, destroying the temple of God and taking the people away from the Land into exile.

In exile, the prophets began bringing a different message, one of hope and restoration. As a call back to the theme that God had always been faithful to Israel even when Israel was repeatedly unfaithful in return, the prophets told of a time when God would bring Israel back to the Land. In that day, a faithful representative of God would appear, one who would bring God's dream into reality. The people would return to trusting Yahweh, and Yahweh would accept them back with open arms.

New Testament

God stayed faithful to the promise made to Abraham and through the prophets, and became human in Jesus. Jesus did what humans in general, and Israel in particular, were always supposed to do—he lived in a way that showed the world what God was like. He showed in his life, death, and resurrection how the way to life was a way of self-sacrifice and love, and he encouraged his followers to trust that was true, choosing to walk that path with him. The church, then, is meant to continue carrying this on, not as a replacement for Israel, but as a fulfillment for what Israel was always supposed to be.

CREATION

GENESIS 1

The Main Idea: There is one God who created everything and made it good. God made humans to be God's helpers in taking care of the world so that it would be filled with goodness and justice and life and joy—a world that works in ways that match who God is.

In the world of the Bible, God's people lived together, and wherever they were, all around them were other groups of people. Each group had their own stories about the gods, about who made the world and how they did it. Many of the stories from those groups go something like this: The world was made when the gods got into a great big fight. The god who won split open the god who lost, stretched their body out tight, and that's what holds up the sky.

The Bible tells the **creation story** differently on purpose, because our God is different from those other gods, and it goes a bit like this:

The story begins in the beginning, of course. In the beginning God created the heavens and the earth. Before there wasn't much at all, except for God's Spirit hovering over the **waters**.

Then God said, "Lights on!" God spoke and there was light and dark. And God saw the light and the dark and God said, "Ooooh, that's good."

Okay, God didn't say exactly that, but nearly.

Genre—Creation Story

There were lots of other creation stories in the Ancient Near East, from people like the Babylonians, Egyptians, and Assyrians. Genesis 1 shares some features with those stories, which has led some people to dismiss the Genesis story as just another myth copied from the others.

But what's especially interesting in the Bible's creation story are the differences from those other stories. One God creates everything. God does the creating peacefully, and with a word, not through a violent battle with other gods and monsters. God cares about all humans, not just men, and not just the king. Humanity is created to be God's partners, not God's slaves.

The picture that emerges as you put those differences together is of a God who is different from the other gods—powerful, yes, but also loving, desiring relationship with people, sharing power instead of hoarding it, loving peace, and full of grace.

Fun Detail—Water

Genesis 1 says that God separates the waters above from the waters beneath. This might seem a strange way of saying things unless you know that in the ancient world, people believed that if you were able to go up past the sky, you'd find a massive body of water. After all, the sky is blue. And rain comes out of it. So there must be water up there, right? They also believed that, since you couldn't find the bottom of the ocean, it must be water all the way down. Waters above; waters below. This is important for two reasons: One, it's fun. But two, it is another clue that what we are reading is not a science textbook; it's a story. The author is using their current understanding of the world to make a point about God's power and goodness, which is a far more important thing than where water is or isn't.

Fun Detail—The Sun

A sharp-eyed reader might notice that plants appear on day three, but the sun doesn't appear until day four. Um…what? The scholar Terence Fretheim points out that Ancient Israel's botanists hadn't yet figured out the role of the sun in plant growth, but instead thought it was the earth that did all the work. Since dry land had appeared, plants could now grow! (Fretheim, "Genesis," 37)

Historical Context—Order

You may have been taught to read Genesis 1 as a story of how things came into existence, because medieval and modern philosophers were most concerned with questions like: "Why is there something instead of nothing?"; or "Where did the universe come from?" Scholars like John Walton have found that in the Ancient Near East (the cultural region the Bible was written in) these weren't the questions people were asking. Rather, they were much more concerned with order and function, with questions like: "What is the purpose for the world and the things in it?"; or "Who is in charge of keeping things as orderly and nonchaotic as possible?" When we read Genesis 1 with those questions in mind, we get answers much closer to what the original author was actually trying to say.

And God said, "Daytime, nighttime, sun, moon, stars!" God looked at the day and the night, at **the sun**, moon, and stars. And God said, "Ooooh, that's good."

God spoke and sky and land, the rivers and the seas, mountains and valleys were made. God looked at it all and said, "Ooooh, that's good."

And God said, "Plants, your turn! Sprout and stretch. Flower and fruit." God said, "Animals, your turn! Crawl and climb, swim and squawk, fly in the sky and flip-flop in the sea."

Every time, God said just a word and things were made. The earth formed all the spaces it needed, and those spaces got filled up **just right**.

And **everything** that was made got the same response from God: "Ooooh, that's good."

A sky filled with birds, fields filled with grass and animals to munch on it, and oceans filled with fish.

Good, good, and good. But something was missing.

People.

Key Number—Seven
The number seven is one that shows up a lot in the Ancient Near East in general, and the Bible in particular. Like many numbers in ancient writings, it's not meant to be taken literally in the counting sense, but is instead used to make a more important point about what it all means. A 7 is often used as a symbol for unity and completeness, for example. Here, seven days does not mean seven twenty-four-hour periods, as if what was important was how many minutes it took God to work. Seven days means the time necessary for the whole act of creation to be truly complete, and for God to finish all the work, not leaving anything out. Which, I think we can agree, is far more important than what a stopwatch would have told us.

Key Word—Good
Genesis 1 repeatedly deems creation to be "good" before calling it "very good" after humans take their place within it. The scholar John Walton encourages us to hear a slightly different note than we might be used to in that word. He points out that in the ancient world, goodness was usually related to order. Chaos was bad. Order was good, because order is what allows things to work out the way they are supposed to. Chaos is always getting in the way. For God to be good, and for creation to be good, God needs to make creation orderly, and one of the main points Genesis 1 is trying to make is that that is exactly what God does (Walton, *The Lost World of Genesis One*).

The Bible says God said, "Let us make people in our **image**, according to our likeness. Let them rule over the fish of the sea, over the birds of the sky, over the cattle and over the earth, and over every creepy thing that creeps along the earth.

"So God created people in God's own image. In the image of God, God created them."

People are made last in this **special poem**, because people are special. Have you ever heard someone say, "Save the best for last"? That's happening here. God saved the best for last. The whole world God made was good. But people? Of people God said, "Ooooh, that's *very* good." People are called "very good" by God.

Key Word—Image of God
People have discussed what Genesis means by humans being made in the "image of God" for thousands of years, often by bringing in all sorts of outside concerns that do more to reflect what *they* value, not what the story is saying. As we read Genesis 1, a big piece of the answer is included. Immediately after it says that God created humans in the image of God, in the very next verse, it tells us what that means: "fill the earth and govern it" (Gen. 1:28). Humans are made to be God's representatives on earth, taking care of creation well. Unsurprisingly, this is exactly what we see in other ancient stories that talk about an "image of God." Except in those other stories, only one human is given that status—the King. The King is described as the representative of the gods, meant to rule over their people. But Genesis democratizes it, giving all people, male and female, the status and dignity of being God's representatives and partners.

Literary Feature—Poetic Structure
Genesis 1 can be called a poem not because it rhymes or has a consistent meter, but because it uses a tight structure and other literary features as part of how it communicates what's important. While there's some debate as to whether Genesis 1 officially "counts" as an Ancient Near Eastern poem, its intentional and artful style is part of how it shares its main message.

Take the repetition of "evening and morning" and "it was good," for example. The structure of the days is very significant. In days one through three, God creates spaces that are then filled on days four through six, and in fact they line up with one another exactly. Day one's day and night are filled with the sun, moon, and stars in day four. Day two's ocean and sky are filled with day five's fish and birds. Day three's land is filled with day six's animals. It's all very neat and tidy and purposeful, which is exactly the truth the author is trying to communicate. God creates an orderly, purposeful world in an orderly, purposeful way.

God told the people, "Your turn! Fill things up, care for these creatures, expand this good start." Image bearers, after all, get to act on behalf of the one they are like. So people were invited to care like God cares, create like God created, and fill up the world like God first filled it.

And when God had **finished** all of God's good world, God rested.

Your Kid Asks: What about evolution?
We can have both! Genesis is a story about who made things—God—and what God is like—good. It's not a story about the details of how creation happened. The writer wouldn't have known anything about natural selection. This is a *who* story, and science helps tell us the *how* story—how the world changed over vast amounts of time.

THE DREAM IS DISRUPTED

GENESIS 3

> **The Main Idea:** This is a story that speaks to the questions about how the world is versus how we know it should be. Because God shares power, people make real choices about whether to trust (or not) and those choices have real consequences. Regardless, God always loves us, no matter what, which is where the story ends and is a key takeaway for kids.

The Bible actually has two creation stories, and in the second one, the people enjoy God's amazing creation from a garden. Let's imagine it together:

If you walk through this garden, soft grasses are under your bare feet, unless you stroll near one of its rivers to feel the mud squish between your toes and the cool water wash it away. The sun warms your face and arms as it shines on so much green from all the plants that grow. Each plant grows fruit like jewels—bright red pomegranate rubies, deep purple fig amethysts, caramel-brown date topazes.

This is a happy place.

This is a place that works in ways that match who God is. The people walk with God in the garden, enjoying their friendship with God. They live together as a team, as helpers, care for creation, and know deep inside themselves that they are loved.

This is a place where people live connected to God, each other, their inside selves, and creation.

Our world doesn't always feel like this, though, does it? We know there are hard and sad things happening near and far. Why is that?

If God dreams of a world that works in ways that match who God is, why is the world so often the exact opposite—greedy instead of generous, mean instead of kind, hurt instead of happy?

This is the story to help us with that very question. To understand, we want to activate our skill of time-hopping, jumping from our world to the world of the Bible writers, who have characters and symbols to share.

Our characters include a snake who is twisty and tricky, and a man and a woman who live in the garden, who will say and do things that you and I would likely do, too, if it were us.

And our main symbols are two **trees**, one that stands for life and one for wisdom.

Key Word—Helper
The biblical account, you may know, includes the woman being created out of the man, and called Adam's helper. I didn't include it simply for length. Some have taken these to mean that women are forever and always inferior to men by God's Supreme Design for All Things. This is wrong. For one thing, Adam is made out of dirt, but that doesn't make him inferior to dirt. For another, the person most often described in the Bible using that same Hebrew word, "helper," is...God. Patriarchy in this story occurs after, and directly as a result of, Sin. It is very much not God's Supreme Design.

Key Image—The Trees
This story is the first instance of a theme that runs throughout the Bible, that humans have the choice of two paths, one of which leads to life, the other to death. In this story that choice is represented by the trees of Life and Knowledge. As John Walton points out, in the ancient world life and wisdom were thought to belong to the gods. In most of the surrounding nations, the gods jealously guarded them. But in this story, both life and wisdom are offered freely to humans as a part of their intimate relationship with God. It is only when humans try to grab them on their own terms that they get removed from reach (Walton, *The Lost World of Adam and Eve*, 127).

So as we time-hop, remember our big question: Why is this world so different from God's dream? Perhaps a story can help:

One day in the garden, the **snake**, crafty little critter, asked the woman about something God had said.

(What God had said was: Enjoy the whole garden, except you should not eat the fruit on this one tree. It was called the tree of the knowledge of good and evil.)

The snake asked, "Did God really say you must not eat the fruit from any of the trees in the garden?"

And the woman said, "Oh, we can eat from all the trees! We just aren't meant to eat or even touch the one. God said if we do, we will die."

The snake was quick to reply, "Die? No! You won't die. You'll become like God."

He didn't say it aloud, but the snake was claiming that this one little fruit would make it so the people wouldn't have to listen to God all the time. They could do what *they* wanted. After all, what if God was holding out on them, keeping good from them, not letting them be free?

The woman was convinced, and took a fruit from the tree of the knowledge of good and evil and ate some. She gave some to the man who was with her and he ate.

And things changed quickly.

Historical Context—Snake
It's not until close to the time of Jesus, many hundreds of years after this story was first written, that people started connecting the snake to Satan. In this story it's just, well, a snake. The scholar John Walton thinks the original readers would have seen this creature as a kind of "chaos agent," similar to the sea serpents that show up in other creation stories and need to be tamed by the gods (*The Lost World of Adam and Eve*, 128ff). Think less "supreme evil being" and more "trickster like the character Maui in *Moana*."

The Bible tells us they did see things differently, but not in a good way. They realized they were **naked** and felt ashamed of it. So they made clothes from leaves.

They had spent time right up close with God, but now they wanted to hide from God. So they went into the bushes.

And God did what God does—**God came** to find them. "Where are you?" God called. "Over here," the sound came from the bushes as the man called back.

"Why are you in the bushes?" God asked.

"I heard you coming and since I was naked, I hid," the man answered.

"Oh. You ate from the tree I told you not to eat from, didn't you?"

"It was the woman's fault—she gave the fruit to me!"

The woman jumped in now to say, "The snake tricked me, and I ate."

At this point, God responded to them all. Because true knowledge of good and evil? God has that. God is the one who knows what leads to life…and what doesn't. And God could describe just how things would work and feel now that things had changed.

The connection to their inside selves? Now they didn't feel good in their bodies.

Their connection to God? They went and hid.

Historical Context—Naked
In the ancient world, nakedness was seen as shameful. This went beyond the sexual to the broader way nakedness showed someone to be vulnerable, exposed. It's a beautiful way of portraying the world God dreams of that Adam and Eve are naked and unashamed. Their trust in God at the beginning of the story means they are completely invulnerable, secure, free, and safe.

Literary Feature—God Walking
This story includes God doing two things that might seem a bit strange to your ears: walking and asking questions. Both of these actions serve to portray a God who cares deeply about relating with creation and with humans on our own terms. The scholar John Goldingay points out that asking questions, even questions we already know the answer to, and hearing another person's answers are indispensable parts of any relationship (*Old Testament Theology*, vol. 1, 137).

Their connection to each other? Now they were accusing and blaming each other. And they would keep trying to use power over each other for their own benefit.

Their connection to creation? It was going to change from harmony to hardship.

But just after God described the **consequences** to them, God also made them clothes. God cared for them right in the middle of this very hard moment. And it was indeed hard—the people were sent out of the garden, now guarded by **angels**. They were not sent away from God, though. Even if all four very good connections—to God, themselves, each other, and creation—had been broken, the story was far from over. God's love is far too big and strong to let this be the end. It was just going to take some time.

Key Word—Consequences
After God discovers what the humans have done, God speaks a series of what are often called "curses." Some have interpreted these as *punishments* that God brings down for people's sin. Instead, we might see them as accurate descriptions of the *consequences* of humanity's actions. They are describing reality, not prescribing a punishment. Not trusting God inevitably results in what is sometimes described as a four-way breakdown of the good and harmonious relationships that God intends.

    First, there is a breakdown of relationship with God, because the closeness and mutuality God hopes for is not possible without trust. Second, within ourselves as anxiety and fear creep in (see note on "Nakedness"). Third, with one another as power dynamics creep in (see note on the woman as "Helper"). And fourth, with creation, as humans toil and struggle and exploit instead of living harmoniously with nature.

Fun Detail—Angels
People's first reaction when angels show up in the Bible is usually fear. Picturing them like the angels at the end of this story—as winged warriors wielding flaming swords—helps explain why!

I wonder why trees are the symbols
of life and wisdom?

I wonder how a snake sounds when it talks?

I wonder why people have a tendency to
think God is keeping good from them?

A PLAN FOR A TOWER OF PROTECTION

GENESIS 11

> **The Main Idea:** When humanity tries to gain security and status on their own terms, it always fails and often backfires, becoming self-focused and power-driven. But God is working to bring life and blessing to the world, and people are a key part of that plan. God is a God who makes and keeps promises, and when people trust that reality, they find life and security that are better than any they would have achieved on their own.

Many years passed after Adam and Eve left the garden, and the number of humans got bigger and bigger. But not too big, because our story begins by telling us that "all the people of the earth" got together to make a plan, and that they all "spoke the **same language** and used the same words."

Literary Feature—One Language
One of the clues that this is more a parable than a historical account is how it starts, with "the whole earth" having "one language" and *all* building a city together (Gen. 11:1 NASB). Since chapter 10 has already told us about many different nations and cities being built, this is kind of doubling back on the story, a bit like Genesis 2 doubles back on Genesis 1, highlighting different ideas.

And, even though they had left the garden, they hadn't wandered too far, because they found themselves in "the **east**," which is also where the garden was. God, remember, had given humans a job to do, to go out and fill up the whole world, making every part of it good and lovely.

But these people weren't sure that was such a good idea.

"That sounds pretty dangerous," one said. "How do we know we'll be safe?"

"Yeah, and what's in it for us?" asked another. "I want to **be important!**"

"Ugh, it's way too much work to go traveling all over the face of the whole earth. I want to stay right here!" complained a third.

Then, one of them came up with a plan, and everyone agreed to it. The plan was to build a great **city**. In this city there would be a soaring **tower**. And this city and tower combined would keep the people together in this place.

Key Word—East
Genesis 11:2 tells us where this story is happening with words that are identical to those in Genesis chapter 2 for where the garden is located. It's possible the author is giving a little hint that Babel is a story of humans trying to get back to the security of the garden before it all went wrong, but going about it the wrong way.

Key Word—Make a Name
The first reason the people give for wanting to build their city is that they want to make a name for themselves. They're looking for prestige and fame, and probably the security that comes with those things. The people get a name, all right, but ironically, it's not the one they were looking for. "Babel" is related to the word for "confusion." Their name isn't great; rather, it's confused. The author then calls back to this in the story of Abraham, because in 12:2 one of God's promises is that God will "make [Abraham's] name great." In simply trusting God to keep Their promises, Abraham gets exactly the thing the people of Babel tried, but failed, to get despite (or maybe because of) their great effort.

Fun Detail—City/Tower
The people decide to build a city with a tower that will reach "the heavens". The problem with all of this is not the building. Cities are fine and have shown up already in the opening chapters of Genesis. The problem is with the reasons (see notes on "Scattered" and "Make a Name"). One funny detail is how the author makes a point of telling us that God "came down" to see what the people were up to. Apparently their tower was not *quite* as tall as they'd imagined it, not even coming close to reaching the heavens.

They would be safe as could be inside the huge city, where no wild animals could get them.

Their tower would be the tallest one that ever existed, with a top that reached all the way to the heavens as high as where God lived. They'd be known all over the world as the greatest of great people who had built the tallest of tall towers.

And, best of all, they could do it all right there, in the east, without traveling dusty miles, spreading out across the whole earth.

They started building. Bricks were shaped and stacked. Higher and higher. Until the tower was close to done, and the city was taking shape.

And all this time God was watching them work, saddened by the people's decision not to trust that if they listened to what God had told them, everything would be okay. What God saw was people who were invited to fill the world, but instead, they all clumped together. They were invited to use God's image in them to shine out in their own unique and creative ways, but instead, they built a structure for themselves, to protect themselves and make themselves seem great.

But God's dream of the whole world being good and right and lovely is too important to just shrug off and give up on. So, eventually, God came among them and changed things up.

God came down to get a closer look. God had to come waaaay down, because as tall as the tower was, it maybe came a teensy bit short of reaching the heavens.

And then, God took their one language and scrambled it. Now, instead of all being able to speak and plan together, the people found they couldn't understand each other. Which made it really hard to keep building, as I'm sure you can imagine.

They had to give up their dream of building a great city to protect themselves and make themselves important. In the end, the people were left doing

Key Word—Scattered
The second reason given for building a city is so that they would not be scattered "over the face of the whole earth." You may hear an echo of Genesis 1, where God commands humans to *fill* the whole earth. That's intentional on the part of the author, and gives us a clue as to what's going on here. The problem isn't that people are building a city; the problem is that the *reason* they are building the city is an explicit rejection of God's dream for the world, as well as humanity's place in it. This is like Jonah not only *not* going to Nineveh, but going the exact opposite direction. Again, ironically, their plan backfires, and scattered is exactly where they end up.

Fun Detail—Terah
Abraham's dad, Terah, shows up at the end of chapter 11. Terah's roots are in "Ur of the Chaldeans" which is not too far from where the Babel story took place. That's one of the many ways the author refers back to Babel in the story of Abraham. It says that Terah took his family and set off for Canaan but then stopped halfway. Abraham then completes the journey when God calls him after Terah's death. Did God call Terah, but then he got cold feet partway and God had to try again with Terah's son? Maybe?

Key Word—Blessing
With the start of chapter 12, we get a picture of God working to get the dream back on track. Through the first 11 chapters, we've seen glimpses of the dream God has for all creation, only for that dream to be repeatedly rejected by humanity. But God doesn't give up, and in 12:1–3 we see God's plan for renewal, and it centers on blessing. God is calling a family. Actually, God is going to create a family where one doesn't exist, but that's next week's story. God is going to bless Abraham, but not so Abraham can hunker down with a nice, inward-looking, blessed chosen people of God. No, God will bless Abraham's family, *so that* his family will bless the whole world. Blessing is a key theme in Genesis that shows up throughout because it captures the dream, not that one family would be blessed, but that all of creation would know the blessings that come from Yahweh God.

Connections—Pentecost
There are echoes of Babel in the story of Pentecost in Acts 2, when the Holy Spirit comes to the disciples and allows them to speak and understand foreign languages. In some ways, Pentecost is a reverse of Babel, God bringing unity back to humanity out of the diversity that divides us. But Pentecost does not achieve unity by reinstating one universal language. Instead, the diversity of human language and culture is preserved; but there is unity in that diversity, which is what God has intended all along.

what they were meant to do in the first place—**spreading out** over the whole earth, filling it up.

And if you could push "fast-forward" on the story, as families grew and spread, and grew and spread some more, you'd leave the unfinished city in the east and come at last to a place called Haran and a man named **Abram**.

Abram and his wife, Sarai, didn't know it, but God was going to team up with them to help the dream come true. That group in the east wanted to make their own names great. God was going to make Abram's name great, as his family grew and **blessed** the world. The dream is too important to let it die, and **God is too good to give up** on the world God made.

I wonder what the city and tower were planned to look like?

I wonder what made God decide to get involved instead of just watch?

I wonder what the first hour was like when they went from one language to lots?

WAITING FOR BABY ISAAC

GENESIS 17; 18; 21:1–7

> **The Main Idea:** God didn't become a relational God when Jesus showed up. All through God's interactions with humanity, God has shown a deep desire to be with us, to relate to us. Part of any genuine relationship includes the mutual obligations, responsibilities, and promises we make to one another. And so, God makes promises. And, just as in any other relationship, it matters that God is a God who can be trusted to keep promises, no matter what. God willingly takes on the obligations of relationship with us and then fulfills those obligations.

Long ago a man named Abram and a woman named Sarai lived in the lands called Ur, Haran, and Canaan. Over their lives in these lands, they got to know God more and more. They learned God would at times speak to them. God would at times lead them to a new place. One time, Abram made a choice that put Sarai in danger, and God protected her.

But perhaps the biggest thing they learned was this:

This God is a promise-making, promise-keeping God.

God dreams of a world that works in a way that matches who God is, and so God decided to form a group who would help that happen. This group would be a family—a huge one. And as this family took care of each other and the world, they would show the world what God was like. That would be their purpose.

Have you ever taken a flashlight and a mirror into a dark room? You can shine the light on the mirror and it will reflect out to make the whole room brighter. This family God was making would be like the mirror, brightening the world as they filled it with love and justice and… what else?

What else do we know about who God is? Would you name something? What would it be like if the world matched that?

Back to our story: In order to make this big God-family possible, God made a promise. God promised Abram and Sarai a baby. This baby would begin the family.

There was a problem, though: no **baby**.

Abram and Sarai did not have children, and they thought they could not have children. Some people can have children and don't want to. Some people cannot have children but also don't want to. Some people can have children and do want to. Some people cannot have children but do want to. Abram and Sarai were in that last group, especially because they lived in a time when their community and culture valued having babies a lot.

So this is the conversation Abram had with God one night.

GOD: Don't be afraid, Abram. I'll protect you and care for you.
ABRAM: Well, God, I'm not so sure your protection and care do me

---

Historical Context—Descendants
It wasn't just important to Abraham to have children because "Oooh, cute baby!" People in the Ancient Near East didn't, for the most part, believe in an afterlife—a heaven or a hell. At most, they believed in a kind of shadowy netherworld that was a pale imitation of this life, but most just believed that when you died, you were dead. Descendants were quite literally seen as a person's life after death. They carried on that person's bloodline and memory after they died. Think something along the lines of the Disney movie *Coco*, where being forgotten is the real death. In this light, God is promising Abraham true, maybe we might even say eternal, life.

much good. I don't even have a son (let alone lots of kids to start this family you promised me).

GOD: You will still have a son. Look up at the night sky. Look at the **stars**—really look. Try to count them if you'd like. Your children, their children, the children after them—your descendants will grow until they are as many as those stars.

If you were Abram, and you'd been waiting for a very long time for God to keep God's promise, what might you be thinking or feeling right now? Would this be easy or hard to trust? Why?

Abram trusted God. That's all the Bible says to us. We aren't told exactly what helped him trust, just that he did.

The conversation continued:

GOD: Remember, I've been with you since you lived in Ur, and in Haran, and here in Canaan, which will be your land someday. I will give it to you and your descendants.

ABRAM: Yahweh God, how can I be sure this will actually be our land?

How do you think God responded to this question?

Fun Detail—Stars
Abraham is told to count the stars in the sky and trust that God will give him that many descendants. A more literal-minded kid might wonder at this, since the actual number of stars in the universe is many, many times greater than the number of all the humans who have ever lived, or since the number of stars that can be counted with the naked eye is actually much smaller than the number of Abraham's descendants. It's better to think about this as a figure of speech—just as it isn't possible for you to count the stars in the sky because you would inevitably lose count, so you won't be able to count the number of descendants.

God did not get mad or impatient. God did not say, "Since you questioned me, I take it back."

God instead invited Abram to be part of a special ceremony where Abram made an **offering** and God came to him in the night, looking like smoke and fire. The ceremony formed what's called a "**covenant**." When God makes a **covenant**, it's like a super promise. Impossible to break, not that God would break a promise anyway.

Even so, if you read the Bible after this story, you'll find that Sarai and Abram struggled to trust God to keep **God's promises**. They worried God was taking too long. They tried to force the promise to come true with their own actions (and hurt some people along the way).

Still, God kept God's promises. One day they did have a baby boy, the promise in a body, Isaac.

Key Image—Animals
The actual ceremony of the covenant described in the Bible is one of the stranger details of this story, especially for us so many years later. It's one you might not get into with younger kids, and I chose to omit it here, but older kids may think it's interesting.

The animals are split in half and arranged with half the body on one side and half on the other with a path in between. This is so the flame representing God's presence is able to pass through the middle of the carcasses. This is a symbolic act, which in a nutshell is saying, "May I be split apart like these animals if I fail to fulfill the terms of this covenant." It's striking that God is the one who passes through the animals and accepts these terms, symbolically accepting death if the covenant is unfulfilled. It's also striking to see the connection that, in the end, Jesus' death is a central part of how God ultimately fulfills this covenant.

Key Word—Covenant
A covenant was a binding agreement between two parties, a contract of sorts. It is an official way of setting out the obligations, responsibilities, and benefits that each can expect. It's a super promise. And what's striking in this story is that it is one-sided. God is the only one who makes promises or takes on obligations. Our God is one who willingly and freely ties Themself to this particular person and family, no matter what.

Connections—Covenants
God makes more than one covenant in the stories of Scripture, and the scholar Terence Fretheim points out some interesting parallels between how this covenant with Abraham comes about, and how the future covenants with the Hebrews post-Exodus, with David and with the followers of Jesus (the "new covenant"), come about. In each case the order of events is consistent, and important. First, God chooses people (in this case, Abraham) not on the basis of any of their characteristics, but just because. In fact, usually these people very much lack the positive characteristics we might expect. Second, God delivers them (here, God has already saved Abraham from a couple of tight spots in previous chapters). Third, the people show their trust in some way, often worship. Crucially, their trust is not "blind faith." God has gone first (step two, deliverance) to show them that God can be trusted. And fourth, God makes promises to bring life to God's people (Fretheim, "Genesis," 120). The foundation of the covenant is never the people's behavior, nor even their obedience. The foundation is God's choosing and deliverance. Trust and then obedience arise out of God's actions in each case.

Key Word—Righteousness
Abraham believes God's promises, and the story says that God "reckoned it to him as righteousness." (Gen. 15:6 RSVUE). The word "righteous" can have some less than positive connotations these days (think: "self-righteous"), but most of the time we use it to mean something like "being a good person." That doesn't really make much sense in this story—Abraham believed God's promises and that meant he was a good person? The New Testament scholar N. T. Wright, among others, argues that there is a better way of understanding this word when it shows up (*Justification*, 207ff).

Righteousness, more broadly, means something like "being in right relationship," that the relationships we are in are in a good place. It can apply to any number of human-human relationships—including within a family, with an employer or employee, and in a legal sense with other citizens. But it can also apply to human-God relationships, or to human relationships with creation. Being a good person is related to all of these, of course, but that's not quite what the word is getting at.

In the Bible, Wright argues, "righteousness" is usually related to the covenant, as it is in this story. God makes a covenant with people, and those promises are the foundation for God's relationship with God's people. So, believing in God as a promise-keeping God *is* being in "right relationship" with God; it's how a person opts in to those promises. It's a way of saying, "Yes, I want to be part of this covenant, this family."

In other words, being considered righteous means basically the same as being part of God's people. And the way one gets included in the people of God is not genetics or behavior, not even "being a good person"; it's belief, trusting that God will, in fact, keep Their promises.

I wonder if they thought God lied to them?

I wonder how Abram felt at the
beginning of the conversation with God?
Or at the end?

I wonder what other promises God keeps?

GOD IS WITH JOSEPH

GENESIS 37–45

> **The Main Idea:** The repeated theme throughout the story of Joseph is that God was with Joseph. This did not mean, however, that things went great for him. This story offers a fantastic opportunity to highlight that through it all—when he was his father's golden child, when he was sold into slavery, when he was in charge of Potiphar's house, when he was falsely accused and imprisoned, when he sat in a cell for years and years and years, and when he was in a position of great power in the greatest empire of the day—God was with Joseph, and God will be with us, too. No matter what happens, God can be trusted to be with us in it.

This is a bit of a long story, and even as we try to focus on some of the biggest parts, we're leaving some details out. Someday you might enjoy taking any of these sections and hearing even more about them! But for now, our story has four big parts, so let's dive in.

Part 1: Meet Joseph, who is in a pit. How did he get into a pit, you ask?

Let's rewind. Joseph is one of twelve brothers who all have the same dad, a man named Jacob. These brothers don't all get along, to put it mildly. In fact, the Bible says they hate Joseph. Some of that isn't Joseph's fault, really. Jacob loves Joseph most, and they know it. For example, Jacob once gave Joseph an incredibly special gift of a colorful robe, and the others received nothing.

On top of the **coat** incident, though, was the dream incident. See, Joseph had two **dreams**, and he told his brothers what they were. What's the big deal about that, you ask?

In these dreams, there were symbols—bunches of grain in the first one; the sun, moon, and stars in the second. And there was **bowing**—the brothers' grain bunches bowing to Joseph's grain bunch; the sun, moon, and eleven stars bowing to Joseph.

You know who doesn't want to bow to Joseph? His brothers.

Now, let's fast-forward.

Key Image—Coat
Jacob, Joseph's father, gave him a special robe. We aren't told many details about the robe or why it was given, but it was certainly a symbol of Joseph's status as his father's favorite son. This may have included an implication that when it came time for inheritance, the young Joseph was going to jump to the front of the line as well, which would help explain his brothers' anger. When they throw Joseph into the pit they strip him of the robe, symbolically stripping him of what they see as his undeserved status and taking it for themselves.

Historical Context—Dreams
Kids sometimes wonder whether God still speaks through dreams in the way that we see God do several times in this story. I tend to think that God can speak to people in any way God wants to speak to people, so…probably? It might be helpful, though, to point to the cultural context of this story. In the Ancient Near East, it was just an accepted fact that the gods spoke through dreams. This wouldn't have been seen as strange at all. One thing we see with God is that God speaks in ways that people will understand. God wants to be in relationship with us, and that includes using the words, the language, the symbols, and the methods that fit with who we are and where we live. So in a culture where it was normal for the gods to speak through dreams, God spoke through dreams. In our culture where that isn't expected, it's no surprise that God doesn't seem to use this method quite as often.

Historical Context—Bowing
Joseph starts the whole fiasco with his family by putting himself above not only his older brothers but his parents as well, and in a way that would have been massively culturally offensive. While the brothers certainly are in the wrong, the storytelling reveals that Joseph is not at all innocent. The whole saga of Joseph and his brothers is a great example of why I advocate for God-centered storytelling. Sure, Joseph does some good things, and there are aspects of his character and actions we might want to emulate. The good that comes from this story comes not because Joseph is so great, but because God is with him.

Joseph was sent to check on his brothers and report back to their dad, but when they saw him coming, they made a plan to kill him and blame a wild animal. His brother Rueben tried to help by getting them to instead throw Joseph into the pit. Then later, he could come back to save him.

They agreed that a pit was less involved and troublesome for them, and so when Joseph arrived they ripped off his colorful robe and threw him into the pit.

Part 2: Here's Joseph again—he's in an **Egyptian** prison. How did he get into prison, you ask?

He didn't do anything wrong, in case you're wondering. Someone lied about him. We'll get back to that in a minute.

While Joseph was in the pit, a group of traders came along, and the brothers adapted their plan again. They sold Joseph into slavery. Now, the Bible doesn't tell us a lot about these conversations, but I bet you can imagine that even though this is simple to tell you, it was very complicated to be living.

It gets even more complicated as the story goes on. Joseph went from the pit to the traders, from the traders to Egypt, and then to a man named Potiphar who was quite powerful. And somehow, despite all Joseph had been through, he was able to adjust to life in this new place. He was able not only to work hard, but to be good at his work. And Potiphar noticed. In fact, Joseph was eventually put in charge of all of Potiphar's household as second in command.

Connections—Egypt

The story ends with Jacob, Joseph, and the rest of the family in Egypt. For those who remember the story of Abraham, they might hear an echo of the time when God told Abraham that his descendants would end up as slaves in Egypt for four hundred years. Right now, Joseph is in a position of power and favor, but if this were a movie, we'd be hearing the shark music in the background right now, giving us some foreshadowing that the good times aren't going to last for the people of God. However, as this story has shown us, God will be with them even in slavery.

It all seems really good, right? How does a person go from second in command to a prison? Just like the pit before, this is another hard part of our story. There was a time when **Potiphar's wife** came to Joseph, and she touched Joseph when he did not want to be touched. He was able to run away, but he left a piece of clothing behind. She turned the whole story around, lied, and told Potiphar that Joseph had tried to touch her and to hurt her. She showed the left-behind clothing as "proof." Potiphar believed her, and that was that. Joseph was sent to jail.

Part 3: Here's Joseph yet again—he's in a palace. How did he get into a palace, you ask?

It took a few years for Joseph to go from the prison to the palace, but during his time in the prison, somehow, he adapted to his new life. In fact, the Bible says, "But the LORD was with Joseph in the prison and showed him his faithful love" (Gen. 39:21). The guard eventually put him in charge of many of the prison responsibilities. He was second in command.

One day two men who had worked for the king, Pharaoh, were put into the prison, because they had made Pharaoh unhappy. And after a time, each of these men had a dream. Joseph found them talking about the dreams one day because the men were confused about what they might mean. And God had

---

Your Kid Asks…About Potiphar's Wife
While I'd advise that the attempted rape is a detail to skip and save for later with most kids, eventually it's likely to come up, either because they hear it or read the text for themselves. When it's time to dive into this, or if your kid has heard this part of the story on some occasion and wants to know why it's such a big deal that she wants Joseph to lie next to her for a cuddle, here's what I'd say: Potiphar's wife is someone with power who wants to touch Joseph, but he doesn't want to be touched. Sometimes people with power think that it's okay for them to make other people do things that those people don't want to do. And sometimes the powerless people get hurt whether they go along with it or not. That is, unfortunately, the way our world works sometimes. But it's not the way God wants the world to work. God wants powerful people to use their power to bring life to other people, like Joseph does later in the story, not to use their power to get things for themselves or force others to do things those people don't want to do.

given Joseph the ability to know what dreams meant, so he told them. For one of the men, the dream was bad news; but for the other, it was good news, and it meant that he would be back in the palace, doing his old job again. Joseph asked that once the man got there, he would remember Joseph.

Unfortunately, the man returned to his old life and forgot all about Joseph. Until one day, a couple of years later, who should have two dreams but Pharaoh himself? And who should remember Joseph but the man who'd been in prison with him before?

So Joseph was brought to Pharaoh, where God gave him the ability to tell him what his two dreams meant. And it was a good thing Joseph did, because the dreams meant that seven good harvest years were coming, but they'd be followed by seven years with hardly any crops at all.

What do you think Pharaoh did next? If you know this story, imagine it was new to you—what might you guess Pharaoh would do? Maybe say, "Thanks, Joe!" and send him back to prison? Maybe panic about the news?

Pharaoh thought about how Joseph was clearly being given wisdom, and he decided to put him in charge of crop management, so to speak. Joseph would make sure that extra grain was saved from the good years so food would be available in the bad years. And so Joseph went from prison to the palace.

Key Word—Shalom
When Pharaoh asks Joseph to interpret his troubling dreams, Joseph assures him that Yahweh God would give Pharaoh the interpretation, and that the interpretation would be, to use the Hebrew word, one of "Shalom" (Gen. 41:16). This word is often translated as "peace," although in this verse it's often translated as "favorable" or "desired." It's a big word in the Bible, one that means much more than the absence of conflict. Shalom is the world as it should be, with goodness all around. Shalom is a world that reflects God's character. In this case, Shalom is found in the economic and political policies that Joseph wisely implements that save not only Egypt, but the surrounding nations, from famine and death. God's people bringing Shalom to the world is God's dream, part of the promise God made to Abraham that his family would be a blessing to the nations, and something we can still participate in today, in our own ways.

Part 4: Here's Joseph's BROTHERS. You thought I'd say here's Joseph again, didn't you? Nope!

See, there wasn't enough food during the bad years not only in Egypt, but all around, including where Joseph's family lived. When word got around that there was food in Egypt, Jacob sent ten of Joseph's eleven brothers to get some. Brother number eleven, Benjamin, stayed back. He was the baby of the family, and was the most special to his dad (who clearly still could learn a bit about not having favorites).

They arrived in Egypt and came to Joseph, but they didn't recognize him. And they bowed down to him as they asked to buy food for their families. Joseph did recognize them, though.

If you were in Joseph's place, what might you be thinking or feeling at this point?

Joseph was full of feelings, and even needed to leave them to have time to cry about everything. He actually set up a whole scheme to try to find out if they had changed at all over the years by telling them to bring Benjamin to him. This time, they protected Benjamin and cared about their father's sadness—things they had failed to do that day in the fields. And eventually, Joseph revealed his identity to them.

I want you to hear from the Bible how the story ends.

"I am Joseph!" he said to his brothers. "Is my father still alive?" But his brothers were speechless and frozen in fear! They were stunned to realize that Joseph was standing there in front of them.

Literary Feature—Irony

Joseph's brothers sell him into slavery in an attempt to ensure that his (to them) offensive dreams do not come true. "There," they must have thought as the dust of the slave trader's caravan disappeared over the horizon, "we won't be bowing down to that brat." And yet that's exactly what they end up doing, after a series of events that never could have transpired if they hadn't tried to keep it from happening. Their attempt to prevent the dream from coming true is exactly what made the dream come true.

"Please, come closer," he said to them.

If you were one of the brothers, what might you be thinking or feeling at this point?

So they came closer. And he said again, "I am Joseph, your brother, whom you sold into slavery in Egypt. But don't be upset, and don't be angry with yourselves for selling me to this place. It was God who sent me here ahead of you to preserve your lives."

It's always a good idea to ask: What do you notice about who God is or what God is like? But I also wonder: Hearing what Joseph's life was like, and hearing what he said to his brothers when they met again, what do you think *Joseph thought* about who God is or what God is like?

I wonder how long it took Joseph to trust that God was with him?

I wonder if Joseph had people to talk about things with along the way?

I wonder what Joseph's brothers thought about God once they were all together again?

A CONVERSATION WITH A BURNING BUSH

EXODUS 3

The Main Idea: The God who appears to Moses and talks out of the burning bush is one that makes promises and then keeps them. God is a God who is always there, as the name Yahweh indicates, and God will be with Moses and with the people throughout the dangers and fears they are about to face. God is not just powerful; God is present.

Our story begins in Egypt, where God's people were enslaved, forced to work for Pharaoh and his empire. It was a hard experience for them, and they suffered very much.

At this time, every nation had their own gods and goddesses. For example, Egypt had a sun god and a rain god and a river god, and they were in charge of Egypt. People thought that a god was powerful in their own nation but nowhere else. In other words, the Hebrews would have thought they were stuck, because who could possibly save them from the powerful gods of Egypt?

Outside of Egypt, in a land called Midian, there was a man named Moses taking care of sheep. But Moses was not a Midianite. He was a Hebrew. He was also not a typical Hebrew, because he had been raised in Pharaoh's own household, like an Egyptian. Moses was a shepherd in Midian because he'd

Genre—Theophany
"Theophany" is a fancy word for the appearance of God in some sort of tangible way. This happens in various ways in the Bible, but one common feature is fire. In fact, any time you see fire show up in a story in the Bible, your first thought should be that God is present. Later in the Exodus, God will be a pillar of fire protecting and guiding the people; at Pentecost, the Holy Spirit is like small fires descending on the disciples' heads. Fire is a physical phenomenon used by God to say something about who God is. Fire is wild, unpredictable, potentially destructive, and terrifying. It's also warming, life-giving on a cold winter night, and a provider of hot, nourishing meals. Fire also serves as a light in the darkness, protection from wild animals and the unknown. God is all of those things and more.

Literary Feature—Conversation
One of the most striking aspects of how this story is told is how UNheroic Moses is. God did not call an action figure ready to lead the charge in battle. God called someone who had spent the bulk of his life as a shepherd in the boondocks, who was well past his prime, and who didn't speak so good. And Moses proceeds to let God know all this in no uncertain terms. And because of all that, this story is so important in how we think about who God is and how God relates to us. God takes Moses seriously through all his objections, excuses, and fears. God engages in the back-and-forth, changes the plan to help Moses feel more comfortable, meets Moses' present-tense fears with future-tense promises. And sometimes, God raises Their voice when Moses' legitimate objections turn more toward pure whining. Which is all, when you think about it, how a real conversation goes in a real relationship. And, again like a real conversation, Moses' pushback leads to deeper relationship, as God reveals the name Yahweh in response to only one of Moses' questions. The healthy back and forth leads to more intimacy. God is establishing a mutual relationship based on trust, not a dictatorial one based on fear.

Key Words—Hebrews, My People, My Child
The term "Hebrews" ended up becoming more or less synonymous with "Israelites," but Old Testament scholars point out that the word is one that showed up in one form or another in a number of different Ancient Near Eastern languages, and always had the same basic meaning. Hebrews were low-class, usually foreign (not one particular ethnic group, but any of the minorities that might exist), and manual laborers. "Hebrews" is a slur, in other words, for, you know, "those people." And Yahweh describes Themself in this story as "The God of the Hebrews," calls them "my own people," and then, upping the ante even more, calls them "my child." This mixed-ethnic rabble of slaves are the ones Yahweh chooses to call Their children. We follow the God of the riffraff (Alter, *The Hebrew Bible*, vol. 1, 363n.).

run away from Egypt after doing a bad thing. Moses' whole story is very interesting, but today, we're going to meet him on a mountain in Midian.

Because on this day on a mountain in Midian there was a bush on fire that did not burn up. A talking bush on fire that did not burn up.

Okay, it was not a talking bush. In the Bible, fire is a symbol of **God's presence**, and the voice was God's voice, and **God said**, "Moses!"

"Here I am!" Moses replied.

"Do not come any closer… Take off your sandals, you are standing on holy ground."

"Holy" is a word that means "set apart." So, imagine you are making cookies, and you take some of the dough to eat with a spoon, and then you put the rest on the pan. You set apart that spoonful of cookie dough for the purpose of eating a yummy treat.

In the Bible, a group can be holy, like God's people were holy—they were set apart and different from all the nations around them. God is holy—different from every other god around. And places were sometimes holy—set apart for a specific message or job.

Moses is on holy ground, a place God has set apart so that God can share an important message with him.

The message was this:

"I have certainly seen the oppression of **my people** in Egypt. I have heard their cries. I am aware of their suffering. So I have come down to rescue them from the power of the Egyptians and lead them out of Egypt into their own wonderful land…

"Now go, for I am sending you to Pharaoh. You must lead my people Israel out of Egypt."

If you were Moses, how would you react to this message?

Moses said, "Who am I to appear before Pharaoh? Who am I to lead the people of Israel out of Egypt?" In other words: Me? Really? Not, like, someone else?

Moses wasn't happy or excited. He was overwhelmed and afraid.

God answered, "**I will be with you.** In fact, I have a sign for you: You and all my people will be back, free, and worship God at this very mountain."

Then Moses said, "If I go to the people saying, 'The God of your ancestors has sent me to you,' they will ask me, 'What is his name?' Then what should I tell them?"

See, not only did every god or goddess have a territory; they also had a name. These names told you something important about what they were like.

So God gave a name to Moses, "I am who I AM. Tell the people of Israel: I AM has sent me to you."

I AM, "**Yahweh**" in Hebrew, is our God's name. Remember, the name of a God tells you something about what they are like. Yahweh, I AM, is a name that means "always there." Not just at the burning bush, but even in Egypt, even though that is supposed to be some other god's territory. God would be there, too.

Then God gave Moses some directions for what would come next. He would go first to the leaders of God's people and tell them what God had said.

Key Word—I will be with you
This continues a theme from Joseph's story, and will continue to be a key theme throughout the Bible. Throughout the conversation with Moses, God repeats, "I will be with you." It's God's trump card whenever Moses' objections and fears threaten to derail the whole plan. The promise is not that everything will go perfectly without any trouble; it's the assurance of God's presence.

Key Word—Yahweh
The name of a god in the ancient world told about their character. Who is this God, and what are They like? The name Yahweh is something of a puzzle, but it seems to be a form of the verb "to be." It could be "I Am what I Am"; or "I will be there"; or "I will be who I will be." It's all of these things, because how else can we capture all of who our God is? Yahweh is about being. This is a God who is, was, and will be; who is consistent and can be counted on. Yahweh is about presence. This is a God who will be with the people and with Moses no matter what, and no matter where they find themselves. Yahweh is about action. This is a God who will be whomever They need to be, who will do whatever They need to do in order to fulfill Their promises. Yahweh is a name that can be trusted.

Then he would go to Pharaoh, the king of Egypt, and say that God, Yahweh, I AM, said to let the people go.

God gave Moses signs—special things he'd be able to do to show the people God really appeared to him, like throw his walking stick to the ground where it would **transform** into a snake, only to become a stick again when he picked it back up. And God gave Moses his brother Aaron as a companion to help him. Then God gave one last **sign** to Moses: "One day you'll be here again, with all my people, worshipping me at this exact same mountain."

But God also knew this: People who worship power do not give up power. People who build empires unjustly cannot simply start being just. That's not how it works.

Pharaoh was not going to listen to Moses or this god Yahweh. I mean, who's this Yahweh anyway?

But Pharaoh was about to find out.

Historical Context—Magic
God gives Moses a sign to take to Pharaoh that is, basically, a magic trick. In fact, there are Egyptian stories from around the same time that seem to indicate that turning a staff into a snake was par for the course for an Egyptian magician. In other words, Pharaoh would not have been overly impressed by this trick, and it's no surprise that later Pharaoh's magicians replicated it. It's almost like a trap, luring Pharaoh into the contest, and is another clue that perhaps Yahweh has bigger goals in mind than just freeing the Hebrews as quickly and easily as possible.

Key Word—Sign
God gives Moses a sign as a guarantee that all God has promised will come true. The sign is that when all is said and done, Moses and the people will worship God on the very spot that Moses is standing upon. In other words, Moses gets no guarantee on the front end, except God's word. He has to go on faith, trusting that God will bring him through safely, no matter how dark things get in the midst. And when he does that, he'll be able to look back and see that God was trustworthy and had been with him all along.

I wonder what God's voice sounded like?

I wonder what Moses was most worried about when it came to God's message?

In this story, God appeared in a burning bush. At other times in the Bible God appears in a pillar of fire, a pillar of cloud, a dove. I wonder, if you could pick a way for God to appear, what would you pick?

YOU ASK

I KNOW IT'S IN THE BIBLE,
BUT DO I NEED TO TELL IT TO MY KID?

Let's talk more about skipping—skipping details and skipping stories altogether, using two guiding principles:

- Make stories kid-accessible, but not kidified.
- If you can't do that, skip it and save the story for the future.

Principle 1:
Kid-Accessible Storytelling

There are resources that change the story so much to make it kid-friendly that it's far from the point. I call this kidifying a story.

Kid-accessible is when we can share a story with a child at their level.

When we make an idea kid-accessible, we may do things like choose simpler words, or summarize a story rather than read it verbatim from the Bible. When deciding what it means to be at a kid's level, this is what we're thinking of. Can I be faithful to the story's meaning but present it to a child? When I'm ready to build on this later, will the next layer of depth or complexity fit in with what I've said so far?

Two brief examples from *Wonder*:

- The burning bush is a long conversation. Moses objects four different times. I included just two instances for one simple reason: to keep the length manageable. Over time, I can add more details.
- I included God parting the sea, but skipped Passover, because theologically and thematically it raises questions that are beyond most kids' development. But I did not kidify the story to be all about Moses' obedience. When kids are older, I can tell about the Passover, and it will fit with the contest theme I already established.

When a story is kidified, the meaning gets changed from something authentic to the passage to something different (often something that tells a child how to act). Kidifying is a helpful tactic for obedience training. Almost any Bible story can be lifted from its time, place, and genre and converted into some tidy axiom.

We help kids engage the Bible well as we BOTH tell the story in alignment with its meaning, faithful to what it's about, AND tell it in a kid-accessible way, including paraphrases, humor, and creativity.

We want kid-accessible. We'd like to avoid kidifying.

If you can't tell an accurate version of a Bible story, in a kid-accessible way, save it until you can.

Which leads us to…

Principle 2:
Skip-and-Save Stories

This is a point of debate when it comes to kids and the Bible, but I don't think kids can or should "get the whole Bible" in one swoop. Instead, I advocate for adults to use a skip-and-save approach with kids for several reasons:

- Our goal is not biblical literacy, where our kids know as much of the Bible as their little brains can hold. Our goal is for kids to get to know God, and to be their guides as they explore Bible stories that help them discover who God is and what God is like. Sometimes skipping is as simple as helping point out certain themes, knowing you can highlight other themes in other stories at a future time.
- The Bible is not a children's book. It is full of content that is not appropriate for or understandable to children. That may be because some of the content is not appropriate thematically, or because it uses metaphors and imagery while kids are concrete, or because the themes are complicated enough that children need to be older to understand them.
- Just because a Christian should learn it "someday" does not mean a kid needs to learn it today. (In fact, I'd argue it's a bit superstitious to act as if a kid will meet God via the Bible only if they're told every Bible story, as if God cannot meet a person through myriad ways.)
- Saving some Bible stories until kids are older respects not only a child's unique development but also the Bible itself.
- It respects your kid as someone who can meet God, grow into understanding the story of our faith, and doesn't have to be pressured to "get it" by some deadline.
- It respects the Bible as a book whose faithful testimony of who God is comes through a story told in a context, a genre, a culture, and a specific moment in history.

It's not, to my mind, a problem that kids can't engage the whole Bible. There's plenty there for them now, and they can get to the rest later on.

So as we encounter parts of the Bible our kids can't access or understand, what do we do?

We simply skip it for now, and save it for later.

GOD SPLITS THE RED SEA

EXODUS 5–15

> **The Main Idea:** The Exodus is fundamentally a story about a contest: Yahweh, whom we would now just call "God," against Pharaoh and the rest of the gods of Egypt. The prize? The trust of the Hebrew slaves (as well as any others who decide to join them, even Egyptians). Yahweh is showing Themself to be a God who is worthy of trust—one who provides, protects, cares, guides, loves. As we will see in some of these commentary notes, seeing the story in this light, as opposed to simply being about setting people free, is the key to understanding some of the harder aspects of the story. Freedom is included in God's goals, but there is more going on in addition to it.

This is my God, and I will praise Them—my father's God, and I will exalt Them! Yahweh is a warrior; Yahweh is Their name!" These words are part of a song that was raised from the far side of the sea. On the freedom side of the water, opposite of Egypt, the Hebrews followed Miriam's lead as she celebrated and thanked Yahweh God for where they were, as well as where they weren't.

God had set them free. It was wonderful. It was amazing. It seemed like it couldn't be done.

You see, the Hebrews had been enslaved in Egypt for a very, very long time. So long it was all they knew. So long that while they may have remembered the old stories of God making promises to their ancestors, they didn't have any new stories of that God showing up. So long that they didn't really know Yahweh God for themselves. In Egypt, **Pharaoh**—which means "son of Ra," the sun god—is god. He can make their lives easier or harder with just a word, like saying, "Make your bricks, but you can't have straw for them anymore."

When Yahweh God sent Moses and his brother Aaron to the leaders of the Hebrews and to Pharaoh himself, a contest began. A contest God intended to win, not to simply show off God's power, but to show the Hebrews what God's like. Yahweh God was coming to fight for Their child against the empire that kept them trapped in their suffering.

Things began fairly simply: Moses told Pharaoh, "Yahweh says, 'Let my people go.'" And Pharaoh replied, "Yahweh who? I don't know any Yahweh and I'm not letting them go."

As if to prove who was really in charge, Pharaoh made everything harder for the Hebrews. The contest was on—who would win? Pharaoh or Yahweh? We may know now that God would come through in the end. But they didn't know that then.

Historical Context—Pharaoh

We might read this story and see Pharaoh as a political figure, a head of state. But at the time Pharaoh was much more than that. Pharaoh was a god in his own right. And crucially, Pharaoh, along with the Egyptian pantheon he represented, would have been the only god the Hebrew slaves had any experience with. They had been slaves in Egypt for hundreds of years at this point, so any memories of the true God would have been legends and stories from the distant past. What good is that when the power of the gods of Egypt is seen and felt and suffered every day? This is why a contest is needed. Yahweh needs to prove Themself to a people who either don't know God at all or have only long-ago stories for reference. We, knowing the end, might see this as an unfair fight—God bullying a human. If anything, the people at the time would have put it down as an unfair fight, too, just in the opposite direction. Who is this Yahweh that They would dare challenge Pharaoh? This helps us understand why things drag on so long. It's important for the people to see that Pharaoh did not willingly allow the slaves to go free, that he fought with all his might to keep them. It's only if the most powerful figure on earth puts up as much of a fight as possible that the people will be able to see the comparable power and character of Yahweh, and choose to trust this new God instead.

Pause and ask: Have you ever wondered if God was really there, would really help you, or was really real? Have you ever felt like the Hebrews felt? Tell me about it.

Back and forth it went—Pharaoh showing his power; Yahweh showing Theirs. Well, Pharaoh's main power was to simply have power. See, every time Yahweh did something to show this was serious, these are called the plagues. Things like swarms of frogs or flies. Pharaoh would say, "Okay, you can go!" But when the plague ended, he would change his mind and refuse. Again and again this happened.

But it never happened in Goshen, the area where the **Hebrews** lived. No plague came near them. Ultimately, Yahweh won the contest. Pharaoh let the people go, and they left Egypt. God led them from there, away from the empire that had held them for so long.

God appeared, always in front of them, as a pillar of **cloud** in the daytime and a pillar of **fire** at nighttime until the people came to the Red Sea.

Meanwhile, in Egypt, Pharaoh changed his mind one last time. "What have we done?" he and his officials were saying. So he harnessed his chariot, called his troops, and they chased after the Israelites in one final, all-out display of the power of Pharaoh, son of Ra, god of Egypt.

Key Word—Hebrews
In the last story, we talked about how this word is functionally a slur for low-class, mixed-ethnic slaves and manual laborers. It did not, at the time, mean "Israelite." That's important here because the group that flees Egypt, and whom God delivers at the Sea, are said to be a "mixed multitude," including many different ethnic groups, even some Egyptians. From the very beginning of Israel as the people of God, the genetic borders are blurry, and God's ultimate goal of forming a family that includes *all* who choose to put their trust in Yahweh shines through.

Key Image—Cloud and Fire
These were common images at the time to represent the presence of a god. We touched on fire as a symbol in the last story with the burning bush, and all that symbolism applies here too. "Cloud" should probably be understood to be more like "dense smoke" than a thin wispy sort of thing floating in the sky. In this story it functions both as an unmistakable guide for the people as they flee and as impenetrable protection from the enemies pursuing them.

Key Word—*Suph*
This word has often been translated as "red," as in the "Red Sea" we know today. It more likely should be translated "reed," as in a reedy body of water. We don't know the exact location, but we can make a guess from the context. It could be a fork of the northern Red Sea close to where the Suez Canal would be today. It could be a large body of marshland, which is very common in that area. It might be used metaphorically to mean something like "end," as in "a sea at the very border between Egypt and the wilderness." What's important is that this is a sea the people can't cross. They're stuck and need God's deliverance. Knowing the exact geographic location doesn't really add anything important to that theological truth.

Historical Context—Wilderness
When the people start panicking, they say that they would have rather died back in Egypt than die in the wilderness. This isn't because they could have avoided a long, dusty walk that way. At the time, the worst fate imaginable was not to die. It was to die and be unburied, food for the scavengers. The people are saying that Moses (and Yahweh) has taken them from a bad situation to the worst possible situation.

Key Words—"See" and "Know"
As the Egyptian army closes in, the people, understandably, panic. They do not trust that Yahweh is going to deliver them; they have no faith. And yet. God's command is striking: "Be still and watch"; in Hebrew it's not too far from "Shut up and watch." This is the moment when Yahweh is going to show the world They can be trusted. The story has been building to this: the most powerful empire on earth, advancing with everything they have on one side; Yahweh God of the Hebrews on the other. It's no contest.

Today it's understandable for us to wonder about the violence of the exodus story. Was it all necessary? The reasons given for it in the story itself revolve around the words "see" and "know." God, again and again, says that all of this is so that "they [sometimes the Hebrews, sometimes Egypt, sometimes the whole world] will see/know who I am." The violence toward the Egyptians is part of this. God is showing, in the only language the people at the time would have understood, that They are trustworthy. We might prefer different methods today, and no doubt today God *would* use different methods to get the point across. But in this time and place, these were necessary parts of the point God was wanting to make.

Connections—Creation
There are echoes of the creation story from Genesis throughout the exodus story, too many for us to cover here. The important one for us right now is that the exact same words are used for God splitting the Red Sea to allow the Hebrews to cross on dry land, and for God splitting the waters in creation in order for dry land to appear. It's a hint to what the author wants us to see—God is doing more than freeing a group of slaves, God is creating a people, a family, to carry on the work that was begun in creation.

God Splits the Red Sea

As the army drew near, the people began to panic. With an army on one side and a **sea** on the other, there was nowhere to go, and they were certain they would die. "What? There aren't graves for us in Egypt? Since we're going to die either way, why'd it have to be out here in the **wilderness**?!"

But Moses told them, "Yahweh Themself will fight for you all. Just keep quiet and watch."

The pillar of cloud that had led them there moved from in front to behind, and not just behind, but between. It blocked the army from reaching them. Then Moses stretched out his hand over the sea, and Yahweh sent wind across the waters. Slowly the water parted until there were two walls of it, with a path right between.

God split the water, and as they walked through, it was as if they were being remade, no longer enslaved, but free; no longer subject to Pharaoh, but belonging to Yahweh.

The Egyptians chased them into the middle of the sea. But when all the Israelites had reached the other side, the Lord said to Moses, "Raise your hand over the sea again. Then the waters will rush back and cover the Egyptians."

Despite all of Pharaoh's power, it was God who rescued them. It wasn't that they were more powerful than Egypt and saved themselves. God is more powerful than the evil empire of injustice. God came. God saved. God fought for them. God set them free.

The Bible says that "when the people of Israel saw the mighty power that Yahweh had unleashed against the Egyptians, they were filled with awe before him. They put their trust in Yahweh."

I wonder why God did all this instead of just instantly freeing them?

I wonder what it was like to walk through the walls of water?

I wonder if this changed how the people thought about Yahweh or the gods of Egypt?

GOD PROVIDES MANNA AND WATER IN THE WILDERNESS

EXODUS 16

> **The Main Idea:** These stories give us a vivid picture of God's goodness not in some abstract, theological way, but in the very concrete act of providing for people's everyday needs. The people have just come from a place in Egypt where food and water were earned in exchange for backbreaking work. No work; no bread. One of the first lessons God hopes Their people will learn after having been set free is that a new day is here. Their God is different from Pharaoh. Yahweh gives bread from heaven, abundantly, consistently, and graciously. No work required. No earning. Just grace. That's who our God is, then and now.

God's people were newly freed from slavery in Egypt, and they began a journey through the wilderness in a dry, desert place. Since they were journeying, they weren't growing fields of food. Since they had left Egypt, they weren't right by the Nile River, so they didn't have water.

You may remember that it was also common to think a **god was only in charge of their one spot?** The gods of Egypt in Egypt, for example? Now, in this wilderness, was this Yahweh God still great? Still helpful? Still there?

Historical Context—Many Regionally Bound Gods
These stories often get told with an exasperated tone of "Ugh, those dumb Israelites, how could they *possibly* be so clueless as to not trust God? I mean, they just saw the Red Sea get parted!" And really? Fair enough. One of the Old Testament's favorite ways of describing the Israelites is as a "stubborn" and "stiff-necked" people. But their reluctance to trust might make a bit more sense than it first seems. Remember, every culture around Israel at the time was polytheistic, and the Bible introduces two revolutionary ideas about God.

First, as far as we know, Israel is the first group of people ever to worship *one* God. And second—the key idea for us right now—Israel is the only culture to believe that their God is the God of the *whole earth*. In every other culture the gods were geographically limited. The gods of Egypt, the ones Israel would have been used to, were powerful only *in Egypt*. They had no power, or at best limited power, outside the borders. So yes, Yahweh had just parted the Red Sea and set the people free. But they still had to learn that this Yahweh would be with them *everywhere*. It was revolutionary to say God is the God of the whole earth—in Egypt, in the wilderness, in the Promised Land, everywhere.

Key Word—Yahweh
The name God gives Themself is often translated "I Am." It also can mean something like "I am there" or "I will be there." It's a name both of existence, "I Am," *and* presence, "I will be there." These stories help both us and the Israelites know that God being present with us isn't a sometimes thing, but an always thing, because it's part of who God is, a part of Their very name. See the note on page 46 for more on this.

Genre—Miracle Stories
Miracle stories show up all through the Bible, and they are meant to make us say "Wow" at the power of our God. But we aren't meant to stop there, because the stories also, and always, point us to something true about who God is. In this case, we see that God's power and goodness extend throughout the world, even to the mundane details of everyday life. God isn't just about doing battle with Pharaoh in Egypt. God is about caring for God's people day-to-day in the wilderness.

People who read miracle stories like these sometimes get sidetracked into trying to explain how they happened. Is there a natural explanation for the seemingly supernatural? For this story, as an example, a favorite "natural" explanation is that there is apparently an insect that secretes a sweet, white substance that melts in the sun. The problem with this is not that it is bad to speculate about such things, but that it can distract from what the story is trying to tell us. These stories are not about how God can do magic tricks; rather, they are intended to point to who God is. In this case, God's actions show that God is one whose power and goodness extend throughout the world, even to the mundane details of everyday life. So yes, wonder away at how God accomplished providing for the people in the wilderness, but without losing sight of who that provision shows us our God is.

Could they trust this God? Should they trust this God? Or should they trust someone else?

This was the first thing God was helping them learn in the desert: to trust **Yahweh God** and not idols. How did God help them learn that? By feeding them.

In a desert place it would be harder to find food, and the people began to be hungry. They worried and whined, saying, "It would have been better to die in Egypt. In Egypt we had pots of meat; in Egypt we had all the food we wanted. Out here we are just going to starve."

So God said, "Here in the desert, I will **rain down food** for you. Each morning it will be there; go out and gather what you need for the day."

The next morning, there it was—sweet flaked food on the ground. They didn't know what it was, really. So they named it "What is it?," or **manna** in Hebrew. Whatever it was, God sent it every single day for them. And they had the food they needed.

God was **providing** for them. They could trust God. And part of how they practiced that trust was that the manna lasted only one day. Some people tried getting more for the next day (even though they were told to just take food for one day), and what did they find the next morning?

Fun Detail—Manna
It's a fun detail that the word "manna" comes from the Hebrew for "What is it?" The manna is described as sweet, and it melts away in the sun. How cool is it that God's bread from heaven comes presweetened and melts in your mouth?

Connections—God Provides
This story is one of so many in the Bible where God provides food and water for people in the wilderness. In Genesis 21, God hears the cry of little Ishmael and provides for Hagar and her son. In 1 Kings 19, God provides for Elijah when he flees from the wrath of Ahab and Jezebel. In Luke, God provides for Jesus after he is tempted, then later Jesus provides bread and fish for the crowds. In John 6 and 7, Jesus refers back to this story by saying that he is the bread of life and living water. Why do these stories keep popping up? Because providing the good things that we need, over and over again, is central to who our God is.

Worms! But as they practiced taking the day's food, they learned that God would always take care of them tomorrow.

So that was the first thing God was helping them learn in the desert: to trust Yahweh God, not idols.

The second thing God was helping them learn was how to be holy. "Holy" means "set apart or distinct." It means "unique."

What are some words that describe God?

Those words you just named make God holy—different from other things you can worship or trust. So God is holy and was inviting them to be holy, too. They could live differently than the others, especially by living in a way that matches who God is.

How did God help them learn that? Well, every day the manna came… sort of. It came six days in a row. But it didn't come at all on day seven! Instead, on day six, everyone collected double. Half was for day six; half was for day seven. On day seven, everyone rested.

I wonder what they did on rest day?

Taking a day to rest and not work was very different from what other groups around them did. But that was the point—they would be different, and even without working, they would be okay. God was helping them practice living holy—different in ways that matched God. They rested on day seven, just like God rested on day seven of the creation story.

The third thing God helped the Hebrews do was to remember.

**Fun Detail—Maggots**
When the people don't trust that the manna will show up each day and try to save some for later it ends up filled with maggots. God has a sense of humor. I mean, it could have just disappeared. Sometimes people see this as a punishment or as evidence of God's anger at the people. But God doesn't take away the next day's food; God keeps on providing whether the people trusted the previous day or not. It's not a punishment; it's a reminder. A reminder that God is inviting the people to learn to trust God's goodness, every day.

What do you think was important to remember?

God was helping them remember who God is and what God had done: God was the compassionate one who **heard** their cries in slavery. God was the powerful one who freed them. God was the caring one who fed them every day. God was the holy one who would help them live in good ways.

So to help them remember that, Moses told the people to take some of the manna and keep it in a jar. This manna stayed good, because God had told them to keep it as a reminder of **all God had done for them**.

The manna was not just food; it was a gift, a gift that helped the people learn to trust, to live holy, and to remember. It was a gift that helped them know Yahweh God more and more in their new lives of freedom.

Connections—God Hears
Exodus 16:8 tells us that Yahweh "has heard" the people complaining. We shouldn't think of this as if God were a mother about to scold her fighting children, because God "hearing" is central to the story of the Exodus. Back in chapter 3, one of the first things God tells Moses is that They have "heard" the people crying out for help, and that God has come to save them. At that point in the story, the grumbling God heard was against Pharaoh; this time it is against God. God's response is the same in both cases: to care for them. God hears the cries of people in trouble, and God responds, always, even if not always in the way we might expect.

Connections—God is…
In future conversations, this story can also help highlight how God cares, God provides, God hears, God is powerful, God is faithful and consistent, and God is always with us. These are all aspects of God's goodness; of course, they show us *how* God is good. As your kid grows, they will be able to add to their understanding of God's goodness, and how it might show up in their own life.

I wonder if kids like you helped
get the manna in the morning?

I wonder what the very first manna day was like?

I wonder what God's goodness
looked like for us this week?

THE LAW—LOVE GOD, LOVE YOUR NEIGHBOR

DEUTERONOMY 6:5

The Main Idea: The starting place for understanding the Law is relationship. It is a reflection of a relationship between Yahweh God and the newly freed and reshaping Israel, all oriented around the purpose of loving one another.

After God freed the people from enslavement in Egypt, they began a new chapter in their story together. You might title the chapter "Learning to Live Together" or "How to Become a Group Now That We're Free." Okay, these aren't very catchy titles, and maybe you can come up with a better one after you hear more of the story, but the point is the same: Now that the Hebrews were free, how could they live together in ways that matched who Yahweh, their God, was? Life together could be so *different* than in Egypt. It could be so much *better* than in Egypt, mainly because Yahweh God was so *different* from the other gods, so much *better* than the other gods.

Not only that, but their life together could work in ways that showed the world what Yahweh God was like. They could be like stars that shone out, glittering and lovely, inviting others to stop and notice the light.

Connections—"For you were slaves in Egypt"
Another phrase that keeps popping up is this one. The reason given for some of the laws is explicitly tied to the people's own experience of slavery. Unsurprisingly, these are often the laws that have to do with justice, especially economic justice and the treatment of the vulnerable. The people know what injustice feels like; they have experienced it. But now, instead of replicating that system of oppression, they are to live differently in this important respect. They will treat the vulnerable with justice. They will structure their community in ways that promote economic equity and dignity. They will live like people who remember what slavery was like.

Historical Context—Not Egypt
The Hebrews had been slaves for hundreds of years in Egypt at the time of the Exodus, which is a lot of cultural momentum. While minority communities *can* retain aspects of their distinct culture in the midst of a dominant culture, as time goes on and future generations are born and live and die in *this* culture, it becomes harder and harder to do so. The dominant culture begins to take hold more and more, shaping what life looks like and how it is lived. For many of the Hebrews, the way things worked in Egypt would have long since become simply the way things work, period. Egypt's oppressive, violent, unjust culture of slavery and domination and economic exploitation would have just been the way the world is, how it should be. But Yahweh's vision is for a new people, a distinct people who operated completely differently. Yahweh is not freeing the people to set up a culture just like Egypt but with different people in the positions of power. Yahweh envisions a whole new culture entirely, and the Law is God laying out what that culture could look like.

Key Word—Holy
Another repeated command is to "be holy," often with the added phrase "because I am holy." Today, when people use the word "holy" they often mean "moral" or "perfect" or something along those lines, but that's not actually the root of the word. The main sense of the word "holy" in Hebrew is "set apart," "distinct," or "different." Often it is used to describe a person or thing that is set apart from normal life so it can be used in religious rituals. The point is not that the thing is "moral," but that it has a specific purpose. It's not an everyday object anymore, but a special one. This fits exactly with what we are saying about the Law. The people are to be a distinct, or set-apart, people. They are to *live differently* than the culture of Egypt or Canaan or Babylon. They are to show the world a different way of living, one that reflects the character of God, because Yahweh is a God unlike all the other gods. And yes, that will include moral living, but not in a rigid, rule-based sort of way. We live in that way because it's who Yahweh is.

God led the people through the wilderness to the mountains, where they set up camp. Their leader Moses climbed the mountains, and the Bible says God's presence was like a thick cloud.

God said to Moses, "You've seen all I've done—how I freed you and you flew from Egypt like you were riding on an eagle, brought to a safe nest with me. Now, I want you all to be my people, and I'll be your God. You all will be like treasure to me, so special, so dear. And your lives as a group will be special, too."

Then God gave Moses guidelines, teachings, and rules for the people. Together they are often called "the Law," but they didn't work like laws do nowadays. In fact, we're going to call it "Life Together Teaching." Because that was the point—life together as God's super-loved people.

There are three books in the Bible that are full of details about their Life Together Teaching, so now let's read them all, mmmkay? Just kidding! Here's what you really need to know about them. They can be summed up like this:

Love Yahweh your God. Love one another.

You may feel like, *that's it?* If that's all, *why* are there three whole books of details?

The details help for the times when people don't. When they don't love God. When they don't love each other.

Key Word—Torah

For Jews, the word "Torah" is the word for the first five books of the Old Testament. While it is often translated "the Law" in English, it refers to not only the rules and regulations but the whole story of God and humans that those passages only play a part in. Many scholars prefer translations like "teaching" or "instruction" for this reason, as opposed to "Law." To our twenty-first-century minds, "Law" refers to rules that we must obey or be punished, but that isn't really what Torah is. Even the rules and regulations parts that we're talking about this week and next are best seen as contextual guidelines rather than rigid legal requirements. They are guidelines intended to help the community of God's people live together in their specific time and place in ways that reflect who Yahweh is. In other times and places, the specifics will change, not because God's character has changed, but because the cultural setting has changed. This is why Jesus seems to change aspects of the Law from time to time, sometimes in more strict ways, and sometimes in less strict ways, because he is living in a much different cultural setting.

Like, say, what if someone doesn't take care of their ox, and then their ox gets loose and hurts someone? Or what if a stone is marking the edge of somebody's land and then they decide they want more land, so they move the stone into their neighbor's land to make their own land bigger? Or what if someone from another land comes to live here and after your field of food has been picked, they want to walk through to grab leftovers and fallen bits but the field owner wants to send workers back in to pick up every last crumb?

What then, hmmmm?

These **detailed** books of Life Together Teachings came together to help the people agree on how they could respond to these situations—and so many others—in ways that would match up with who God is and being God's people. They were the ways that this group would love God and love each other in their time, place, and community.

And while we may not have to think about our ox, or the rocks that mark off the edge of land, or our harvest plans, we do get to ask, *How might* we *love God and love others in* our *time and place?*

Literary Feature—Details and Specificity
Even a cursory reading through Leviticus will highlight the level of detail and the highly specific situations these teachings address. This reminds us of the "ancientness" of the Torah, and can, understandably, be a source of confusion for interpretation. In short, how should we, now, not only read this section but connect it to our world or lives today? While there are those who lean toward "timelessness," others advocate that these are deeply time-bound, meaning that in other times and places, the specifics will change.

This is not because God's character has changed, nor the invitation for the people of God to love God and love one another. However, when the cultural setting has changed, the expression of being a community that lives in ways that match who God is will look different.

I wonder which is easier to practice: love God or love your neighbor?

I wonder who that stone-moving law or grain-picking law helped the most?

I wonder what you would want to be a Life Together Teaching for our time and place now?

YOU ASK

WHY ARE WE DEVOTING TWO WHOLE "STORIES"— BECAUSE C'MON, THESE AREN'T FULL STORIES— TO THE CHAPTERS WHERE "WALK THROUGH THE BIBLE IN A YEAR" PLANS GO TO DIE?

Fair question. Here's why:

For one thing, I hope the paraphrase will help you and your kids hear the ways these chapters are actually embedded in a story, the story of God with God's people. And second, I hope this essay will frame in a helpful way what the chapters we call "the Law" are about.

To that end, here are three things the Law is and isn't:

First:
The Law is about becoming a community that reflects God's character. It is not about individuals knowing how to be good.

This reality becomes clearer when we look at the Law in its literary context, when we read it as part of the overarching story. There is no separate section of the Bible that is "the Law." Or, at least, not how we usually mean it—the rules and principles and thou shalts and thou shalt nots and such.

Let's do some quick Hebrew translation here. It'll be painless. The Hebrew word translated "Law" is "Torah," and if you asked a Jew which part of the Hebrew Scriptures was "Torah," they'd point you to the entire first five books, what we sometimes call the Pentateuch. From a Jewish perspective, the whole story of Genesis–Deuteronomy is Torah, and the part we usually are referring to when we say "the Law" is *embedded in* that overarching story. (This is why some scholars argue that "teaching" or "instruction" might be better English translations of Torah, getting away from the purely rule-based connotations of the word "Law.")

And in that context we get a glimpse of its purpose, so let's review the story so far:

The people are freed from slavery in Egypt by a God who is, to them at least, unknown—Yahweh. Yahweh overpowers the most powerful gods and empires in the world and leads the people through the waters to freedom. It's a symbolic new birth signaling a new family, a new people of God. God then provides food and water for the people in the wilderness and leads them to Mount Sinai.

In other words, God has shown that God can be trusted to protect and provide for the people, bringing them life like any good God should. But, again, this is a new God, or at least one the people haven't known for hundreds of years, for generations. The people would be wondering: What is this God like? What does it mean to be the people of Yahweh, as opposed to being the people of the gods of Egypt? How should we live together in light of these amazing things that have happened? What does this Yahweh expect of us?

Which is why the Law, beginning with the Ten Commandments, is the very next thing that happens. It is like the founding charter, or constitution, of the people of Israel. It's the answer to the question: What should the people of Yahweh look like? And sure, individual acts and decisions matter in that, but the focus is on becoming a community that reflects the character of this God Yahweh. A family whose life together shows the world what *this* God is like.

This is why Jesus can say that the Law is summed up in love God; love your neighbor. It's not that the individual laws are unimportant. It's just that they are specific examples of what loving and representing *this* God *means* in everyday life.

Second:
The Law is contextual, set in a particular time, place, and culture. It is not timeless.

You've probably noticed that Jesus sometimes puts a very different spin on the Law when compared with the wording of Exodus or Deuteronomy. Sometimes in ways that seem more lax—like when he lets the woman caught in adultery off the hook entirely. Sometimes in ways that seem far more stringent—like when he rejects reasons for divorce that the Law specifically allowed for.

In fact, Deuteronomy, which is a repetition of the Law right before the people enter the Promised Land, sometimes puts a different spin on things than Exodus, just a couple of books earlier. If we see the Law as timeless—giving us rules that are for all times and places—then this is confusing. But it isn't if we see it for what it is—contextual.

The chapters we call "the Law" are intended to show what it would mean to be a community that reflects God's character *in that time and place and culture*. Which is inevitably going to be different, sometimes very different, than being a community that reflects God's character in *our* time and place and culture. Not because God's character has changed, but because the cultural context has changed, and so the ways we live out God's character should, too.

Third:
The Law provides guidelines to help the community think for themselves. It does not provide rules to be blindly followed.

This leads to our third thing, which is to see the Law more as guidelines than rules. The word "Law" makes us see these chapters as ironclad rules to be followed, like how we think about laws today. We aren't really supposed to *think about* the laws of our state; we're supposed to follow them. But many scholars don't think that is how the Law would originally have been read at all.

The scholar Christopher Wright says that "ancient Near Eastern lists of laws and cases functioned more as *collections of legal wisdom*, lists that would provide paradigmatic illustrations of what justice should look like, guidelines that would educate and assists judges" in doing their duty (*Exodus*, 387, italics in original). These were examples of justice that were always intended to be built upon and developed.

And this means that we can read and use the Law in exactly the same way it was always intended to be read. We can, as Christopher Wright says, "allow them to shape our overall orientation to God, our neighbors, and the wide range of life" (*Exodus*, 427). Seeing the character of God reflected in the Law, we can use it to help us think for ourselves about what it would mean to reflect God's character in *our* everyday context, even as that context is so very different from that of Exodus.

THE LAW—
FESTIVALS AND JUBILEE

EXODUS 20; 23; 31; LEVITICUS 23

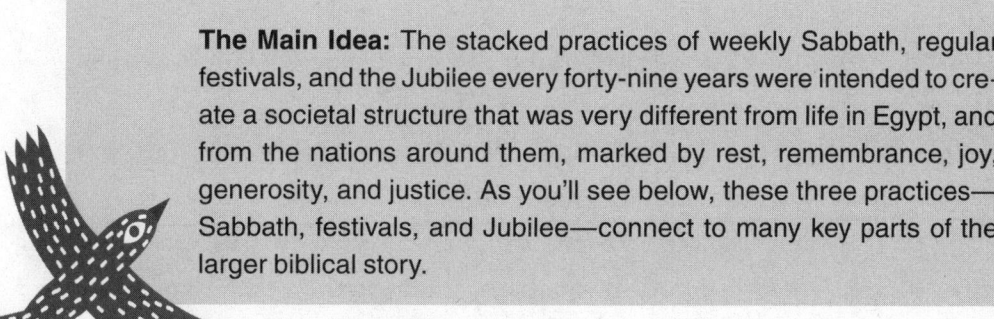

The Main Idea: The stacked practices of weekly Sabbath, regular festivals, and the Jubilee every forty-nine years were intended to create a societal structure that was very different from life in Egypt, and from the nations around them, marked by rest, remembrance, joy, generosity, and justice. As you'll see below, these three practices—Sabbath, festivals, and Jubilee—connect to many key parts of the larger biblical story.

Right now we are taking a big chunk of the Bible—three whole books!—and summing up some important things we find there. Specifically, we find God commanding the people to do three things that they never would have, never *could* have, done in Egypt. What we want to think about together is: Why?

Why would God tell the people to do these things?

Why would God tell them to... practice Sabbath?

When God first sent manna for the people in the wilderness, it came with specific directions, including this: "This is what the LORD commanded: Tomorrow will be a day of complete rest, a holy Sabbath day set apart for the LORD. So bake or boil as much as you want today, and set aside what is left for tomorrow." Every seventh day, the people stopped. They didn't collect manna at all.

And then a bit later there's a little more on how this is meant to work. Listen for who is included in this practice. Exodus 20:10 says, "The **seventh day** is a Sabbath day of rest dedicated to the LORD your God. On that day no one in your household may do any work. This includes you, your sons and daughters, your male and female servants, your livestock, and any foreigners living among you."

These few books mention **Sabbath** forty times! That's quite a lot.

So back to our big question: Why? Why would God tell them to practice Sabbath?

(Need a hint? Think about what kind of work the people did back then. Think about what work was like in Egypt. Think about what else you know about what God's like.)

Why would God tell them to... hold festivals?

See, weekly Sabbath leads to something else. Listen to this verse from Leviticus 23:4: "In addition to the Sabbath, these are the LORD's appointed festivals, the official days for holy assembly that are to be celebrated at their proper times each year."

Festivals took place throughout the year, and they were for everyone in the community, including servants and foreigners, and often involved bringing **offerings** of food. A little bit of the food was given to God, as a way to remember and act out that God gave it to them first. The rest became a meal for everyone to share together. Each festival celebrated or remembered something unique, and together they were a regular part of the year. It's similar to how we might break up the year by holidays.

So back to our big question: Why would God tell them to hold festivals?

(Need a hint? Think about what might have made them afraid and how festivals may help with that. Think about who God's people were invited to be. Would this help? How? Think about what the group would be like if they did this together year after year.)

Why would God tell them to... **have Jubilee**?

The Law—Festivals and Jubilee   77

Key Number—Seven
Another story, another seven, this time recalling the creation story as a reminder that life is not complete with only work. It is complete when the seventh day, the day of rest, is included. The sevens here show that Sabbath and Jubilee are not to be seen as add-ons or optional; they are key parts, and Israel's life as a community would be incomplete without them.

Connections—Sabbath
The Jubilee year arises right out of the concept of Sabbath. When the Law gives the Sabbath to the Israelites so that they would have rhythms of work and rest, it makes clear that this rest is also meant for the servants and even the animals. They *all* are meant to have time for rest and play. The rhythms of God's goodness are for every-body. Then, even the *land itself* is given a sabbath every seventh year. The rhythms of God's goodness aren't just for every*body*; they are for every*thing*, all of creation. Then, added on top is the Jubilee year, the year after the seventh seven, when land is to be returned to the original owner's family. How is this related to Sabbath? The logic of both is based in trusting God to give us enough. We don't need to maximize productivity to guarantee we will have enough. We can rest. We don't need to hoard more and more land to guarantee we will have enough. We can return it to its original owners. And we will have enough because of who God is. And in so doing, we will ensure that the original owners also will have enough.

Historical Context—Sacrifices
In the festival descriptions we also see sacrifices. This is a great reminder that sacrifices are not really about appeasing an angry God or addressing sin. In this case, the sacrifices are literally making the festival feast. Symbolically offering a portion of them to God is an act of remembrance and gratitude for the person they trust and who is with them. It's like inviting God to symbolically pull up a chair and eat.

Connections—The Land
When Israel enters the Promised Land, one of the first jobs the people have is to divide up the land. This process is described in the long, boring section that takes up the second half of the book of Joshua and consists of endless lists of place-names and tribes, chapter after chapter. Yes, it's boring to read, but it's actually a really important moment. It's laying out God's intention of economic justice, wherein every family would have the means to support themselves, which in that time and place meant having their own land on which to grow food and raise livestock. Jubilee is the way that intention was meant to be sustained in the real world where people fall on hard times, whether due to bad luck or bad choices. According to Jubilee, economic justice means giving families a new chance, restoring their land no matter why they lost it in the first place, so that no one person would have too much, and everyone would have enough.

Okay, we have one more command to talk about—the most super Sabbath of them all, the most festive festival of them all: Jubilee.

Jubilee was meant to happen every forty-nine years and was also known as the Freedom Year. There were lots of pieces to this. If in the past forty-eight years a family had needed to sell their land to survive, in the Jubilee year, they would get the land back. If a person had needed to become a servant because they had no money, they would be freed. Even the land would rest—no one would plant things and people would eat whatever grew on its own. How would they eat if the **land sabbathed**? It was a great big reset for the whole community.

And the question we want to talk about again is: Why? Why would God tell them to have a Jubilee every forty-nine years?

(Need a hint? Think about what might happen without Jubilee. Think about what God hoped Israel would be or do for the world. Do you see any connection between Jubilee and the **Exodus**?)

Do you know what all three of these things—Sabbath, festivals, and Jubilee—have in common? They ain't happening in Egypt. There isn't regular

---

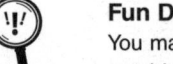

Fun Detail—Volunteers
You may wonder, *How would they eat if the land sabbathed?* Well, if you let crops go to seed independently, some portion of them will sprout on their own the next year. These non-planted crops are called "volunteers" and could have provided the people with grain while not requiring a proper planting and harvesting process.

Connections—Exodus
Right in the middle of the Jubilee laws in Leviticus 25 is this, from verse 38: "I am [Yahweh] your God, who brought you out of the land of Egypt to give you the land of Canaan and to be your God." Exodus is the reason the people would do such a ridiculous thing as give land back for free. After all, God set the people free from Egypt and set up laws intended to prevent any of them from falling back into slavery. Our God is an exodus God, one who sets people free from oppression. And that means we are a jubilee people, who do what we can, even if it's as radical today as returning land to the original owner back then, to make sure people can have life, freedom, dignity, and joy. We don't ask questions about who deserves what, or whether they brought it on themselves, because our God doesn't ask those questions of us.

rest, or collective celebrations where no one is left out, or ways to get out of the debt, slavery, or poverty built into life in Egypt. Without God's commands, the people might have just copied *now* what they were used to *then*, and that would not make them into a community that worked in ways that match God at all. God is a life-giver, a freedom-bringer, and an invites-everyone kind of God. And so God gives them life-giving, **freedom-bringing**, everybody-in kinds of practices together.

Connections—Jesus
"The Messiah set us free so that we could enjoy freedom!" Paul says in Galatians 5:1. In Luke 4, Jesus stands up in the synagogue and reads from Isaiah that he is setting the captives free and announcing the year of the Lord's special favor. While the word "Jubilee" is never used in the New Testament to describe what Jesus is doing, it's right there under the surface. Jubilee was about the forgiving of debts and restoring people to their rightful place as full members of the community of Israel, no matter what they had done to lose that status along the way. In the same way, Jesus was bringing about the ultimate restoration of all people to their rightful place as members of the family of God.

I wonder what they did together on a Sabbath day?
What do you like to do on a rest day?

I wonder what you would put on the menu
if you were in charge of a festival?

I wonder why Jubilee never happened.
You see, as best we can tell, the people never did do
that one. There is no evidence or stories that talk about
it taking place outside of these original directions.
Why not?

PART II

LIFE IN THE LAND

RAHAB

JOSHUA 2

> **The Main Idea:** The story of Rahab is about a person who might seem to be as far from a "good child of God" as you could imagine. If Israel was looking for recruits, she'd be no one's first choice. And yet all that matters is her unqualified trust in Yahweh. She and her family are accepted, no further questions asked. This is one of many stories in the Bible that remind us that however much people try to barricade the doors, God's table is for whoever wants to pull up a chair.

Our story begins with two spies who were sent to a town called **Jericho**, because the town was at the edge of the land God had promised to the people. That land's very fancy, official name? The Promised Land. Clever, eh? (Okay, it also had the name Canaan.)

These spies found their way into the city and stayed with a woman named Rahab. Within her community, Rahab was a woman who was looked down on and held no power. But these men were about to need her help in a big way.

See, the king found out about the spies and he found out they'd been with Rahab. So he ordered Rahab, "Bring the men who've come to you and been in your house. They're here to search this land out."

Rahab had a choice to make: Obey the king or help the spies?

If you were her, what would you be thinking about or feeling?

Historical Context—Jericho
The city of Jericho was one of many loosely connected, but mostly independent, Canaanite city-states in the Promised Land at the time of Joshua, and it was logical for the Israelites to target it first in their conquest of the land. It was located around a lush oasis in the midst of barren wilderness, and because of said oasis, was at a crossroads for major north-south and east-west highways.

Key Word—Prostitute
What's maybe most surprising is not Rahab's profession, but the completely matter-of-fact way the Bible tells us that the spies...uh...spent the night in her house. Ahem. The story seems to be completely uninterested in her (or the spies') morality, because what matters is her message about the people of Jericho in general, and her own faith in particular. The scholars Robert Coote and John Goldingay both tell us that her profession is included mostly to indicate her place in society. Coote says that "Rahab's prostitution is the narrator's way of addressing indebtedness, for in most instances in the ancient world prostitution alternated with debt slavery" ("Joshua," 47); in other words, for many poor women the choice was one or the other. "A marginal figure," says Goldingay, "part of society, but not really part of it" (*Joshua, Judges, and Ruth for Everyone*, 13). There's no reason to include her profession when telling this story* to kids, but if your kid *has* heard it, you can decide to what degree to explain what that particular profession entails, or to what degree you can emphasize instead what that would mean for her social standing, which is what the Bible is more interested in.

Connections—Midwives
Aka Those Lyin' Women. Rahab, like the Hebrew midwives who deceive Pharaoh when he commands that they murder baby boys, isn't entirely truthful when the representatives of the king show up (actually, she isn't at all truthful). But the author doesn't seem terribly concerned about this. In fact, it seems more like a praiseworthy thing. As John Goldingay puts it, "Like the midwives in Exodus 1 or other women in Israel's story, she does not feel obliged to tell male authority figures the truth when there is nothing truthful about the way they are behaving" (*Joshua, Judges, and Ruth for Everyone*, 13).

Fun Detail—Flax
The spies are hidden by the flax drying on the roof. This would be part of the process of producing linen material for clothing (feel free to pull some out of the closet as an object lesson if you've got some!). The presence of flax makes for an interesting hidden connection, though. Flax was harvested just before Passover was celebrated, which means this story is happening right around Passover. The sign the spies give to Rahab that will protect her house—a red rope tied to the window—echoes the lamb's blood over the doorway at Passover.

---

*   (You'll see in our paraphrase the choice to describe her status.)

Rahab responded to the king by saying, "The men were here before, but they're gone now. They left right before we closed the city gate for the night. I don't know where they came from, I don't know where they were going. But I bet if you hurry and go after them, you can catch up to them!"

So the search party went out of the city to find the spies...who were actually under piles of **flax plants** on Rahab's roof.

Once the search party left the city, the gates were shut for the night. The spies were safe for now. But how would they escape?

Rahab came to find them once the coast was clear, and she told them some very interesting information: "Everyone is scared of you all—we heard what your Yahweh God did at the **sea by Egypt**." Then she said something unexpected, given that she was a Canaanite in Jericho: "Yahweh your God is indeed God in heaven above and on earth below."

Rahab had made a choice as she hid the **spies**: to put her trust in their Yahweh God, not just as the God of their group, but as the God of all places.

As amazing as that was, though, there was still the teeny-tiny problem of how to escape the city. So Rahab explained. She could help them get out because her home was built right into the walls. They could climb out of a window and...literally...head for the hills. But she wanted their help: Would

---

Connections—Red Sea
Rahab, when she tells of the people's terror, directly quotes from the song sung by Miriam after the crossing of the Red Sea in Exodus 15:15–16. It's a reminder to the reader that God is being faithful to the promises made at the time of the Exodus. Another connection to the exodus story is that Rahab fits in perfectly with the ethnically mixed, but universally poor and marginalized, multitude that Yahweh freed from Egypt.

Connections—Spies
There's a clear contrast in this story with the story of the spies who went into the land back in the book of Numbers. (We didn't cover that here, but you may have heard it.) In fact, the situation has reversed. In Numbers, all the spies, except Joshua and Caleb, are quaking with fear because of the size and strength of the inhabitants of the land. Here, Rahab reports that the inhabitants of the land are quaking with fear because of the power of Yahweh. One of those two groups puts their fear in the right place, and it ain't the Israelites.

they promise to keep her and her family safe when the army came back to Jericho?

"Yes," they said, "We will keep you all safe." They agreed to a secret sign—a red cord to show where Rahab and her family were—so they could be protected. And with this agreement in place, the men slid out the window, down the wall, and ran to the hills, where they could hide out for a few days before returning to the Israelites.

Before we end our story, let's time-hop allll the way to **Jesus'** birth.

One way writers told a biography—someone's life story—was to list their ancestors, their family from the past. And when the gospel writers went to tell Jesus' biography, they did this, too. The list is called a genealogy. It can be a bit dull to read, but it did an important job: It told readers and listeners why this person was important, based on where they came from.

Jesus' genealogy includes great people, like kings. But it also has some weird stuff. First, it includes some women when the lists were usually all men; and second, well, take a guess.

It includes Rahab.

She's not family! She's not even from the Israelites! She's a Canaanite! And she's not important or powerful. She's the opposite. What's she doing on this list?

It comes back to what she decided as she hid those spies in the flax: She would trust Yahweh God as her God. Anyone can be part of God's people, because joining isn't about anything other than who you trust.

Connections—Jesus

Rahab makes another appearance in our Bible, in the New Testament, when Matthew makes a point of including a certain Canaanite prostitute in the genealogy of Jesus. You can't get much more a part of the family of God than that! (Yes, she also shows up in the books of Hebrews—which says she was saved by her faith, and James—which says she was saved by her works—but that's not a debate we need to get into today!)

I wonder what Rahab told her family after the spies had left the city?

I wonder when the search party decided to give up and go back to Jericho?

I wonder what the spies told their leader, Joshua, or their families when they got back?

THE NO-FIGHT BATTLE

JUDGES 6

> **The Main Idea:** The story of Gideon is one of a preposterously powerful enemy—so numerous, they swarm like locusts—against a comically weak Israel—a handful of men who sneak out of the hills where they have been hiding, "armed" with nothing but torches and trumpets. God comes through, but not because of the might of the Israelites, or the power of Gideon's leadership, but because that's who our God is. No matter the enemy, God is with us and will save us. Believing that is the heart of what putting trust in Yahweh is.

God's people were living in the land God had promised them. It was a great land, and even the fact that they lived there was a sign that God kept promises. Except, as we begin this story, things are not so great. They're awful.

Despite living in a land that meant God kept promises, God's people had been ignoring God for a long time. They'd done enough ignoring that they'd forgotten who they were, which led to acting in ways that didn't match who God was at all, which of course always meant people were getting hurt by those actions.

There were also enemies who would come to fight them, attack their land, or even move in and live there, too. One of these enemy groups was the

Midianites, who would raid their homes and steal their food; the people were starving.

And the Bible says this little phrase, "The Israelites cried out to Yahweh God for help."

Imagine you're God right now. You've told the people, suuuuper clearly, that trusting you leads to life. Now, they've got no life because they have not trusted, but here they are asking for help. What would you do? Why?

Here's what God did do—not just this time, but again and again—God showed up.

God came to a man named **Gideon** and said, "Mighty hero, **Yahweh God is with you!**"

Historical Context—Midian
The Midianites were not actually residents of the land of Canaan. They were desert nomads from east of the Jordan River. This story takes place when there was something of a power vacuum in Canaan itself, allowing the Midianites to make regular raids over the river, taking what they wanted from the overmatched Israelites. Of special note to the author, apparently, since he mentions them several times, are the Midianites' camels, which were not native to Canaan.

Key Word—Jerubaal
Gideon has two names through the story. Most likely the one that appears partway through—Jerubaal—was his given name. It means something like "Baal Fights" (as in "the god Baal fights for his people") and is a clue that Gideon's parents weren't exactly loyal to Yahweh alone. In the story, that name is repurposed to mean that Gideon is one who fights against Baal. And Gideon is given a new name that is from the Hebrew verb for "cut down," as in how Gideon cuts down the poles used to worship pagan gods. One of the key questions the Bible is asking is "Which God are you trusting and what are they like?" These cultures assumed that there were multiple gods, and the Bible is comparing and contrasting Yahweh with these other gods. Gideon comes from a family that trusted Baal, but he chooses to switch his allegiance to Yahweh alone.

Connections—Call of Moses
The moment when God approaches Gideon has a lot of similarities with how God calls Moses. There's fire. There's skepticism on the part of the human. There's bargaining and objections. John Goldingay writes, "As was the case with Moses, God determines to use someone who is a failure, without obvious potential and without religious insight, because God's using someone does not depend on that person's leadership qualities or spiritual insight" (*Joshua, Judges, and Ruth for Everyone*, 109).

Let me tell you something. At this moment Gideon is far from a mighty hero. He's a hiding zero. Literally, he's hiding out trying to work with some grain and not get it stolen. And he seems to have some thoughts and feelings about Yahweh God at the moment, because he replies with a question that many of us feel when things are hard and sad and awful.

"If God is with us, why have all these terrible things happened? We've been told stories from the past about all God has done. But now? Yahweh God has abandoned us."

Bold answer, isn't it? And God's reply is, maybe, just as bold:

"Go in the strength you have and save Israel out of Midian's hand. Am I not sending you?"

This began a back-and-forth between Gideon and God. God kept saying that They would be with Gideon. And Gideon, for his part, kept trying to do something like get out of it, or, if that was not possible, to be sure it really was God. Gideon **asked for signs**, and God gave them to him, not just once, but three different times.

So Gideon gathered an army to take on the Midianites, trusting God's promise to be with them. He gathered more than **thirty thousand** men

Connections—Bargaining and Faith
Gideon is one of many characters in the Bible who bargain with God and doubt God in ways that seem far from "faith." And yet God uses him anyway. John Goldingay writes helpfully on this topic: "Gideon's action points to another Old Testament assumption. Its attitude to doubt is that what ultimately matters is not whether you are doubting or believing in God but whether you are doubting or believing in the real God. It's okay that Gideon is doubting Yahweh; the important thing is that it is Yahweh he is doubting, not Baal" (*Joshua, Judges, and Ruth for Everyone*, 113).

Key Number—Thousand
As is usually the case in the Bible, numbers are symbols. The sizes of the armies here, in the tens of thousands of soldiers, would be utterly preposterous from a historical perspective, where armies tended to be in the hundreds or maybe thousands at the most. The Hebrew word for "thousand" can also mean "clan" or "unit," meaning Gideon's army started with thirty-two "units," not thirty-two thousand. The point is not the actual number, so much as the smallness compared with the size of the Midianites' army.

together, ready to send Midian packing. Only, God had other ideas. God had Gideon shrink down the army. Then, God had Gideon shrink it down again! And not just by a little bit—there were just three hundred fighters in the end.

I imagine Gideon is wondering if God will *really* be with them now. Because if not, they're surely going to lose.

Not only was the army now tiny, but their battle plan was…unique, to say the least. They didn't bring weapons to the fight. They brought **horns**, and each man had a clay jar with a **torch** in it.

What ideas do you have for a non-weapon to use in a battle? What would you bring and how would you win (e.g., "I'd bring rubber chickens and the squeaking would annoy them into surrender")?

In the middle of the night, the three hundred men snuck into the Midianite camp. They broke into three groups, spread out, and waited for Gideon's signal. Then it happened.

**Fun Detail—Drinking Like a Dog**
One of the ways Gideon pares down the army in the biblical text is by watching whether the soldiers drink by lapping water from cupped hands or by lowering their face to the water. If you're like me, you've heard sermons about how the way the soldiers drink tells us which ones are more watchful, or better soldiers, or some such thing. But the whole point of the story is that God is making sure it's crystal clear to all involved who is responsible for victory…and it ain't the soldiers. If anything, it would make more sense for God to choose the most bumbling and clumsy men to make up the army. This is just an arbitrary way to whittle down the numbers so that God's point is clear.

Key Image—Fire
The first sign God gives to Gideon to show that this bizarre message is truly from God is to burn up some food with fire. Fire, as always in the Bible, is a symbol of God's presence. It's a call back to the burning bush, and the pillar of fire at the Red Sea, and a foreshadowing of the time many years down the road when God will consume the offering of Elijah in the contest with the prophets of Baal.

**Fun Detail—Torches and Trumpets**
The army that Gideon ends up leading doesn't even bring swords to the battle. They bring torches and trumpets. Talk about putting your trust in Yahweh to the test! But they don't need swords, because Yahweh can bring them victory without violence.

Gideon's group blew their horns and broke their jars. The other two groups followed and did the same. As the massive noise surrounded the camp from every direction and the fires cast shadows everywhere, the Midianites were shocked. They panicked and ran about every which way in confusion, fighting each other or fleeing the camp, until…

The battle was over.

Gideon's army won, and they didn't even fight. This began a time of peace and goodness for God's people that lasted…until they forgot or ignored God (**again**). And then they did stuff that made life hard and things got bad (again). And then they cried out to God for help (again). And God would hear, and come, and help, and be with them. Always.

 Connections—Cycle of Faith and Unfaith
This is part of an ongoing cycle in the book of Judges and in the Bible more broadly. Israel calls out to God. God saves Israel. Israel trusts God. Things go well. Israel stops trusting God. Things stop going well. Israel calls out to God. Repeat. Throughout, there is a contrast between the faithlessness of the people, who keep forgetting the good things God has done for them, and the faithfulness of Yahweh, who keeps coming through when the people call out, even if, as is the case here, the people don't repent and turn back to Yahweh until after the deliverance comes.

I wonder why God shrunk the army?

I wonder if it matters that they won the battle with instruments instead of weapons?

I wonder if you've ever felt like God was asking you to do something, like Gideon?

GOD SPEAKS TO YOUNG SAMUEL

1 SAMUEL 3

> **The Main Idea:** Yahweh is a God who speaks to people, a relational God who wants to be present with us and partner with us. One important aspect of this is that God's speaking is about more than our one-on-one interaction. God speaks with a purpose, inviting Samuel into a lifetime of interaction and action, experiencing God's light and then bringing it into the world. When God speaks, new beginnings come into being.

This is the story of a kid like you learning to hear from God. His name was Samuel, and even though his experience will not be just like yours, it's helpful as we wonder together about how God speaks to people.

Samuel was learning to serve God and had a teacher, an older man named Eli, who loved God very much, and who helped Samuel learn about the work he did helping in the tabernacle (which was a bit like a church, if that church was a really fancy tent you could take down and put back up again). One unique thing about the process was that Samuel and Eli both lived there.

At this point in the story of God's people, there weren't many experiences of hearing from God. The Bible says it was a rare thing. Which made what happened one night so unusual. In the middle of the night—the part of night so dark the tabernacle **lights** could still be seen burning—Samuel was asleep when he heard someone say his name: "Samuel!" He woke up and went to Eli, thinking Eli had called him. Who else could it have been anyway?

"I didn't call you," Eli said. "Go back to bed." So Samuel went back to his own room, lay back down in his bed, and was just getting cozy under his covers when... "Samuel!"

The Voice again. Off with the covers, up from the bed, and back over to Eli's room.

But again, Eli said, "I didn't call you. Go back to bed."

What was going on? Was Eli tricking him? Was there somebody else hiding in the tabernacle?

Back to bed again. The Voice, again. "Samuel."

This time, when Samuel returned, Eli realized what was happening. Eli knew God very well. So Eli wondered if God was speaking to Samuel.

Do you think God speaks to people? Why or why not?

Eli told Samuel what to do: "The next time you hear your name, say, "Speak, **Yahweh**, for your servant is listening."

I imagine Samuel walking back to his bed, practicing his response over and over, so he was ready: "Speak, for your servant is listening." "Speak, for your servant is listening." "Speak, for your servant is listening."

Back to bed. The Voice again: "Samuel!"

And Samuel said, "Speak, for your servant is listening." Wouldn't you know? The Voice was God. What do you think it sounded like?

God had a message for Samuel. See, Eli's sons had been doing some really harmful things, and Eli wasn't stopping them. God cares a lot about people being hurt, especially by more powerful people. So God was upset, and was going to step in to stop things.

When morning came, Eli asked Samuel what God had said to him. Uhhh...with such a hard message, Samuel wasn't sure he wanted to share.

If you were Samuel in this situation—what would you be thinking or feeling?

Key Word—Light
Light is a very common symbol in the Bible for God's presence, and the help God's presence offers (like when God's word is described as "a light for [our] path" in Psalm 119:105). When the story tells us that the light in the sanctuary had not yet gone out, on one level it's telling us what time this story happened: It was still night. On another level, though, it is giving us more important information: Even though a word from God was rare, and the people were therefore in darkness, God hadn't abandoned Israel entirely. God's presence was still there, even if it was just a little lamp flickering in the night, and God was preparing to do something new.

Key Word—See
A theme throughout this story is sight. The people as a whole can't see the word of God in verse 1. Eli the priest cannot see. God speaks to Samuel while it is still night. Then Eli "sees" that God is the one speaking. All of these could be just ordinary descriptive details in the story. But they're more than that. They are giving us clues about the bigger picture of what is going on. Israel has lost the ability to see God, to see what God is up to, and to see how they could join in, at least in part because their leaders have lost that ability. God speaking to Samuel is about more than an interaction between one boy and God; it's about restoring sight to God's people.

Fun Detail—Yahweh
On the third time that Samuel comes in, the priest Eli "sees" what is happening and gives the boy instructions. The next time the voice calls out, Samuel is to say, "Speak, Yahweh, for your servant is listening." But when Samuel responds to the voice he says something slightly different, "Speak, for your servant is listening." He drops God's name. It's a fun little detail showing that Samuel really didn't know God at the beginning of this story, that Samuel's preexisting faith or holiness or any characteristic of his own are irrelevant.

Historical Context—Scorn
If you read this story from a Bible, you find that the chapter before this one makes sense of the harsh message God gives to Samuel. Eli's sons are engaged in corrupt and oppressive practices toward the people who come to worship at the sanctuary. Their actions—abusing their position of authority for their own gain—are the equivalent of "scorning" God, as verse 13 tells us. The word can also mean "showing contempt for" or even "damning" something. When those who are supposed to represent God abuse that position, it's the equivalent of *damning God*, and God will not allow it to go on forever. Consistently, the Bible saves its harshest words not for the "worst sinners" (whatever that might mean), but for leaders whose unjust actions lead people away from God. This state of affairs needs to end, and God speaking to Samuel is the start of a new era.

Eli's love for God was bigger than his concern about **the message**, so Eli insisted Samuel share, and he did. Eli accepted what he heard, leaning into his trust in God.

As for Samuel? This was the first time he heard from God, but it would not be the last. And just like God spoke to Samuel, God still speaks. We don't usually hear a voice out loud like Samuel did; God often speaks in other ways. God speaks to us as we pray, through the Bible, inside our minds, through music, in nature, when we're with others who love and trust God (like how Samuel had Eli). Speaking of Eli, God gives us adults to help us practice hearing from God. It took them a few tries, and that's often true for lots of people. But God speaks, not just to important people or powerful people, but to ordinary people, and kids like Samuel, and you.

Connections—The Prophets
Samuel's calling has some similarities to the call stories of Moses, Jeremiah, Isaiah, and other prophets. And, as is true in those cases, this word from God is coming at a time of dire need. The pattern of the people forgetting what God has done and who God is, and then needing to be called back, happens time and time again. Each time, God is ready with a new beginning for whoever chooses to listen and return.

I wonder how often Samuel heard from God?

I wonder how many different ways God "speaks" to people?

I wonder how we know if it's really God or not?

THE PEOPLE WANT A KING

1 SAMUEL 8–13

> **The Main Idea:** God listens to people's requests, concerns, and ideas even when they're off base or just plain bad. God doesn't *always* act the way people want, but remarkably, sometimes God *does*. It's a striking part of this story that the one who is outraged by the people's request, and what that request says about their inner thoughts and commitments, is not God but Samuel. God seems to meet the people's desire for a king with a shrug and goes along with it, even while knowing that it isn't a good idea. God takes us seriously, and God knows that part of partnering with us humans is working with and through the mistakes we make.

As God's people settled into their life in the land, they began to notice a few things. For example, they noticed that enemies often invaded, making things very hard. They also noticed that these enemies were led by kings, while Israel had no human king.

They also forgot a few things. They often forgot how Yahweh God had taken care of them, or promised that trusting God was the best path to life. This was especially common when the people felt afraid, which I bet you can understand. That's when they most wondered if God would really be there, and what if God wasn't, and would they be okay?

What about you? When you feel afraid, is it easy or hard to trust that God is with you? Why?

It was during a time of fear when not one, but two big enemies kept threatening them, that the people came to Samuel, the judge of Israel. They said, "You're getting old. Your sons who have become judges are not good like you are—we can't have them running things. Here's what we want: Instead of judges, we want a king, **like all the other nations** have."

Like all the other nations? But the whole point was to be different from the other nations. They were supposed to be holy, and that's what "holy" means–set apart, or unique.

This was a huge, bold request—replacing Yahweh God as king with a human king instead. The request left Samuel feeling discouraged and sad, and so Samuel went to talk things over with Yahweh God.

Literary Feature—Irony
A part of the people's request for a king is noting the ways in which Samuel's sons do not follow in their father's footsteps. They are described in ways that call our minds back a few chapters to how Eli the priest's sons are described. Both sets of sons are abusing their father's position of power for their own gain. The people don't want Samuel's sons to take charge; they want a king instead. The irony here is that by setting up a monarchy, they are putting themselves in the position where they will be stuck with future bad sons.

Key Word—Like the Nations
The people's rationale for wanting a king is simple: They want to be like all the other nations. I mean, who ever heard of a nation without a king? For someone who has paid attention to Israel's story, these words are tragic, a complete rejection of the whole purpose God has for Israel from the beginning: to be a holy nation, *different* from the other nations with that very difference being the way in which Israel would *bless* the other nations. Scholars note that Samuel's warnings about what a king will inevitably do are very close to the way the Canaanite kings operated historically. In other words, the people would get exactly what they wished for—not a military commander to lead them to victory after victory, but the injustice and oppression that all kings bring with them.

Key Word—Justice
The word "justice" keeps showing up in this story. Samuel "judges" Israel, and we are told he "administers justice." But then his sons pervert justice instead, and the people want a king as a result. Then Samuel uses the word again to warn of the behavior of kings, telling them exactly what "justice" they will get from a king. The king's justice will not be just at all. The author is wanting us to see that Yahweh, and only Yahweh, is the source of true justice.

Now, the Bible does not tell us as much about how God felt, just Samuel. So what is your guess? How do you think God felt about this request?

God told him, "Give them what they've asked for. They aren't actually rejecting you, you know. They're rejecting me as their king. It's not like this is the first time. They've done this over and over—ever since **Egypt**! They see the other gods and they trust them instead of me.

"So do what they've asked, but also, warn them: This won't go well at all. Be sure they hear from you a reminder of what a king will be like."

When Samuel talked to the people again, he did warn them. Or at least he tried. "A king will make all your sons soldiers and workers! He'll make all your daughters do palace jobs! He'll take **10 percent** of what you grow just to enjoy himself or give to the important people who work for him, and won't share it with you at all. I'm telling you—this is how it will be with a king, and

Connections—Exodus
God tells Samuel to emphasize the serious downsides to the people's plans. Their sons will be sacrificed to the king's military ambitions and building projects. And the words Samuel uses—"chariots," "slaves"—are intentionally meant to bring to mind Pharaoh in the exodus story. Whether it's an Egyptian pharaoh or an Israelite king, the end result of monarchy will be the same: "You will be slaves." The people will in this sense be choosing to go back to Egypt.

Connections—Exile
The language of Samuel's warning sounds much like the words the prophets will use to warn of the coming exile. In other words, the judgment of exile hundreds of years into the future is the inevitable result of setting up a human king. The king is, after all, nothing but an idol, promising the power and security the people feel they lack. Instead of trusting God's promise that they will be okay, they want a powerful king—preferably tall and handsome to look the part—whom they can look to for comfort. But while idols promise life, they inevitably fail to come through.

Key Number—10 percent
Samuel warns that the king will take a "tithe" of all they have. This is an intentional reference to the tithe the people are supposed to offer to God in certain festivals and sacrifices. It's one of the ways they are replacing God with a human king. They'll be giving 10 percent either way; it's just that one way is voluntary and the other by force. There's another key difference: When a king takes his tithe, it all goes into the royal storehouses. When the Bible describes the tithe the people bring to God it's as part of a celebratory feast that the people themselves get to share in.

when I'm right and you're sorry, God isn't going to bail you out from your own choice and its **consequences**."

Then it was time. Time for them to think about this warning and decide what to say back.

It was a chance. A chance to remember that Yahweh God was a trustworthy king, and being different from the nations was their actual job. It was a chance to change their minds.

"Even if you're right about all of that, we want a king! We want someone to go before us in battles!" they said.

Now it was God's turn to decide what to say back. *What would you say if it was your decision?*

God **listened** to the people. Not only did God let them have a king, God even helped Samuel pick a good man, named Saul, to be the first one. Saul had the potential to be a good king if he trusted Yahweh as he ruled. And Samuel reminded the people: This could work, even if it isn't what God wanted for you

---

Your Kid Asks—If God knew it would go bad, why did God say yes?
A recurring biblical theme is the genuine power God has given to people, and that partnering with God is always, only, by choice. When the people have decided they don't want to listen, God still listens. Sometimes I say to kids, "God has given power to people, and even if they use it in not-good ways, God doesn't take it back."

What's more, God's warning carries a big "if" with it (as is often the case). "This will go badly if you trust your king like a god or make your king an idol. This could be okay if your king, and you, trust me through it." God isn't going to be the cause of the negative consequence; God simply knows what God knows about how kings (and their power-grabbing, self-serving, militaristic ways) can't give the people the life they promise.

Connections—God Listens to Us
Other stories that show God listening (and at times God even changing God's mind) include: Abraham bargaining for Sodom (see Gen. 18); Moses asking God not to destroy the people after the golden calf incident (see Exod. 32); Jesus calming the storm (see Mark 4); and Jesus healing the Gentile woman's daughter (see Matt. 15).

all, if you will still trust God and not idols. If you will follow God's ways, not the ways of the **nations nearby**.

So Saul became king, and the years of being led by judges ended. Still, God's dream for the world never changed, and God's invitation to the people to be part of making it come true stayed open in case they wanted to say yes.

Connections—Solomon
The things Samuel warns will happen when a human king is on the throne are not empty threats. In 1 Kings 10–11, the reign of King Solomon is described in terms that closely mirror Samuel's warnings. And this was during what was in some ways the golden age of the monarchy in Israel! God is not warning the people about individual "bad guys"; God is giving them insight into what *always* happens when power is concentrated in one person or group.

I wonder how the people decided who got
the job of telling Samuel their decision?

I wonder why the people had trouble believing
they didn't need a king?

I wonder why God let them have
what they asked for?

ANOINTING DAVID TO BECOME KING

1 SAMUEL 16

The Main Idea: God makes a habit of choosing to work through unlikely people. This story is one of the few that give us a clear reason why. While humans decide things based on external characteristics like age, height, beauty, or personality, God looks at the heart, particularly the degree to which our hearts are committed to trusting and following God alone.

Our story starts during Israel's first time of being ruled by a king. It was going…poorly. Once the first king, Saul, had power, his potential to be a king who trusted and followed God seemed to be covered up by his desire to get his way and be in charge. He didn't know God, and he didn't care to get to know God.

Back when Israel first asked for a human king instead of God as king, the prophet Samuel had warned them, "When this all goes bad (and it will) and you don't like it (and you won't), God isn't going to stop the consequences of your own choices."

And here they were.

So…would God just leave them to suffer the consequences? That would be fair.

But God cares more about being faithful than fair. Even though God wasn't the one who created the trouble, God wasn't going to abandon Their precious people.

Samuel, who had first anointed Saul, was terribly sad about how it was turning out. God, who had first picked Saul, was terribly sad as well. But the time had come to let go of the hope that Saul would be a good king. Maybe there could be another king, a king who might trust God.

And so God asked Samuel to go find the next king and anoint him, sending him to Bethlehem to find a man named Jesse. One of his sons would be the second king.

As Samuel began to meet the sons of Jesse, he could not help but notice: These were strong, tall, good-looking men. They looked, well, like kings, each one of them! Samuel met the **first son** and thought, "Well, this is it!" Except then he heard God say, "Don't get caught up in his height and his appearance;

Connections—Lying
When you read the full account in the Bible, you find Samuel frightened that King Saul will get word of what he's up to (it's never a good idea to anoint a new king while the old king is still living!). So God gives him a simple plan: Lie. Or, at least, give a highly misleading account of your plans. It reminds us of the Hebrew midwives of the Exodus story who lie to Pharaoh to protect the baby boys, or of the spy Rahab lying to the Canaanite king to protect the spies. There's a pattern here: God seems not to be too worried about lying in matters of life and death to kings who have forfeited their right to the truth through their own violent actions.

Historical Context—Eldest Sons
This is one of many biblical stories where God passes over the eldest son in a culture where birth order mattered quite a lot. Jacob, Joseph,* Moses, and now David are all youngest sons. That isn't the only way God subverts expectations in this story. The expectation was that the king would be an impressive figure, one that reassures the people of their own safety and security, that they are in good hands. It's the role of an idol, in other words, and unsurprisingly God wants no part of it.

---

*   (Joseph is technically second to youngest and Benjamin is the very youngest, but Joseph's narrator would like us to let that slide, mmmkay?)

I've rejected him. I don't **see** things the way you see them. People judge by outward appearance, but I look at the **heart**."

As Samuel met the others, one at a time, he kept hearing God's voice saying, "No, not him." Again and again, until he'd met seven sons and heard seven no's.

What was going on?

"Are these all your sons?" Samuel asked.

"No," Jesse answered, "there's one more. The youngest is off with the herds."

"Send for him right away," Samuel said, "We'll wait to eat until he comes, too."

Eventually the youngest, named David, arrived from **shepherding** in the fields, likely with his hair stuck to his head by sweat, drying his hands on his robes from a quick dunk in a stream in an attempt to wash up.

Key Word—See

This story, like the story of God calling the boy Samuel, hinges on seeing: who can see and what they can see. When Samuel was a boy it was Eli the priest who couldn't see. Now, Samuel himself is the one who can't see what God is up to, but he at least listens to what God tells him. In an image-obsessed culture such as ours, it's an important reminder that in God's eyes what matters is not the outward appearance but whether or not our hearts are committed.

Key Word—Heart

In Ancient Israel the heart was not the place of emotion like we often think of it today. Instead, it was seen as the place for decision-making, will, commitments, and understanding—almost like how we would see the brain. This matters because in this story, God looking at the heart is not saying that God sees David as "a good person" in the vague sense we might mean if we said someone "has a good heart." God is seeing that David is fully committed to Yahweh and not turning to idols.

Connections—Jesus

David is shepherding the sheep when Samuel comes to anoint him king. The image of a shepherd was fairly common in describing kings at the time. To our ears, we might hear echoes of Jesus being described as a good shepherd. This is just one of many ways the New Testament describes Jesus as being like David, just more so.

"This one," God told Samuel. "I've picked him." So Samuel took some olive oil he'd brought and poured it on David's head, anointing him with the oil as a sign of God's choice and his future role as king of Israel.

With **eight** brothers to choose from, the youngest one would have been guess number eight for anyone trying to guess God's choice. But God chooses unlikely people, inviting them to say yes.

Have older kids? You might add: Now, here's an interesting thing. If you fast-forward in David's story, two things are true at the same time. He did trust only Yahweh God. And he did some really terrible things. Listen to God's words from earlier again: "Don't get caught up in his height and his appearance; I've rejected him. I don't see things the way you see them. People judge by outward appearance, but I look at the heart." Keeping in mind how David made quite a few bad choices, what do you think these words might mean? There's no right or wrong answer here.

Key Number—Eight
You thought I'd say seven again, didn't you? This eight is meant to be ironic. Samuel looks at seven sons—surely his job is complete, right?—but then God tells him to look at one more. David isn't just a youngest son, he's coming from out of left field, an outsider even.

I wonder if David wanted to be king or not?

I wonder if we can think of other unlikely people God invited from the Bible or other times?

I wonder what makes a person unlikely? Back then? Nowadays?

ELIJAH, THE WIDOW, AND THE LAST CUP OF FLOUR

1 KINGS 17

> **The Main Idea:** Elijah is in a pretty terrible situation: on the run from the king and queen who want to kill him, living in isolated places and depending on birds to bring him food, suffering through the drought and famine that have consumed the land. But Elijah knows that Yahweh is a God who brings life, and so he trusts God and invites the Canaanite widow he meets to trust Yahweh, too. They both find that God cares for us, giving us all we need even when circumstances look as bleak as can be.

Elijah was a prophet, someone who receives messages from God that need to be passed on.

On the upside, you receive messages *from God*. On the downside, the message is for a person who doesn't want to hear it. These messages were often for the leaders, warning them that they were using their power to harm, instead of using their power in ways that fit with what God is like. And often, the leaders would get angry about or flat out ignore what the prophet shared.

In Elijah's time the people were struggling to trust God and not Baal, the rain god of the Canaanites. In this part of the world, it doesn't rain all that much, and because water is so vital, it was tempting to believe that doing certain rituals certain ways would make it certain that rain would come. And

Baal promised that was how it worked. The people could control what happened if they did it just right, and the water would arrive. Baal was promising life.

How had this happened to God's people, this trust in other gods? It was because of King Ahab, who turned from God to idols, and when he married Princess **Jezebel**, that made it all worse. Together, they led the people far from God, all while bringing other gods and goddesses to Israel who were not at all like Yahweh. They were demanding and fickle, ungenerous and violent.

The people were in a drought—a time without rain—because Baal could not actually send the rain.

And Elijah's first message to them was this: There won't be rain until you turn back from these paths that have led you so far from God.

As the drought raged on, there was less and less food. Everyone felt the weight of it. During this time God sent Elijah to a woman who lived with only

---

 Historical Context—Baal
Baal was one of the chief gods of the Canaanites, as you can tell from his name, which means "Lord" or "Master." In a geographic region entirely dependent on rain for crops to grow, Baal was unsurprisingly both the god of storms and the god of life. A drought, therefore, is not some random punishment brought by God on Ahab for not being good. It's a direct confrontation of Baal's power. It's God setting up a contest. "If you think Baal is the one who brings rain and life, let me show you his powerlessness instead." God is inviting the people, as Elijah makes clear, to recognize that Yahweh, and Yahweh alone, is the source of life.

 Historical Context—Ahab and Jezebel
Ahab was the king of Israel when this story takes place. He was not a good guy. Close to the top of the list of why, at least from the perspective of the biblical writers, was that he didn't trust Yahweh alone. Instead, he acted like kings often do, making political alliances with the stronger nations around him to try to protect himself. In his case, this took the form of marrying the daughter of one of the Canaanite nations to the north. Jezebel came with her own gods, and she quickly made sure that worshipping those gods was integrated into normal Israelite practice. It wasn't so much that they were worshipped instead of Yahweh, just alongside Yahweh, as if Yahweh were just one of many gods. Elijah has some harsh words for Ahab and Jezebel, and much of his life is spent on the run from them as a result.

her son, saying, "Go to **Zarephath**, and stay there. I've instructed a woman to give you the food that you need during your stay."

Elijah **found her** while she was out collecting sticks.

"Would you please make me something to eat?" he asked her.

"While I wish I could, the fact is, these sticks are going to light one last fire, that will cook one last loaf of bread, using the very end of my flour and oil. My son and I will eat it, and then there will be nothing left."

"Don't be afraid. Take your sticks home for the fire. Make some bread and bring it to me, then make some for yourself. Because Yahweh God of Israel says that the flour in the jar and the oil in the bottle won't be gone until the day Yahweh God brings the rain back to the land."

Now the Bible tells us only that she went home and made the bread for Elijah.

But that means she had an entire walk back to her house. All the time mixing the flour and oil, shaping the dough. The minutes while it baked in the heat.

Key Word—Zarephath
As the story progresses, Elijah is told to flee to a place called Zarephath. What we might miss (unless your knowledge of ancient geography is slightly better than mine!), but the original readers definitely wouldn't have, is that Zarephath is in the same region that Jezebel came from. It's Canaanite territory, in other words, where the gods of the Canaanites were worshipped. Elijah is taking the fight into enemy territory here by showing Yahweh's power in a place where gods like Baal and Asherah were supposed to reign. It makes it all the more significant that the widow recognizes Yahweh as the true God at the end of the story. Elijah has been rejected in Israel, but finds faith among the Gentiles.

Key Word—Widow
The widow that Elijah meets, it's important to note, is not an Israelite. She is from the territory of Baal. She is, in other words, pretty much the opposite of who a reader might expect to help Elijah. She is powerless, as widowed women always were in the ancient world. She's so poor she and her son are at death's door. She is a pagan. But none of that matters to God. Yahweh can bring life to anyone who puts their trust in God, even a woman like this.

What if this was some sort of trick? What if she was making a terrible mistake? What if this was the last of her food and she was giving it away? What if there wouldn't be enough for them after all?

What if Yahweh God really saw her? Really would make this small pile of flour and tiny drizzle of oil last and last?

What if God really cared, and she would be okay? While Baal was failing to give life day after rainless day, Yahweh God was providing, **scoop after scoop, drizzle after drizzle.**

Until the day the sky, too, began to drizzle, then drip, and the land began to drink, and the grain began to grow again.

Connections—Jesus

Elijah's story, and miracles, have several echoes in the stories the gospels tell about Jesus. Usually, the gospel writers are showing how Jesus exceeds the miracles of Elijah. Jesus also goes out into the wilderness and is provided with food miraculously (see Matt. 4). He multiplies bread for thousands, not just three (see Matt. 14). Jesus goes and meets a pagan woman, asks her for water, and then brings her to believe in the God of Israel (see Mark 7). He raises to life the son of a widow (see Luke 7). He reaches beyond the people of Israel, finding faith among the Gentiles, and even references this story in Luke 4, proclaiming that his ministry is like that of Elijah in this way. Jesus is God continuing on the story of Israel and Elijah, bringing that story to completion. It's not something entirely new.

I wonder what kind of bread you'd want
her to make you?

I wonder what Elijah and this unnamed woman
thought of this situation as it continued on?

I wonder why God helped Elijah through
another person's action?

GOD'S STILL, SMALL VOICE

1 KINGS 19

> **The Main Idea:** There are times, like for Elijah in the preceding story, when things are going great. There are times, like for Elijah in this story, when everything seems to be falling apart. God is with us in both. Sometimes God is with us in power that causes us to stand back amazed. But often God is with us in the silence, when we are alone in the wilderness feeling sorry for ourselves, and we need someone who loves us to wrap us up and care for us.

Elijah was done. Beyond discouraged. He was a prophet, someone with messages from God. But it didn't matter how often he gave the message: These fake gods cannot help you. Because the terrible king and queen—who worshipped the fake gods and commanded the people to do the same—didn't want to hear it. They didn't care that the people needed help. It didn't matter what was true. The people with power didn't want the truth. Instead, they wanted Elijah dead.

How could it be that Elijah knew what was true, had even shown them, and instead of accepting it, they were attacking him?

Elijah **fled** King Ahab and Queen Jezebel, out to the wilderness. Then he found a bush, crawled beneath it, and curled up, and told God the truth. "I have had enough. I want to be done living."

Then Elijah fell asleep. What woke him was a touch. An angel told him to get up and eat, and as he looked around there was **fresh bread and a jar of water.** He ate and ate, and as soon as he was full, he went back to sleep. But again the angel woke him and encouraged him to eat even more to regain his strength.

And the sleep and the snack gave Elijah just enough strength to continue on until he reached **Mount Sinai.**

Historical Context—Conflict and Flight
This story exists in the middle of an extended story about Elijah's conflict with the current king and queen of Israel, Ahab and Jezebel. Elijah is devoted to Yahweh alone, while Ahab and Jezebel have led the nation into a sort of blended faith that includes the worship of Baal and other gods from the surrounding nations alongside Yahweh. Yahweh had just sent down fire from the sky as part of a competition between Elijah and the prophets of Baal. But despite this, Ahab and Jezebel are not impressed, and Elijah is forced to flee for his life into the wilderness. Having to run away after such a high point must have only enhanced Elijah's sense of loneliness and isolation. Even after *that*, after fire coming down from the sky, Ahab and Jezebel are still in power, and no one is on Elijah's side.

Connections—God Provides
This story is one of so many in the Bible where God provides food and water for people in the wilderness. In Genesis 21, God hears the cry of little Ishmael and provides for Hagar and her son. In 1 Kings 19, God provides for Elijah when he flees from the wrath of Ahab and Jezebel. In Luke, God provides for Jesus after he is tempted, then later Jesus provides bread and fish for the crowds. In John 6 and 7, Jesus refers back to this story by saying that he is the bread of life and living water. Why do these stories keep popping up? Because providing the good things that we need, over and over again, is central to who our God is.

Key Words—Wilderness and Mountain
Both of these are consistent places God's people go to meet with God in the Bible. The first place the people go after the Exodus is to meet with God at Mount Sinai, which is also called Horeb at times. In fact, Horeb is where Elijah goes in this story. This story has so many connections to the exodus story that it cannot be an accident. There is some sense that Elijah is being taken back to the start, back to that foundational story where God set the people free and then made a covenant with them to be with them and to protect them. Elijah is being reminded of the bedrock of who God is.

Once he got there, **God asked** him, "What are you doing here?"

And importantly, Elijah told God the truth. "I have been committed to you, but no one else is. Israel doesn't care about you at all. It's like they are stomping on top of your promises, grinding them into the ground while they walk far away from you. And us prophets? Well, everyone but me has been killed trying to remind them what is true, and I'm next, if Queen Jezebel gets her way."

And God replied, "Go out to the side of the mountain, my presence will be there."

When Elijah made his way to the side of the mountain **three amazing things** happened.

A wind rushed with such noise, such power, that you could hardly stay standing. But God was not in the wind. An earthquake shook so that your feet came right out from under you. But God was not in the earthquake. A fire

---

Genre—God Appears
As we've talked about before, the fancy theological word for stories like this is "theophany," stories in which God appears. One of the most interesting features of these stories is how confusing and seemingly contradictory they are. Sometimes, as here, God is a still silence. Other times, God is a raging earthquake or a fire. Sometimes God seems to show up in human form, walking in the garden, wrestling with Jacob; or definitely shows up in human form in Jesus. Other times we're told that Moses can't see God's face and live to tell the tale. Sometimes God speaks audibly. Other times, God speaks through dreams or visions or people, even animals. When we are met with these sorts of differences, we can look at them as adding needed tension to our picture of who God is, rather than trying to "solve" them and tie them up into a nice, neat, understandable bow. Our God is not going to be fully understandable for us humans. But that's not the same as saying God can't be known at all.

Key Images—Wind, Earthquake, Fire
All three of these are common symbols of God's power. God had just sent down fire, after all, in the previous story. God sends mighty winds to split the Red Sea and the Jordan River in other places in the Old Testament. God takes the form of a pillar of fire in leading the Israelites out of Egypt in Exodus. Later, in the New Testament, an earthquake goes along with Jesus' resurrection, and tongues of fire come down on Pentecost. At the same time, these are all fundamentally destructive symbols in which power is used to destroy. Perhaps Elijah needed to see that God was more than symbols of power and destruction, that God's presence is quietly there in the everyday as well.

burned so that your eyes were seeing spots and your skin was warm all over. But God was not in the fire.

Then there was a gentle whisper.

Elijah heard it, wrapped his cloak over his face, and moved out toward it.

Again God asked, "What are you doing here?" Again, Elijah answered with the truth. And this time, after he did, God gave him a **friend**. He told him to find a young man named Elisha, and to anoint him to be the next prophet after him. Elijah would not need to go forward alone.

Fun Detail—Friendship
Elijah complains about the isolation he is feeling, that he is the only person still faithful to Yahweh. Not only does God tell Elijah that there are others out there who are faithful, but the very next thing God does is give Elijah a companion, Elisha. God's comfort is not only abstract words, but also the concrete presence of a friend.

I wonder why God is hard to notice sometimes?

I wonder if there are ways we can notice God is with us more often?

I wonder if Elijah expected God to be in the big, fancy events more than in the whisper?

JOSIAH AND THE LAW

2 KINGS 22–23

> **The Main Idea:** This story invites kids to consider how Scripture helps us know, connect with, and respond to God. We can imagine how Josiah and the other leaders grappled with their discovery (and its critique of what they'd been doing) and notice that nevertheless, God is inviting them to turn back. God always invites us back. In that way, this is also a good sample story of repeated themes through Israel's life together.

You might remember how God first gave the people a set of Life Together Teachings—what the Bible calls the Law. But it's not a law like a government sets up today. It's the most important stories of what God has done; it's directions for solving certain problems that might come up; it's teachings for how to live together in ways that will be life-bringing for the whole community.

And the stories had been forgotten. So forgotten that they were shoved in some corner of the temple, buried and unseen for a very long time.

But there came a day when the king, whose name was Josiah, began a new project at the temple—a restoration. He told a priest named Hilkiah, and some of his other trusted advisers, to take the money that had been given to the temple and use it to hire repair workers who would fix the temple again.

126   Wonder

The work began, but along the way, what should be discovered but a scroll of teachings from the **Law**? Hilkiah brought it to King Josiah, and right away, Josiah seemed to know what it meant. He felt very upset and concerned, because he knew that the people's real life together had not looked like these Life Together Teachings, not for a very long time.

Josiah told Hilkiah to take some time to ask God what to do with what they'd found. What did it mean for Josiah and the people? Did God want to say anything to them about this now? As it turned out, God did have things to say to them.

A prophet named **Huldah** told Hilkiah what God had said to her. God was upset that the people had, for so long, trusted idols and worshipped them. In fact, the Bible says God was angry about it.

Let's pause, because it can be challenging for us to hear about times when God feels mad. We know God loves us and the world. We know God cares about us and the world. Is that still true when God is angry? Is it okay for God to be mad?

Historical Context—Deuteronomy
Most scholars believe that the scroll Josiah finds was either the book of Deuteronomy itself, or at least an early form of that book that then was edited and completed under Josiah's orders. The reason for this is that a lot of the language and themes in this story are very closely related to the language you would find in Deuteronomy itself. Second Kings 23:3 is a good example of this.

Key Word—Huldah the Prophet
When Josiah finds the scroll, he realizes that Israel has not been doing the things this scroll says to do at all, and he realizes that might be a problem. To figure out what God wants him to do next, he sends a group of officials to Huldah the prophetess, who gives them a word from God to take back to the king. Of all the people he could have chosen to help him hear from God in this crisis, Huldah was his choice. For those of you keeping score at home, Huldah is one of many women in the Bible who preach, teach, lead, and speak God's words in ways exactly like their male counterparts, but whose existence has been ignored or explained away for centuries. To quote John Goldingay, "The casual way that the story refers to Huldah indicates that it takes for granted the activity of female as well as male prophets" (*1 and 2 Kings for Everyone*, 182). We should too.

Here's something that is important to remember at this point in the story. When it came to worship, the questions were:

- **Which gods** do you trust?
- What are those gods like?
- How do you show that trust?

If a king led the people to trust idols, those idols were very different from Yahweh God, and the way the people showed their trust in *them* often led to people being harmed.

For instance, back when Ahab was king and worshipped Baal, there was a time when Elijah confronted him and all of Baal's so-called prophets. They decided that they would each call on their god, and whoever received fire must be serving the truest one. Baal's prophets actually hurt their bodies as they were calling out for Baal to listen to them! They trusted Baal, and he was a god who was demanding and far away, and to show their trust they had to do something harmful. Meanwhile, Elijah simply spoke to Yahweh God, who did indeed send the fire.

Connections—Idol Worship
One of the things that's easy to miss when it comes to idolatry is that in the Bible, it's as much a practical matter of justice and life as it is a theological matter of which gods you worship. The story of Elijah's contest with the prophets of Baal is a good example of this, with his opponents resorting to self-harm when their gods don't seem to come through. The reason they did this was that *that's what their god asked of them*. The character of the gods we worship has direct effects on the lives we live, and the Bible wants us to see that with idols these effects are not life-giving, much the opposite. The prophets talk about this regularly in their condemnation of the leaders of Israel in their day, that their idolatry has led to injustice—oppression of the poor and the vulnerable, exploitation of creation, the breakdown of social trust and relationships. Worshipping Yahweh alone leads to life—for us, for others, for all creation. Worshipping idols leads to injustice, suffering, and death. That's why it's such a big deal.

We're about to unpause, so here's what's important to know: God is angry *because* God loves and cares about the people who have been hurt and suffered while the kings led them to trust these idols and show that trust in terrible ways.

Unpause.

Josiah heard Huldah's **message** from Yahweh God and listened to her. He began a massive effort to get rid of the idols in the land. There had been spots to worship these idols all over—even in the temple for Yahweh God!—and he **got rid of them** all, one by one.

When that was done, he called the people to celebrate Passover, the holiday remembering that Yahweh God, and no one else, had loved them, heard them, fought for them, and freed them. They were God's people, though

Connections—Truth and Invitation
There is an undercurrent of looming judgment in the story of Josiah, it's true. But the story is ultimately about Josiah seeing things honestly and then returning to God. This is true about most stories in the Bible that feature judgment or consequences for people's choices: The invitation is to return, to repent, and to be accepted back. This is the same as the story of the prodigal son. Zacchaeus is invited to return to God by seeing the truth about the injustice of his actions and then making amends. Even as the prophets warn of the imminent threat of Babylon, they extend the offer of forgiveness if the people will just turn back to Yahweh alone, although it's clear to them that the people will not accept this offer of grace. Consistently it's true: People wander away from God, but God is always eagerly inviting them to return.

Historical Context—Destroying Altars
After leading the people back to the covenant with Yahweh, Josiah goes a step further. We're told that he tears down the altars and other tools used in worshipping the pagan gods, and then he burns them, grinds them up, and spreads their remains over the fields, burning bones on the altars that remain. I mean, he really commits to the bit. It all sounds very over-the-top to modern ears. What he's doing, though, in this context, is trying to make sure these things can never be used to worship pagan gods again. His actions make the objects unusable, and, just as important, ritually unclean. Even if people wanted to go back to worshipping those gods, they'd have to find new tools to do so.

they'd forgotten it. But God's word—this scroll of the Law—reminded them of who they were. It reminded them that they can always come back to God, no matter what, because God is always wanting to forgive and be together. And the Bible says they hadn't celebrated a Passover like that since before the **kings** began or after they all ruled.

Fun Detail—Just Two Kings
Josiah and his great-grandfather Hezekiah are the only kings that the biblical writers have nothing but praise for. Way back when the Israelites had demanded a king, Samuel warned that a king would bring a lot more trouble than good. The people didn't listen, and sure enough, of all the dozens of kings that came after, only two were what you'd hope for (maybe you could include David, too, but he was very much a mixed bag, all things considered).

I wonder if Hilkiah felt nervous, excited, curious, or worried when he first found the scroll?

I wonder how Josiah felt after hearing what God said through Huldah?

I wonder what Passover was like for kids?

YOUR KID ASKS

WHERE'D THEY GO? I THOUGHT THEY WERE IN THE PROMISED LAND.

The Exile might be the most underrated topic in the Bible. It's an event of supreme national trauma for Israel—physically, culturally, and religiously. It makes sense of what's going on in large chunks of the Old Testament, where most of the books are either helping explain *why* the Exile happened (basically, Deuteronomy through Chronicles), warning *about* the Exile (most of the Prophets), or giving encouragement to those *in* exile (the rest of the Prophets, Ezra-Nehemiah, Daniel, Esther). It also helps set the stage for and make sense of what Jesus is doing when he arrives.

So it's kind of a big deal, but not one that is talked about all that often, maybe because there isn't really any *one* story that encompasses it as a whole. So why not remedy that with six questions about the Exile?

What exactly is the Exile?

We'll start with the basics. The Exile is the term used by scholars and historians to describe one part of Israel's history when the empires of Assyria and then Babylon conquered part of Israel and forcibly removed some of the population.

One of Assyria's ways of dealing with conquered nations was to take big chunks of the population and resettle them in another conquered territory. The idea was to mix the ethnicities to the point that there wasn't any strong sense of unity or nationhood, and therefore no reason for pesky revolts.

When Assyria conquered the northern tribes of Israel (the northern and southern tribes having split after Solomon), this is exactly what they did, taking away a large chunk of the Israelites and replacing them with other conquered people groups. The resulting mix of ethnicities in Canaan became the ancestors of what were, in Jesus' day, called Samaritans. The exiles removed from the land never returned, and they are sometimes called the "lost tribes" for this reason.

Babylon's strategy was slightly different, although it was still aimed at destroying the cultural identity of conquered people. They would take the elites, the nobility, of a conquered nation and put their children in what was basically a reeducation camp. We see this happening in the book of Daniel. The youths would live in Babylon, learn Babylonian literature, worship Babylonian gods, and be steeped in Babylonian culture, so that when they then returned to their homeland, they were more Babylonian than anything else. Since they were the nobility, the idea was that the rest of the nation would get in line, too, and Babylon would have nice puppets to keep the peace.

When Babylon conquered Jerusalem, they took the elites back to Babylon for exactly this reason. These exiles, or at least some of them, did return. The commoners more or less stayed in place in the land through this time, except they were now Babylonian subjects, not free Israelites.

When did it happen?

The Assyrian Empire conquered the northern part of Israel around 721 BC. This was somewhere between five hundred and seven hundred years after the Exodus, and maybe three hundred to four hundred years after the reigns of David and Solomon.

The Babylonians conquered much of Assyria a bit more than one hundred years later and, after a siege, burned Jerusalem and the temple in 587 BC.

Why did it happen?

The Assyrians and Babylonians would tell you it happened because their gods were stronger than Israel's and therefore gave their armies victory in battle. That's just the way the world works, after all.

The Bible has a very different perspective. The consistent message of the Bible—from the warnings all the way back in Deuteronomy, through the books that tell about the failures of many of the kings of Israel, through the Prophets—is that the exile was an inevitable result of Israel's idolatry.

Yahweh could protect them from the normal way the world works, in this case that empires gobble up smaller, weaker nations like lions with a sick wildebeest. That's usually how things work, but Yahweh is more powerful than those empires, and will protect Israel. The reason God will protect Israel is that God wants Israel to be a shining example of an alternative to the way empires work. They would trust Yahweh alone, and would live together in ways that showed the surrounding nations the life and goodness and justice that come with trusting Yahweh. They would be God's representatives to the world in this way.

But when Israel instead decided to live like the other nations, worshipping power and violence instead of God, the result was twofold. First, they stopped living in ways that showed who God was. They started to act just like everyone else, with all the injustice and oppression that came with it. And second, this meant they were doing something even more destructive. Instead of showing the world the alternative goodness of the true God, they were making it seem as if Yahweh was just like all the other gods.

Because of these effects, the core sin of idolatry meant that, after pleading with the people for hundreds of years, Yahweh removed Yahweh's protection. And so the world began working the usual way for Israel, and empires gobbled them up.

Why did the Exile matter?

Again, this was a time of national trauma in a number of ways. Perhaps the most important for a nation that had defined itself as God's chosen people was that the Exile seemed to show that Yahweh had abandoned them. Their very identity had been ripped away. They weren't who they thought they were.

And so, it called into question all the rest of the promises Yahweh had made: The promise to Abraham that his descendants would be as many as the stars in the sky and would bless the nations. The promise to David that his kingdom would last forever. Even the promises of return and redemption the later prophets brought rang hollow. How could those things be true when they lived in Babylon?

When did the Exile end?

You'd think this would be a simple question to answer. For the northern tribes, I guess it is: The Exile never ended, because they never returned.

But for the southern tribes, things are a bit more nuanced. Jeremiah the prophet proclaimed that the exile would last seventy years. And, sure enough, a little over seventy years later, the Persians (who had conquered Babylon in the meantime) did allow the exiles to return home. So there you go.

However, while the people had *physically* returned to the land, there were any number of promises that had been made that still hadn't come true. It would take too long to go into detail, but suffice it to say that as long as Israel was under the control of a larger empire and wasn't free, then in some sense the exile was still going on. They couldn't fully be the people of God while serving Persia, or Greece, or Rome.

This is why the book of Daniel reinterprets Jeremiah's seventy years as seventy *weeks of years*, that is, 490-(ish) years, because the people all knew that the exile was still going even though they were technically living back in the Promised Land.

What does that have to do with Jesus?

This understanding—that the exile was still going on, at least in the most important ways—is the cultural setting in which Jesus arrives. The expectation for a Messiah was tightly connected to this sense of exile, and was why the people expected the Messiah to be a military commander who would throw off the yoke of Rome (the empire that had been in control for almost one hundred years at the time of Jesus' ministry).

It is also important context for what Jesus means when he talks about forgiveness of sins. The Exile was the result of the sin of idolatry. The Exile was still ongoing. Therefore, what Israel needed was for their sin of idolatry to be forgiven, so that God's presence would return and they could go back to fully being the people of God they were supposed to be. One of the key things the New Testament writers want us to see is that that's exactly what Jesus' life, death, and resurrection do, even if not in the way the Jewish people of his day expected.

Jesus is forgiving the sin of idolatry, and calling people to turn back to trusting the true God again, and by doing that is re-forming the people of God, ending the Exile once and for all, and getting the whole plan back on track.

DANIEL EATS HIS VEGGIES

DANIEL 1

The Main Idea: God's people often find themselves in hostile situations, in the sense of being asked to put their trust in some other god—*or else*. In Daniel's case it was the gods of the Babylonians. In our own time it might be the gods of money or power or influence or any number of things. In each case the lie is that if we don't trust those gods, then we will die, sometimes literally, sometimes in the sense of not having the life that we want. The truth, the Bible repeatedly assures us, is that when we trust Yahweh alone we will find life.

Our story does not begin in the land God gave the people. It **begins in Babylon**, because Nebuchadnezzar, the king of Babylon, had attacked Jerusalem and won.

"Bring some of the men back with you," the king ordered his chief of staff. "Make sure they're from the leading families, and pick the best ones—strong, healthy, good-looking, and smart. They'll live here and join my courts." So, many of the leaders were taken back to Babylon, including four men named **Daniel, Hananiah, Mishael, and Azariah**.

In order to get them fully ready for royal service, the captives would be taught Babylonian history, study important Babylonian stories, and of course, learn the language. They needed to be nourished, too, of course, to keep up their good appearance. Their food, then, would come straight from the king's kitchens.

But **food** from Nebuchadnezzar's kitchen was also food that was first a sacrifice to a Babylonian god during worship to that god. The food had been an offering to a god who was not Yahweh, and that left Daniel and his companions with a difficult choice to make.

Of course they needed to eat, but they did not want to eat food that was a symbol of trusting another god. And yet, it was very hard to trust Yahweh God at this time, because they'd been taken from the Land, defeated in battle,

---

Genre—Exile Stories
The exile was a national disaster. The temple being destroyed and the people being taken from the Promised Land made it clear as can be that God had abandoned them. The main message of the biblical prophets leading up to the exile was that the sin of idolatry—worshipping other gods alongside Yahweh—was inevitably going to have this result, and so it did. But then those same prophetic books make a remarkable turn once the exile has arrived. They start talking about God's presence returning, about God again being faithful to the promises made. They talk about life coming out of the death of exile. This is the context from which stories like Daniel and Esther appear, stories about what it means to return to Yahweh in a foreign land, being loyal to God alone in the midst of the hostility of empire, and finding that Yahweh is with us and helps us even there, giving hope for the future.

Key Word—Names
Daniel and his friends get a name change as part of their glow-up. Daniel becomes Belteshazzar, Hananiah is called Shadrach, Mishael is called Meshach, and Azariah is called Abednego. In this case those of us who don't speak Hebrew and Akkadian might miss something important. Each of their birth names references God ("El" in Hebrew) or Yahweh ("iah," pronounced Yah). Each of the names they are given has a reference to a Babylonian god. Daniel, for example, goes from "God is my judge" to "Lady [a Babylonian goddess] protect the king." The idea is that Babylon is demanding they switch allegiances to a new set of gods, and then cementing this new allegiance with a new name.

Historical Context—Food
Eating certain foods and not eating others is still one of the markers of the Jewish people. However, most scholars don't think eating kosher is the issue in this story. Daniel and his friends refuse wine, for example, which is not at all forbidden for Jews. Instead, what is probably at issue here is that the meat and the wine both would likely have been involved in worship ceremonies for the Babylonian gods. The defilement Daniel is worried about is not from eating the wrong types of food, but from participating in the worship of idols.

and now **lived** in Babylon. Did all this mean Yahweh God was less powerful than the Babylonian gods? Did it mean Yahweh God was done with them all, since the people had walked so far from God for so long? Did it mean Yahweh would not help them? Or worse, could not help them in this new territory?

What if they didn't eat the special foods from the royal kitchens? It would be a way to trust Yahweh, even here. Could they really do that?

If they did, would God help them as they did?

The four Israelite men asked the chief of staff for permission to eat vegetables instead. (I know! Maybe you just realized what a hard choice this was, because if they skipped the fancy food, that's what was left!)

"Let's say you don't eat from the royal kitchens," said the chief of staff, whose name was Ashpenaz. "What if you become pale and weak compared to all the others? Honestly, I'm afraid of the king's reaction to that—he'd likely have me killed."

"What if we try this?" suggested Daniel. "Feed us vegetables and water for ten days. When time is up, compare us four to the rest of the men and see how we look. If we are doing well, let us continue to eat this way, so we don't have to go against what honors our God."

Historical Context—Exile
This story takes place in the time scholars call "the Exile." After the Exodus, the Israelites made their way to the Promised Land and, over time, established themselves there. The height of their power came in the time of Kings David and Solomon, when Jerusalem was made the capital, and the temple was built there (this was in the 900s BC). After Solomon, the tribes in the north of the land split off from the tribes in the south. Israel (the North) was conquered by the Assyrian Empire in 721 BC, and much of its population was taken off to other parts of the empire, replaced by refugees from elsewhere. This mixed population became the Samaritans of Jesus' day. These exiles never returned, and they are sometimes called the lost tribes for that reason. Judah (the South) held out against Assyria, but it was conquered by the Babylonians in 587 BC, when Jerusalem and the temple were destroyed, and the elites of the day were taken off to Babylon. Daniel and his friends are from this group of exiles. Later, Persia conquers Babylon, and the Jews become Persian subjects before finally being allowed to go home in the time of Ezra and Nehemiah, around seventy years after the exile began.

Key Word—Wisdom
The story says that God gives Daniel and his friends insight and wisdom about all sorts of things. That they end up wiser and more insightful than all of Babylon's celebrated magicians and sages. This is something of a call back to the book of Proverbs, which insists repeatedly that Yahweh is the beginning of wisdom, the fountain from which all true insight comes. The story of Daniel is, in part, meant to remind readers of this fact. Of *course*, Daniel and his friends are the wisest: They're getting their wisdom straight from the source.

Literary Feature—Hyperbole
The book of Daniel exhibits some of the storytelling features that are typical of exile stories. You see similar features in the book of Esther, for example. One very common one is a healthy dose of hyperbole. Daniel and his friends aren't just the wisest in all the land; they are *ten times* wiser than anyone else. In the following story, the king threatens to kill *every single one* of his advisers if they can't interpret his dream *and* tell him what the dream even is without him giving any hints. The authors aren't trying to deceive us; they're telling a good story artfully.

Connections—Joseph
The whole story of Daniel has clear references to the story of Joseph. These climax in the following chapter when Daniel, like Joseph, interprets the king's dream. But even in this first chapter, the idea of God giving wisdom, insight, and favor in the eyes of the Babylonians closely mirrors Joseph's experience in Egypt. The Bible wants to highlight God's consistent presence with and protection of those who trust Yahweh even in challenging, hostile environments, whether the hostility comes from Egypt, Babylon, or the equivalent in our day.

Connections—God Helps Us
God being present with and helping God's people in the darkest of circumstances is one of the most common themes in the Bible, and it allows us to spiral around to it again and again using any number of stories. God helps Joseph in so many situations. God helps the Hebrew slaves in Egypt. God helps the escaped Hebrew slaves in the wilderness. God helps Gideon and his small army. Jesus helps the paralyzed man, and the woman who is bleeding. He helps his good friend Lazarus, the tax collector Zacchaeus, and the Pharisee Nicodemus. In the Bible, God is trustworthy in no small part because God is our help.

Over the ten days, God helped the men, keeping their bodies strong. Ashpenaz admitted they looked perfectly well, and allowed them to continue. From that time on, not only did God keep their bodies strong, but God gave them **wisdom** and knowledge, made them quick to learn new things, and generally made them favorites of the chief of staff and the king. God also gave Daniel the ability to know what dreams meant.

Even in Babylon, so far from home, even for Nebuchadezzar, a king who didn't care about their God, even after something so hard to go through, God was with them and God helped them. Maybe God would **help** them through the rest of this time as well.

I wonder how hard or easy it was for them to decide about eating the king's food?

I wonder what the chief of staff thought after the 10 days were up?

I wonder what God's help looks like nowadays?

THE PROPHETS

YEP, ALL OF 'EM

The Main Idea: The event of the exile was incredibly important and difficult for Israel. Not only that, but it is the backdrop for much of how people heard and responded to Jesus' words. So this story is geared at helping kids get a sense of this piece of the story (without getting bogged down in all of the books of the prophets). While in exile, far from the land and unsure about God, the prophets remind us that God (still) saves us.

First there was a garden, a place of beauty and overflowing goodness. A place that worked so that everything—from the plants, to the animals, to the people—had enough of what they needed. God made that garden and gave it to people so they could enjoy it and care for it. The goodness was meant to go on and on.

Later, there was a land, a place that felt like it was overflowing with milk and honey. God gave that land to Israel, God's people, so they could live there together in ways that would show the whole world what God is like.

And what is God like? Good and creative. Full of grace and kindness. Compassionate and just. The list goes on. *I wonder what you would add to it? What do you think it'd be like for the world to always work that way?*

In the land, the people sometimes really did live in ways that matched who God is. They, too, were good and creative, gracious and kind, compassionate and just. But over time, especially once kings were put in charge, they lived less and less that way.

Τhe kings would decide to worship other gods. And what could everyone else do but follow? It was like coming to a **path** that split in two, and one way led to life, but the other led to power. The kings chose the second path and walked down it. Every step led further and further from God. And the path led the people far away from overflowing goodness and life.

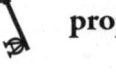God saw all this and knew where it would lead. So God sent messengers to say, "Turn around! Come back!" These messengers are also known as **prophets**.

Like Jeremiah. His message was a warning. They would not be able to stay in the land and stay on this path. They would be conquered and taken

---

Key Image—Paths
A key theme we find in the Prophets is that people walk on paths, and those paths lead where they lead. In this case the choice of paths is between trusting Yahweh alone or trusting idols. Trusting Yahweh leads inevitably to life, with all the good things that reflect God's character. Along that path we will find abundance, joy, peace, justice, goodness, and God's constant presence. That is the promise Yahweh offers: Whatever happens, it will be okay because God is with us. The path of trusting idols leads to death, always. Ultimately, it leads to death because we will get to the end of the path and find that the idols' promises were empty. The gods have no power to keep us safe or provide for us, no matter what lies they tell. And then walking on that path leads to death, because the path is characterized by injustice, oppression, selfishness, violence, and fear. Not because God is punishing us, but because those are characteristics that reflect the idols themselves.

Key Word—Prophecy
Sometimes people think "prophecy" means someone telling the future, but if we come to the Old Testament books known as "the Prophets" with that expectation, we're going to be very confused. Because in ancient Israel, as well as in the nations surrounding Israel, a prophet was not a fortune teller; they were someone with a message from God (or the gods). Now, those messages might *include* information about the future, but far more often they were about current events. Most of the prophecy we find outside of Israel had to do with kings wanting to know whether the gods would be with them in battle (usual answer: Yes, Your Majesty; whatever you say, Your Majesty). Ancient Israel is completely unique in having prophets who are primarily *critical* of the king. The biblical prophets are bringing an urgent message from Yahweh: Turn away from the idols who are leading you toward death, and put your trust in the God who will give you life.

away—exiled. Back then, when a prophet had a serious warning to give to the people, they couldn't just add that to the leadership group text: IMPORTANT: **EXILE COMING** IF THINGS DON'T CHANGE.

So instead, he **carried around a big heavy thing** called a yoke, which is used to keep an ox working the land. It was a symbol of the message: Exile is coming, and you all will be like an ox at work for someone else.

Unless.

You can always turn around. Come back.

Or take Ezekiel. His message was about hope. (Well, okay, it was also a warning.) Back then, when a prophet had a vision or a picture he wanted people to imagine, they couldn't just make a short film and say, "Watch this for me!" So he told it to them: Exile would feel like a desert valley full of bones.

Historical Context—Exile
The prophets come on the scene during a particularly challenging time in Israel's history. They are weaker than in David's day, having split into Israel (the northern tribes) and Judah (the southern tribes). Meanwhile, the constant threat of Egypt (the major empire to the south) has been joined by the rising power of Assyria and Babylon (new major empires to the north). The little kingdoms of Israel and Judah are caught in the middle, the buffer zone that all the empires want to control. And so they are desperate to find some security. Some kings try alliances with one or the other of the major empires, others try worshipping foreign gods who promise protection and victory in battle. The prophets come with a different message: Don't do anything; just trust in Yahweh alone. Yahweh promises to keep you safe. But if you don't trust Yahweh alone, you'll find that these other idols can't be trusted. The prophets were ignored—when they weren't being arrested for disturbing the peace. And just as they said, the idols failed, Assyria and then Babylon conquered Israel and then Judah, and the people were taken away from the Promised Land into exile.

Fun Detail—Weirdness
The prophets were weird. Like, really, really weird. Isaiah walked around naked for three years to embody the shame that the invading armies would bring upon the people. Jeremiah walked around wearing a yoke to display the slavery coming their way. He also hid his underwear under a rock until it was ruined, then brought it out to show people how their pride would likewise be ruined. As an analogy for how Israel has been unfaithful to God, Hosea married a prostitute. Sometimes the weirdness might seem funny, or gross, but it's also showing us the lengths to which God is willing to go to shock people out of their complacency and try to wake up to the reality they've been ignoring.

Key Word—Wrath
Wrath is one of the more uncomfortable concepts that show up in the Prophets. But it's there, and we shouldn't explain it away. Yeah, God's mad about how things are going, but it's important we understand why. Yes, God's feelings are hurt, badly, but the wrath is not God lashing out for being hurt. God's wrath comes for two reasons. First, because idolatry hurts people. The prophets are constantly pointing out the negative impact on the vulnerable that inevitably comes with idolatry. Idolatry leads to injustice, violence, fear, greed, and pain. It leads to the suffering of the vulnerable. And, yes, that makes God angry. God will stand by and watch for only so long before They need to act to protect the vulnerable. Second, idolatry and its negative effects undermine God's plans for the world. God has promised that Israel is going to be a blessing to the nations *through* their identity as God's people. A key part of that is reflecting God's character in their life together, the very thing that becomes impossible when they turn to idols. But God is stuck with Israel because of those promises. And both those things mean God needs to hit the reset button. After centuries of pleading with the people to be the family of God they were supposed to be, something more drastic is needed. The goal is not punishment. The goal is a hard reset that opens up the possibility of life on the other side.

Key Word—Repent
A key theme of the Prophets is that the people are going down the wrong path and need to turn around and head an entirely different way. This is fundamentally what the word "repent" means. It's less about individual wrong choices that the people should feel bad about, which is maybe what some people think when they hear that word today. It's far more about how the people's choice to trust idols has spiraled out in all sorts of ways, negatively impacting their whole life together as a nation. Instead of reflecting God's goodness, they are reflecting the character of the idols. They, as a people, are violent, fearful, greedy, complacent, oppressive to the vulnerable, and on and on. God's people cannot live together in that way. They need to turn around.

Connections—Deuteronomy
Much of the prophets' message parallels closely the words and warnings of Moses in Deuteronomy. The Old Testament wants us to see how the choice placed before the people by Moses at the very beginning of their existence as a people—whether to trust Yahweh or idols—is the consistent choice each generation needs to make. And, just as Moses said, when the people choose idols, the consequences are severe. But, also just as Moses said, the love and faithfulness of Yahweh would extend through and beyond those consequences, with life being on offer even after things fall apart.

Lifeless. But imagine the bones rising up. Imagine them being restored—muscle returning, tendons linking, skin covering, until...life again, even in such an unexpected place.

Exile is coming, and it will feel like hope is gone and life is over.

But there is hope for life again.

There were other prophets as well, and the Bible has long sections telling us what messages they had and how they shared those messages in the hope that the leaders would listen. Because no matter how far the people had traveled down a path that leads away from God, they could always turn around. No matter how long it had been since their community was life-giving and full of goodness, they could be revived.

God would not, could not, stop sending people to say, "Come back home."

I wonder why the leaders usually
did not listen to the prophets?

I wonder how a prophet might give
a message nowadays? And would it work?

I wonder how the leaders felt after
the Exile happened?

PART III

CHRISTMAS STORIES

AN ANGEL VISITS MARY

LUKE 1:26–56

The Main Idea: God keeps promises. The thing the story of the angel and Mary highlights again and again is that the baby she is going to carry is God's answer to the promises made throughout the Old Testament. The time of waiting is over. The new day is here!

There was a girl named Mary who lived in a town called Nazareth in Israel. Like all the people of Israel, Mary was waiting for a promise to be kept.

Hundreds of years ago, people had brought messages from God promising that God would fix all the ways the world wasn't right. God would send a person, called the Messiah, who would bring with them all the joy and life and goodness and justice that God dreams of for the world. The promise was so wonderful, but it had been a long time of waiting. Even so, Mary trusted God, including trusting that God keeps promises. So she waited.

One day, as Mary was doing normal things, something very, very *not* normal happened. An angel named Gabriel appeared, saying, "Hello, **favored one. God is with you.**"

Mary didn't really know what to say to that. It wasn't exactly a typical greeting.

"Don't be afraid," Gabriel said. "Listen to what God is going to do! You are going to have a baby, and he isn't going to be a normal sort of baby. He is going

Key Word—Favor
The angel calls Mary "God's favored one," despite her not being of a prominent family, and a girl, a child. She has no claim to special status, quite the opposite in fact, and yet she is raised up and given a place of honor (see "Mary's Song" below). She is the first of many characters in the gospels for whom status and identity are based not on the usual qualifications, but solely on trust in God/Jesus.

Connections—Joseph and Moses
The angel begins his message to Mary by proclaiming, "The Lord is with you!" Mary herself is said to be a bit confused by this strange greeting. One reason the angel starts this way is to draw on connections to Old Testament stories like those of Joseph and Moses where God being with them is a constant refrain as they partner with God to rescue God's people. God is with Mary in just the same way, and the invitation to her is just the same. She, too, gets to choose to accept God's invitation to be the agent through whom salvation will come to the world.

Fun Detail—Son of God
Our ears, so familiar with Jesus being described this way, don't pick up on something that ancient ears would not have missed. "Son of God" was one of the titles claimed by the Roman emperor Augustus. To say that *Jesus* was the "Son of God" would have been a literally revolutionary statement, renouncing allegiance to the state and pledging allegiance to Jesus instead.

Historical Context—Marriage
The typical age for marriage in Jesus' day was twelve for girls, and the late teens for boys. Engagement happened around a year or so before the marriage itself, so Mary is very likely to be eleven or twelve years old when this story takes place. Unlike today, engagements were not easily broken. The future bride and groom were considered legally joined at the point of engagement (sometimes translations use "betrothal" instead of "engagement" to highlight the cultural differences), with legal documents having been signed and money (the "bride-price") having already changed hands. During this time leading up to the wedding, although the girl would still be living in her father's house, it would take a legal divorce to stop the wedding. The girl showing up pregnant would be…problematic, especially for her own reputation and that of her father.

to be great. He's going to be **God's Son**, the Messiah that God promised. He'll rescue the whole world."

Imagine you are in Mary's shoes—what is going on inside you at this point?

Mary was very excited by this message—God's promises coming true! But she was also confused. "**But wait**," Mary said, "How will this happen? **It seems impossible!**"

"God's spirit will make it happen," said the angel. "Don't worry, with God nothing is impossible."

Mary trusted God with her whole heart, so she said simply, "Okay, I'm happy for God to do whatever God wants to do." And the angel was gone, just like that.

Do you think it was easy or hard for Mary to decide how to respond to this news? Why?

Mary had so many thoughts and feelings swirling inside of her, she felt like she might burst! And do you know what she did? She started singing.

Key Word—Virgin

This is such a familiar part of the story that it's worth taking a second to clear up some misconceptions. First, people in the ancient world were very much aware that virgins did not have babies, and that if this sort of thing were claimed to be the case, there was usually a…let's say, simpler explanation for the pregnancy. Modern skeptics were not the first to see that this was a bit far-fetched. Second, there is no evidence that *anyone* before Jesus read the Isaiah passage about a young girl getting pregnant as meaning the Messiah was going to be born to a virgin. Nor were there similar stories in the pagan world. No one was expecting this sort of thing to happen. Third, it would not be possible to overstate how much of a disaster Mary getting pregnant would have been for her reputation and future life as well as those of her child. In normal circumstances, *no one* would have believed her or been interested in associating with her from this point forward. Taken together, these highlight something important—there was no reason for the gospel writers to make this sort of story up. Like, none. In fact, it would have made more sense to leave it out of their story entirely; it would have hurt their case, not helped it. The simplest explanation for this detail being included is that this is what actually happened.

Mary sang a song about God, about how God loves ordinary people like her and how God helps people who need help. She sang about how much God loves and cares for people and how good God is. She sang about how happy she was. She **sang** about how God was keeping the promises that she and the rest of the people had been waiting for. They were coming true at last.

And then, Mary waited. She waited for the baby to come. But this waiting felt different than the waiting before. She had always hoped God would keep promises, but now, she was seeing God do it with her own eyes.

Literary Feature—Mary's Song
Mary's song—which is not included here but can be found in your Bible—is full of themes of God bringing justice to the oppressed and casting down the powerful from their thrones, and is beautiful and fascinating and important. It introduces themes that will show up again and again throughout Jesus' ministry, and that Luke will highlight throughout his Gospel. The scholar Joel Green calls its message "the very fabric of Luke's whole narrative" (*Gospel of Luke*, 100). What's most striking? These words come from the lips of a twelve-year-old girl. The first to preach the gospel in Luke's story is Mary.

Connections—Psalms
The Old Testament prophets often look forward to a day when God would bring justice like what Mary's song talks about, but the closest parallel is in the Psalms, many of which call on God to bring justice for the oppressed and cast down the oppressors. Mary sees that those hopes are now being fulfilled.

I wonder what Mary had been doing before the angel interrupted her?

I wonder what the tune of Mary's song was like?

I wonder how soon Mary talked to someone about what happened? What would you do?

AN ANGEL VISITS JOSEPH

MATTHEW 1:18–25

> **The Main Idea:** God guides us and can be trusted. The Christmas stories are so familiar to us that we can miss just how hard and frightening the things Joseph is asked to do would have been. He, like many characters in the Bible, has to trust God and follow God into an unknown future that might not turn out the way he wants. God, through the angel, is promising to be with and guide Joseph through it all.

Joseph lived in a small town called Nazareth, in Israel. He was engaged to a girl named Mary, and the time for the wedding was coming soon. Joseph dreamed about what his new life would be like, starting a family, working as a carpenter just like his dad had before him, teaching his sons how to be carpenters, too. There were so many things he was looking forward to.

But then, one day, something happened that changed everything. Joseph found out that Mary was pregnant. This was a big problem, because in those days people did not think it was okay to have a baby before getting married. If he married Mary anyway, for the rest of his life **people would look down on him**. Some would think he was a bad person and wouldn't want to be friends with him. Even some of his family might not talk to him again.

Joseph was hurt. He loved Mary, but how could she do this to him? He was confused. He didn't want to hurt Mary, but he knew he couldn't get married

Historical Context—Honor-Shame
The culture Joseph had grown up in is what's sometimes called an "honor-shame" culture, one in which your status was very much linked to your reputation, and guarding that reputation by accumulating honor and avoiding shame was all important. One of the things this meant was that you needed to be very careful who you associated with because their actions and reputation would reflect on you. If someone had done something shameful, you needed to show without any doubt that you rejected them to prevent their shame from tarnishing you. Shameful things, like, just to pick one random example, an unwed girl getting pregnant. The decision Joseph is being asked to make is not a light one; it's one that is going to have an ongoing negative impact on his reputation and that of his family for the rest of his life in a culture in which, again, reputation was all important. It makes it all the more striking that Joseph wakes up and does exactly what the angel told him to do.

Key Word—Jesus
The name Jesus is the Greek form of the Hebrew *Yeshua* (Joshua in English), which literally means "Yahweh Saves." It was a common name in Jesus' day when all of Israel was waiting expectantly for God to do just that—save them.

Connections—Isaiah
Matthew quotes from Isaiah, saying that Mary being pregnant fulfills Isaiah's words about a young girl having a son who will be called "Emmanuel." What's often lost is that the passage in Isaiah was originally intended to refer to a regular baby from Isaiah's day—possibly Isaiah's own child, possibly King Hezekiah—whom God would use to deliver the people. It was not originally read as a prophecy about the Messiah that needed to be fulfilled, nor was it read that way in Jesus' day. Matthew is noticing surprising and unexpected echoes of Jesus' story in the Old Testament, not changing Jesus' story so that it fits some preconceived Messiah script.

Connections—Psalm 130
The angel tells Joseph that Jesus will "save his people from their sins" (Matt. 1:21). This is a reference to Psalm 130:8, a psalm about waiting for God's forgiveness and rescue. The people have been waiting for those things for centuries, and the angel's message is: The time is now!

Fun Detail—Youth and Wisdom
Who God trusts with the news about Jesus is interesting—a twelve-ish-year-old-girl, a seventeen-ish-year-old boy, and shepherds who were likely teenagers themselves. In a culture where wisdom was seen as going with old age, it's striking that those who show trust in God and an understanding of what God is up to, at least to start, are mostly very young.

to her, either. He didn't know what to do, but thought the best plan was to just break up with her quietly.

He was so sad that he just went to sleep, half hoping it was all a bad dream. Maybe he'd wake up to find it had all gone away.

While he slept Joseph did have a dream, but this was no ordinary dream, because in this dream an angel appeared. "Hello, Joseph," said the angel. "I've come to tell you that you shouldn't be afraid to get married to Mary. Her baby is from God. She is going to have a son, and I want you to help take care of him, even though it will be hard for you. You should name him **Jesus**, because he will rescue the whole world, just like **God promised** would happen. The baby will be the one who makes **God's promises come true**."

If you woke up after a dream like this, how would you try to figure out if it was real and from God or just a dream?

Joseph woke up and thought about the dream. This was God guiding him, but also, God was asking him to do something difficult. Honestly, Joseph wasn't sure how it would all work out. He was worried that getting married to Mary would cause some really hard things to happen. But Joseph also trusted God. If God was guiding him now, then God would also guide him through whatever hard things came. And so the Bible says that when he woke up, Joseph got out of bed and did exactly what the angel had told him to do.

He married Mary. He took care of her, and got ready to care for the baby when he was born. He named the baby Jesus. Later, there were hard times that came, but God continued to **guide** Joseph when they did.

I wonder if Joseph usually dreamed a lot in his sleep?
Do you dream a lot?

I wonder if Joseph had tried some way
of deciding, like flipping a coin?

I wonder what other ways God guides a person?

JESUS IS BORN!

MATTHEW 1:18–25; LUKE 2:1–7

The Main Idea: God is with us! In Jesus, God chooses to be born in the humblest of circumstances, in part to show us something important about God's character. This is a God who is for everybody, who wants to be with everybody, no matter how lowly.

At the time Mary was pregnant with Jesus, Israel was controlled by an empire called Rome. Far away in the city of Rome lived an emperor named Augustus. Augustus sat in his palace one day and thought to himself, "You know what? I'd really like more money. With more money I could have bigger armies, and fancier things, and I like big armies and fancy things."

So Augustus thought about how to get more money, and came up with an idea. He would have his officials **count all the people** in his whole empire. That way he'd know exactly how much more money he could force places like Israel to pay him every year. And when the emperor makes a plan, everyone has to go along with that plan. Augustus sat comfortably in his palace while everyone in the whole empire did what he commanded.

Which is why **Joseph** found himself putting his fiancée—his very pregnant fiancée, Mary—on a donkey for the long trip from their hometown of Nazareth to the town of Bethlehem so they could be counted.

Historical Context—Census

Luke spends more time in this part of the story talking about Augustus's census than he does about Jesus actually being born. Unlike today, a census was not a regular event occurring every ten years. Instead, censuses happened whenever an emperor decided, and they were usually for the purpose of figuring out how much tax money and how many soldiers the Romans could demand from each region in their empire. In other words, they were resented symbols of Roman power, a reminder that however much the people tried to stay loyal to Yahweh, Emperor Augustus was the one who most obviously had power over them. Luke is emphasizing this symbol of Roman power so that we can see the contrast with Jesus—obvious power used to oppress vs. humble power used to save.

Connections—David

Luke tells us that Joseph needs to go to Bethlehem for the census because he is from David's family. This detail is important because the Messiah was expected to be a descendant of David who would restore David's kingly line to the throne, restoring Israel to the freedom and status they enjoyed under David and Solomon in the process. Jesus, we will find, is a different sort of King, a reality that is hinted at in the humble circumstances of his birth.

Fun Detail—Cartoon Christmas

Here's a few features common in children's retellings that don't actually show up in the text (the story itself is *really* short, and mostly about the census). Rather than feeling the need to correct those cartoon Christmases, you could lean into the imaginative side of storytelling when you come across these sorts of things, because that is what allows us to flesh out such a short story to make it feel real.

The Barn: Luke tells us only that Jesus was laid in the animals' feeding trough, not what room they were in. In a village like Bethlehem, this was probably not a separate structure like a barn. Instead, animals were often kept on the ground floor of the family home, with a second story for the people.

The Innkeeper: This character doesn't show up in the story, and even the word sometimes translated as "inn," as in "There was no room for them at the inn," probably means something more like "guest room" or "normal living space." Scholars are doubtful that a small village like Bethlehem would have had anything like an inn.

The Dangerous Journey: The journey from Nazareth to Bethlehem would have taken several days (especially with a heavily pregnant woman), and certainly wouldn't have been easy, but we aren't told anything else about the journey itself. They likely went with a larger group for safety, maybe rode on donkeys, but any other details we'd need to fill in for ourselves.

How do you imagine they felt about this trip?

Mary was going to have a baby any day now, and she really should have been safe at home resting, not bouncing around on the back of a donkey for mile after mile, day after day. But when the emperor makes a plan, everyone has to go along with that plan.

So Joseph and Mary traveled for days and days to get to Bethlehem. When they got there the town was so crowded they could barely move along the streets. The Bible doesn't tell us the exact **details** of how they got from arriving in Bethlehem to having a place to stay for the night, but we know there were challenges.

I imagine that Joseph likely had to push people aside just to get Mary and the donkey to the nearest home that belonged to a distant uncle. He went to ask for a room, but they sent him away. "Are you kidding?" the cousin would say. "Look at these crowds! **We don't have any room.**"

Joseph and Mary and the donkey pushed through the crowds to another home in the family—maybe it belonged to some second cousin twice removed—and the next, and the next. But each time the answer was the same: "No room." Joseph wouldn't know what to do. He had to get Mary somewhere

---

Key Word—No Room

The story tells us that Joseph needs to go to Bethlehem for the census because that's where his family is from. It's likely, then, that he has extended relatives still in town, and that staying with them would have been plan A. After all, showing hospitality to distant relatives was a very important thing in their culture. But there's no room in the guest room for Joseph and Mary, and they're put where the animals live instead. This could just be a practical issue—first come, first served, on the guest bed. It's possible, though, that something else is going on. Certainly word has gotten around the family about Joseph's bride-to-be being pregnant. That means more than a few aunts and uncles would have been shaking their heads at what Joseph had obviously been getting up to, and if that's the case, they probably weren't jumping at the chance to have Joseph (let alone Mary!) under their roof. The story doesn't come out and say it, but it's very possible that the birth of Jesus in an animal space was just the first example of people missing what God was up to in and through Jesus.

to rest. And if it were me, I'd be so mad at the emperor for making plans far away and not caring how he was hurting people like Mary. But that's how emperors are.

Then, Joseph remembered one last home of a relative in Bethlehem; maybe they could help. He went to their house, their last hope, but when he got there, the answer was the same. "We've got no room, Joseph," said the relative. "I'm sorry, I wish I could help… Wait, there is one place, but I'm not sure you'll want to sleep there. There's the room where we keep the animals. It's a bit smelly and dirty, but at least it's warm and dry."

Joseph looked at Mary. Mary looked at Joseph. They nodded. The ground floor with the animals was better than nothing. They made some beds out of the animals' hay and settled in for the night. But they didn't get the sleep they hoped for because instead, Jesus arrived.

While the emperor slept in his comfortable palace, far away from the people who did whatever he commanded, God's son slept in the feeding trough for the animals, wrapped up tight and cozy. This is why Jesus is called **Emmanuel**, which means "God with us," because even at his birth, Jesus was showing us that our God is not like the emperors and kings of our world. Our God wants to be with us, and will do whatever it takes to make that happen.

Key Word—God With Us
Matthew's story begins with Jesus being called *Emmanuel*, which means "God with us." The story ends with Jesus' promise to be with the disciples always (see Matt. 28:20). Matthew wants to make clear that Jesus is the means by which God makes even more true what has always been true—that God wants to be with us and is willing to do whatever it takes to make that a reality. It's also an echo of the same promise showing up again and again in the Old Testament: God being with Joseph, Moses, Joshua, David, Jeremiah, and more. Being with us is central to who our God is and has always been.

I wonder how Joseph's relatives felt about where he and Mary stayed?

I wonder how long it took before Mary was willing to go on a trip again?

I wonder which animals were around?

ANGELS AND SHEPHERDS

LUKE 2:8–20

> **The Main Idea:** God values everyone, and one way that's made clear is because the first people to hear and then tell the good news about Jesus' birth are some of the lowest status members of the community. Just like in Mary's song after being visited by the angel, one of the key themes Luke wants us to see in the story of Jesus' birth is that God values everyone, especially those who aren't valued by the world.

No one else knew that God's plan to rescue the whole world had begun. Jesus was born in the part of the house where the family animals were kept, because there was no room for him anywhere else. And it was just him; his mother, Mary; and Joseph.

And also some sheep and goats and cows.

No one else in Bethlehem knew about the amazing, world-changing things that had happened that night. But that was about to change. God decided to let people know by sending angels to tell people the good news! But the question was, Who should the angels tell?

Should they tell the leaders and important people the good news? The rich and powerful people?

If you were in God's shoes, wanting to get the word out about Jesus' arrival, how would you do it?

"No," God thought. "This news is for everybody, not just powerful people."

So God didn't send the angels to the powerful people in Bethlehem. God sent the angels to ordinary people, maybe the most ordinary people you could find. God sent the angels to some girls and boys who were shepherds taking care of their sheep on a hill outside of town.

Shepherds were often looked down on in those days. They were usually dirty. They smelled like sheep. They were not at all who most people would think to tell important news. But our God cares about everyone, and starting with them was a pretty great way to show it.

The shepherds were settled down for the night, keeping watch to make sure no wild animals attacked the sheep, but also probably getting pretty sleepy on the quiet, dark hillside…

When suddenly the brightest light you've ever seen shone all around them. It was like when a flashlight shines into your eyes in a dark room, but much, much more! They shielded their eyes from the bright light, and when they could finally manage to peek through, they saw an angel.

The Bible says they were *terrified*!

"Don't be afraid," said the angel. "I've come with a wonderful, happy message for you. The best good news you've ever heard! And it's good news that

---

Historical Context—Shepherd

Shepherds in Jesus' day would have been people who were not occupied with farming. This might have been because they didn't have land of their own, or not enough of it to support a family, and so they hired themselves out as laborers. It might have been because they were too young to be doing the heavy labor of farming. In any sense they would have been low in the economic and social hierarchy of the day, and yet these are exactly the people God goes to with the good news about Jesus' birth. This tells us something important about God's character, God consistently raises up the lowly, like the shepherd Moses and the shepherd David.

will bring **great joy to all people**. A baby was born today in Bethlehem. But not just any baby. This is the savior God promised, the Messiah. He is going to do wonderful things and will rescue the whole world!"

"Go, hurry into Bethlehem and look for the baby," said the angel. "You'll find him wrapped up tight in cloths, lying in the trough where the animals' hay is."

The shepherds were squinting at each other in the bright light, wondering what a strange message this was, when all of a sudden, instead of one angel,

Historical Context—Imperial Cult
That's the fancy name given by fancy historians to describe something that was just emerging in Roman culture around the time of Jesus' birth. Starting with the emperor Augustus, people began to worship the emperor as a god. Augustus didn't demand this sort of worship (although later emperors sure would), but he also didn't discourage it. In fact, this historical context gives light to four key words that show up in this story, all of which would have been shots at the emperor Augustus and his propaganda. Augustus wants these words to be associated with him, but they're most truly applied to this baby lying in a feeding trough. Jesus is the true king, but of a totally different sort than Augustus.

Good News: The word that went with official announcements about the great things the emperor had done, especially leading Roman armies to victory over enemies, was "good news."

Savior, Lord: These were two of the most popular titles for Augustus.

Peace: Part of the Roman propaganda was that their armies had brought peace to the world. Unspoken was the amount of violence that was used in order to win and maintain that peace.

Key Word—For All People
Peace, the angels tell us, has come on all the earth and for all people. Luke is telling us a story about the Jewish Messiah, yes, but the implications of Jesus' birth stretch out in all directions, covering the whole world.

Key Word—Peace
The Jewish word for "peace" goes beyond what the emperor of Rome was said to have brought. The Hebrew word "shalom" meant more than the absence of war; it referred to a holistic goodness, all things being well. It meant internal peace for individuals, relational peace between people, intimacy between God and humans, justice in the interactions of the powerful and the weak, and yes, the absence of violence and suffering.

there were hundreds of them! The hilltop was surrounded by them, and their voices filled the air as they sang songs about how great God is.

And then the hilltop became quiet and dark again, like the light and the sound had been switched off. The **angels** were gone. And the shepherds had to decide what to do next.

How do you imagine the conversation went as they decided? Do you think they all agreed? Do you think the conversation was short or long?

"Hurry," they said. "Let's go find this baby and see for ourselves!"

So they ran down the hill into Bethlehem. They didn't stop until they found Jesus, just like the angel had said. They went inside, knelt on the straw, and looked down at the newborn Jesus.

When it was time to leave, they couldn't just go back to the hills. This was too exciting for that. So instead they spent the rest of the night telling everyone they met about what they had seen and heard. They were filled with joy that God's plan had begun, and as they talked about it, their joy spilled out. Jesus was born, and they—the shepherd kids—got to be the first to know.

Your Kid Asks: What's with all the angels?
The stories of Jesus' birth have more angels than just about any other story in the Bible. Angels were usually seen in one of two ways, as God's messengers (that's actually what the root of the word "angel" means: "messenger"), or as members of God's army. We see both of these functions in these stories. After all, when a great king arrives, he arrives at the head of an army, the bigger and more impressive the better, with lots of shiny, dangerous-looking weapons. The word for the group of angels who show up to the shepherds is sometimes "heavenly host," but N. T. Wright actually translates it as "a crowd of the heavenly armies" (Luke 2:13 NTFE) because that's what is literally being described. But the army announcing Jesus' arrival isn't carrying dangerous, shiny weapons; they are singing about good news of great joy for all people. Like any great king, God has an army; it's just that God's army brings news of peace, not war.

I wonder what the song sounded like?

I wonder what brings you great joy?

I wonder if anyone still stayed behind with the sheep? And if so, how'd they decide who'd stay and who'd go?

WISE MEN VISIT JESUS

MATTHEW 2

The Main Idea: God is greater than the great kings of the earth. Even those from far away recognize the greatness of the baby Jesus and come to show honor to him.

At Christmas we tell the story of how God's plan to bring a goodness that matches God's own goodness got started when Jesus was born.

But this part of the story doesn't start with Jesus. It starts hundreds and hundreds of miles away, with some **men** who studied the stars, watching them move day after day and year after year. They thought they could learn what was going to happen on earth by watching what happened in the sky. This is why they are sometimes called Wise Men. They thought there were

Historical Context—Wise Men
As has often been said, the old song is wrong on all three counts—we aren't told there are three of them, they aren't kings, and they aren't from the Orient. They are simply "wise and learned men from the east." Most likely, these were sages from Persia, stargazers and priestly figures who were expected to give wise advice to the king. They would have been expected to know what was going on in the world, and to understand what it all meant, which is why they show up in Jesus' story. While the Bible often connects wisdom with knowing God, it never says that wisdom can't be found outside of God's people. God is always the God of the whole earth, and can interact with that broader world in any number of ways, including giving wisdom and insight.

important secret messages in the **stars**. Maybe that seems like a strange thing to you, but that's what they thought.

The good news that Jesus was born wasn't just for Bethlehem, where it happened. It wasn't just for Israel. It was for the whole world. Given that fact, God decided to use the stars to send a message to the Wise Men, and made a very **bright star** appear in the sky. And the Wise Men, from their homes far away, saw the bright star.

What could it mean?

They looked again. There was the bright star, all right, but they weren't sure what the star meant. They searched and searched through their books about stars to find what it meant, but couldn't find anything. And then, one

---

Key Image—Star
The main question this story might prompt for a curious kid is, Why a star? While astrology still has its devotees today, this is something slightly different. In the ancient, pre-telescope world, they looked at how the universe was put together quite differently than we do today. N. T. Wright points out that "they believed…that the whole world…was interconnected, and when something important happened on earth you could expect to see it reflected in the heavens" (*Matthew for Everyone*, pt. 1, 10). Stars and planets each had their own meaning, and there were people whose whole lives were devoted to studying the movements of these heavenly figures in order to see what that might mean for the connected events here on earth. If a great king was born on earth, then of course the evidence for it would be up there somewhere.

Fun Detail—Which star was it?
A follow-up question, then, would have to do with what specifically the wise men saw. Of course we can't know for sure, which means that naturally about a thousand guesses exist, from a comet to a supernova to a visual phenomenon that God just put there temporarily. My favorite guess comes from N. T. Wright (surprise, surprise!), who writes, "More likely is the fact that the planets Jupiter and Saturn were in conjunction with each other three times in 7 BC.* Since Jupiter was the 'royal' or kingly planet, and Saturn was sometimes thought to represent the Jews, the conclusion was obvious: a new king of the Jews was about to be born" (*Matthew for Everyone*, pt. 1, 10). Is that what they saw? Who knows! Feel free to make fun guesses of your own.

---

*   Note that while the BC/AD divide was *supposed* to be set to make the birth of Jesus year AD 1, the sixth-century monks involved were a bit limited in their historical precision.

day, they opened up a dusty old book from the top shelf that you had to stretch to reach. They looked in the book and found the answer. The star meant that a new king had been born. This king was from a land called Israel, and he was a great king. The book said that this king would be the great king over all kings, the lord over all lords.

A new king was huge news. There was only one thing to do with news like this. Even though they were important, powerful people themselves, they needed to go show their respect for this new king. He was even greater than them.

So the Wise Men got ready for a long journey, packing up food, tents, and clothes. And then they packed something else. They needed **gifts**. When you come to see a king who is greater than you, you can't arrive empty-handed. Bringing gifts shows honor to the greater king. So the Wise Men brought gifts that were beautiful, and smelled good, and cost a lot of money. Gifts that would be good to give to a king, even if they weren't very good for a baby.

They climbed onto camels, because that's what they rode for long journeys, and followed the bright star in the sky. We don't know exactly how long they followed the star, but we do know how they felt on the journey—full of joy. They weren't jealous of a greater king, they were joyful about his arrival and what it would mean when he grew up.

They followed the star until it stopped. It shone down out of the sky onto a little house. The wise men were surprised. This wasn't a palace. Why would the great king be here? But there was the star. And there was the little house. So, they got down off their camels, went up to the house, and knocked on the door.

Historical Context—Gifts

The gifts of gold, frankincense, and myrrh tell us something interesting. These are not gifts that you might bring to a baby. They are, instead, gifts you would bring to show honor to a king, or maybe even more likely to place on an altar to a god. The Wise Men's choice of gifts shows that they understand, in their own way, who this baby is, and what he means for the world.

Mary, Jesus' mother, opened the door. "Hello," said the Wise Men, "we are here to see the new **king**. We saw his star and followed it here. We want to celebrate that he is born! Here, we brought gifts to show him honor."

The Wise Men knelt down next to toddler Jesus and gave him gifts, gifts that showed how great Jesus was. Gifts for a baby who was also the king of kings and the lord of lords. And when they had seen Jesus, and given him gifts, they left and went back home, worshipping God and full of joy about all that was happening. Jesus, the great king, was here!

 Key Image—King
Throughout Jesus' birth stories, a contrast is drawn between Jesus and the kings of the earth. Herod, Augustus, and these great men from the east are all placed alongside this baby lying in a feeding trough. It's meant to show us not only that Jesus is the true King of kings, while these other figures are at best temporary; it's also meant to get us wondering: What type of king is Jesus? Because he doesn't seem to line up with the ways these other kings act. The fact that our Great King comes humbly, to serve and to save, demands that we reorient our own ideas about how power ought to work and how we ought to live.

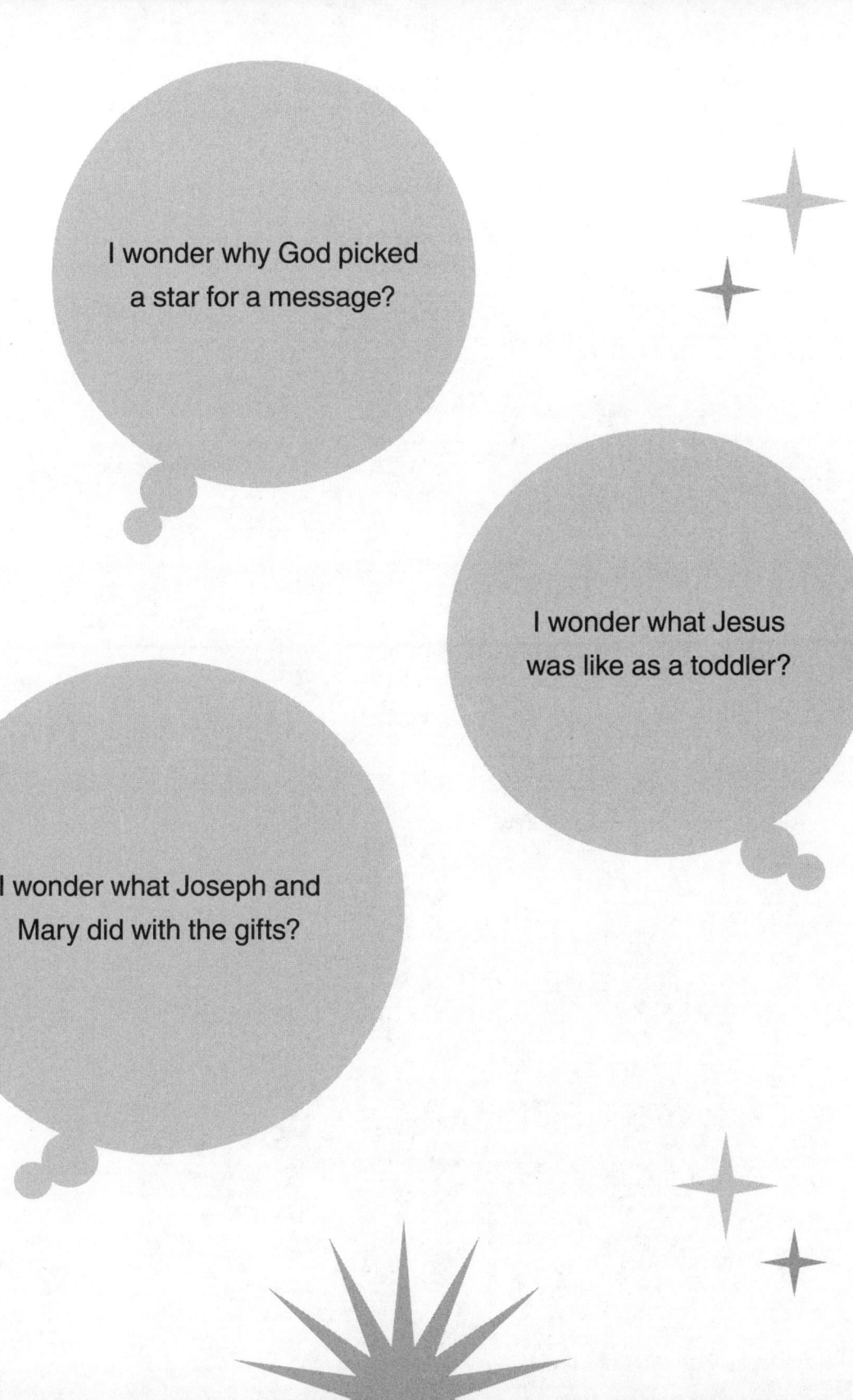

YOUR KID ASKS

ARE MIRACLES REALLY REAL?
BECAUSE THAT ISN'T HOW THINGS HAPPEN.

Kids notice the seeming *lack* of miracles that resemble the biblical variety pretty easily. The waters of the pool never part. Their pizza never becomes more pizza through prayer. And especially for the science lovers, the literalists, and the skeptics, miracles can be a tricky topic.

Given that we have a miracle story next, I thought we could talk about three ideas that may help anyone navigating a miracles conversation with kiddos.

When you hear:
Miracles can't be real.

You might reply: Yeah, it's pretty amazing that God might have done things that go beyond how science usually works.

This is the idea that miracles don't fit with what we know of science because of a God boost. This idea recognizes God as the Great Scientist who set up all that science discovers. But at the same time, God isn't locked into only doing things the usual, earthly way. God can also do unusual things and work outside of science in extraordinary ways.

When you hear:
Why aren't there miracles today?

You might reply: How do you know there aren't?
Okay, this is sort of a two-part conversation. On one hand, I would say there are many trustworthy stories of people experiencing God doing miracles even now. (To be clear, I'm not talking about clips on social media of strange phenomena.)

On the other hand, both at the time of the Bible and now, most people lived ordinary lives. No special miracles. The Bible collects miracle stories *because they were uncommon*, special, and meant to show something to us about God. Each miracle had meaning, and that's why the story includes them.

So it can be helpful to explain that it seems God still does miracles and also the fact they haven't experienced one makes sense.

When you hear:
But why do miracles only happen
for some people but not everyone?

You might reply: I don't know.
In this case, our job is not to prove that miracles can happen, did happen, or are still happening. You might feel afraid of not assuring them entirely, of not assuaging every doubt.

Here's a helpful reframe: You are honoring mystery.

As we uphold here on many things, this is a topic where we do well to practice giving the shortest, true answer we can, then stopping to let our kids respond.

Last thought:
What are miracles, anyway?

You may have been told (I know I was) that miracles are *violations* of "natural law." I remember a class that outlined "true miracle criteria" and such.

My thinking has changed a bit on this over the years. I'm not sure a miracle goes against nature/natural law or that it goes against science.

Now I wonder: What if miracles point to what is *most* natural? That is, what would be most real and natural if Sin wasn't disrupting the holistic goodness of creation? After all, healing, abundance, restoration, and resurrection are all *more aligned*, not less, with the natural way God dreams for the world.

PART IV

JESUS STORIES

JESUS EXTENDS A WEDDING PARTY

JOHN 2:1–12

The Main Idea: This is a story about a good party, but it's about much more than that, too. The sign that Jesus performs brings two things to life. First, the fullness of God's power exists in human form in Jesus. Second, Jesus is using that power to bring God's kingdom into reality with all the life and joy and abundance that come with it.

One time, in a town called Cana, there was a **wedding**. Two people were getting married, and they invited their whole community to come celebrate with them, including Jesus and his disciples. Just like at a party now, weddings then had special foods, music, laughing, and special drinks. You might like lemonade or soda for a special drink. They liked **wine**.

Since the wedding party was for a big group, a big problem came up (at least, it was a big problem when the goal was a great celebration): They ran out of wine. Why was that a big problem? Because the party would be over. All done. End of celebration.

Jesus' mom, Mary, was at the wedding, and she went to Jesus and said, "They ran out of wine!"

At first, Jesus' answer sounds even a little bit sassy: "**Woman**, what does that have to do with me?" he said. Jesus was saying that it wasn't really his concern.

Key Image—Wedding
It isn't an accident that the first time Jesus does something to show who he is and what he's up to is at a wedding. Wedding parties, then as now, were times of feasting and joy; they gave hope for the future and new beginnings. They were the perfect place for Jesus to begin showing that God was bringing a new, and joyful, reality into the present. Wedding parties were also used in the Old Testament to speak about the future joys of God's kingdom. And the image of marriage as a metaphor for the mutual love and faithfulness of God and God's people shows up from the Old Testament all the way to Revelation.

Key Image—Wine
As one of the main beverages of the day (and, in the time before water filters, sometimes the only safe one), wine is often used as a symbol in the Bible. Owning your own vineyard and fruit trees was basically living the dream in ancient Israel. Isaiah 5 speaks about Israel as God's unfruitful vineyard (an image Jesus picks up on in some of his parables, too). And an abundance of good wine is one of the key images used by the prophets to look forward to the day when God would put the world right. All that is why the wine Jesus provides for the wedding feast is about much more than alcohol.

Key Word—Woman
In English, the way Jesus speaks to his mother sounds kind of rude. This may just be a situation where it would sound less dismissive in its own cultural context, but it's a bit of a strange way of addressing your mother even then. The other times Jesus speaks to a woman in this way it's to strangers, so this may be Jesus putting distance between himself and his birth family the way he does at other times in his life. The main thing John is trying to highlight is that Jesus is not taking orders from his mother (or anyone else); he will act, showing his power and identity, when he decides to for himself.

Fun Detail—150 Gallons
The story makes a point of saying that the servants fill up the stone jars "to the brim" (John 2:7 NASB). These are jars that hold twenty to thirty gallons each, so in total they would hold 150 gallons (give or take a few). That's, um, a *lot* of wine. Like, almost eight hundred of today's bottles. And this is *after* they'd already exhausted the original wedding supply!

Connections—Creation
Unlike some of the other stories of Jesus doing the miraculous, here he doesn't touch the jars, or pray, or really do anything but speak. Jesus just speaks, and things happen. It's just like the story of creation, where God speaks and things happen. It's one of the ways John makes clear that Jesus is God in a body, by showing that Jesus' power is of the same strength and quality as God's.

And yet, Mary went to the workers and told them, "Whatever my son, Jesus, says for you to do, listen to him."

Despite what Jesus said to his mom, he went to the workers and said, "Fill these six jars with water." **The jars were huge!** Often a jug of milk in the refrigerator is one gallon. Well, in this case, each jar was big enough for twenty or thirty of those milk jugs! Filled up, they weighed more than you do!

When the jugs had been filled with water, Jesus told a worker to scoop some out, take it to the person in charge of the party, and have them drink.

Can you imagine how the worker might have felt? Perhaps he felt worried. After all, as far as the worker knew, he was bringing a ladle full of plain water to the person in charge of this huge wedding party! Maybe he thought he'd be in trouble: Why would the person in charge want a drink of plain water? Maybe he felt curious about what Jesus was doing.

When the person in charge tasted what was brought to him, he tasted not water, but wine! Good, delicious wine! And he said, "You know, usually people serve the good things first and the less good things later when people don't care so much. You saved the best for last!"

Genre—Miracle Stories
The story ends by saying that this was the first of Jesus' signs. This is a theme in John, where the miracles that Jesus performs are called "signs." What John is getting at is that Jesus' miracles are pointing to something. They go beyond simply showing that Jesus has power to give us insight into who Jesus is and what he's up to. In this story, if Jesus is able to create with just a word, then he is fully God. And if he uses his power to bring to life the abundance and joy that the prophets had promised would one day come to God's people, then that means he is bringing those future hopes into the present. The kingdom of God is here, now, with all the joy that reality brings with it.

Key Word—Drunk
Some translations of verse 10 use a sort of euphemism like "had a lot to drink" (NLT) or "drunk freely" (NASB), but the word literally means "get drunk." While there are some who get a bit squeamish about it, this story is about Jesus providing an extraordinary amount of alcohol for a party.

What had happened? Between the jug and the taste test, Jesus had turned the water into wine! So, so much wine; 150 milk jugs full of wine. Instead of the party having to end, it could go on and on.

Anytime Jesus does a miracle, we should ask: Why? What does this miracle help us see about who God is or what God is doing in the world? If Jesus turned water to wine at this wedding, what does that tell us about what God is like?

It shows us that God is a joyful God, and the community of God should be joyful, a place of more-than-enoughness.

Connections—Feeding of the Five Thousand
One of the key features of this story is the abundance that Jesus provides—more than could ever be needed. This is also true of the story of Jesus providing food for the crowds, when the disciples pick up twelve full baskets of bread and fish after everyone has had their fill. The new era that Jesus is bringing with him will be one that is full of an abundance of good things, because that's who our God is.

Connections—The Prophets
One of the keys to fully understanding this story is recognizing that it's tapping into so many hopes and expectations drawn from the Old Testament prophets. After the exile, when things looked like they had fallen apart and God had abandoned Israel completely, the prophets began looking forward with hope to a new day, a day when God would deliver Israel. Their descriptions of that new day—sometimes called "the Age to Come" or the "Kingdom of God"—had certain themes that kept popping up. It will be time for "a feast of rich food, a feast of well aged wines" (see Isa. 25:6). "The mountains will drip with sweet wine, and all the hills will flow with it. I will restore the fortunes of my people Israel...they shall plant vineyards and drink their wine" (see Amos 9:13–14). "They shall be radiant over the goodness of Yahweh, over the grain, the wine, and the oil...Then shall their young women rejoice in the dance, and the young men and old shall be merry" (see Jer. 31:12–13). Jesus is saying, with this, his first miracle, "The time for those hopes is now!"

I wonder if Jesus picked the servants to help (instead of, say, the hosts) for a reason?

I wonder if there was dancing at the wedding and if Jesus danced too?

I wonder how Jesus might show God's joy and more-than-enoughness if he was on earth today?

JESUS CALLS THE TWELVE

**MATTHEW 4:18–25; MARK 1:16–20;
LUKE 5:27–30; JOHN 1:35–51**

The Main Idea: Jesus' invitation to the twelve disciples was two words: Follow me. And they got to decide if they wanted to say yes, and then literally follow him for years as they considered: Is Jesus for real? Truly from God? Actually bringing God's reign to earth? For us, it's similar: We are invited to follow, and even as we say yes, we get time to keep getting to know who Jesus is and what he's about.

This story is so short that this time we're just going to hear it from the Bible. But it isn't just in there once. **Three different writers** each tell the story, and each has their own style. So listen to these three experiences people had with Jesus. Afterward, I'd love to know what you heard in common and what you noticed was different.

 Your Kid Asks: Which one is true?
When kids start to track with the idea that the Bible has many different writers, they often wonder what to make of the differences between their styles. You might say something like, "They are all true, even when they're different. What if you and three friends all watched the same movie, then told me what it was about? You might take more time on your favorite part, or they might leave something out that wasn't as important to them. But if I asked, 'Which one of you told me the truth about the movie?' you'd say, 'All of us!' It's similar with the Gospels—Matthew, Mark, Luke, and John all tell stories about Jesus in different ways, and it's like getting four tellings of the story."

Mark 1:16–20

As he went along beside the sea of Galilee he saw Simon and his brother Andrew. They were **fishermen**, and were casting nets into the sea.

"Follow me!" said Jesus to them. "I'll have you fishing for people!"

Straightaway they left their nets and followed him. He went on a bit, and saw James, Zebedee's son, and John his brother. They were in the boat mending their nets, and he called them then and there. They left their father Zebedee in the boat with the hired servants, and went off after him. (NTFE)

Historical Context—Fishermen
You might not know many people for whom fishing could be described as much more than a hobby or a money pit. In fact, if your home isn't near the coast of a major body of water, it's possible you've never known a professional fisherman at all. However, it would have been fairly common in the region of Galilee where Jesus spent his time, which is why several of his disciples came from that job. It was hard work and a bit on the dangerous side, but as Mark's detail that James and John left their father "with the hired men" shows us, it could be lucrative enough that you could afford to hire employees (Mark 1:20). It was (as we might say) a solidly middle-class, respectable job, which makes it all the more striking that the disciples were willing to leave it.

Connections—Old Testament
As is true in, well, pretty much every passage of the New Testament, there are layers and layers of allusions in the call stories:

Jesus' call sounds an awful lot like when God told Abraham (Abram at the time) to leave his family and home and go to the place God would show him, and how Abraham immediately trusted and followed. Jesus is like Abraham, the start of God's family who will bless the whole world.

Mark's story follows closely the story from 1 Kings 19, when Elijah calls Elisha to be his assistant prophet. Jesus is like Elijah, calling for a return to Yahweh in a time of idolatry and oppression.

Jeremiah 16:16 uses the image of fishermen to describe bringing the people of Israel back from exile. Jesus is inviting the disciples to be those "fishers of people."

Key Word—Straightaway
This is one of Mark's favorite words. He writes like a breathless toddler recounting the adventures of their day. And then… And then… And then… Here, it helps to highlight how quickly and wholeheartedly the disciples respond to Jesus' call to follow. Jesus is compelling, and his mission is pressing.

Luke 5:27–28

After this Jesus went out and saw a **tax collector** called Levi, sitting at the tax office. "**Follow me**," he said. And he left everything, got up, and followed him. (NTFE)

John 1:43

The next day Jesus decided to go to Galilee, where he found Philip. "Follow me," he said to him. (NTFE)

Historical Context—Tax Collector
There wasn't really an "income tax" in Jesus' day. Instead, the "tax collectors" we meet would have collected tolls from people traveling from one territory to another. Since trade was the most likely reason for travel in those days, it would have functioned almost like a tariff or import tax in most cases. They were representatives of the government, and, as is the case with IRS agents today, would have been viewed with some suspicion. Even beyond that, they were Jewish people collecting taxes for foreign rulers, were often dishonest, and were for this reason universally despised. This is why Jesus calling and eating with Levi (Matthew) causes such a stir.

Key Word—Follow Me
Rabbis would often have followers in Jesus' day, those who would travel with a teacher in order to learn from them. This was more than learning information; it was conforming one's whole life to the pattern of life offered by the rabbi. There is some evidence that the "proper" way for a rabbi to get followers was to allow them to come to him on the strength of his own reputation. Jesus seems unconcerned with his reputation, and stoops to going around and asking for followers, which was apparently "just not done."

Key Number—Twelve
The call stories don't name this, but it does show up later that Jesus ends up calling twelve disciples to be the core of his community. This isn't an accident, as if he were shooting for fifteen, but a few had prior commitments. Any time the number twelve shows up in the Bible, we should immediately think of the twelve sons of Jacob who became the patriarchs of the twelve tribes of Israel. The gospels want to show that Jesus is bringing into reality the promises of renewal for Israel, which would lead to blessings for the world. Twelve disciples is a way of showing that renewal has come through this group of Jesus followers.

What was the same?

What was different?

If these stories are so short,
why do you think they're important?

I wonder why these people said yes?

I wonder why Jesus picked these guys?

I wonder why Jesus only said,
"*Follow me*" and not much else?

JESUS FEEDS A CROWD

MATTHEW 14:13–21; MARK 6:31–44;
LUKE 9:12–17; JOHN 6:1–14

> **The Main Idea:** One thing we see in this story is Jesus' holistic care for people's needs. He feeds them, *and* he points to the life he is offering (here and now, because that's how the reign of God works), a life that would also address the holistic needs we all have. **Jesus is a life-giver**, and this is a story that helps us better understand the kind of life God dreams for us and the world.

One time, Jesus was sitting on a hillside with his disciples when a large **crowd came** to find him. Crowds had a way of finding Jesus. Some people came to hear what he would say about God, while others came to see if he would do something special, like heal someone. In one book of the Bible, John, these special actions are called "signs," which reminds us that they were done to point to an important, true thing about who God is or what God was up to.

Connections—Manna
We might pass right over it, especially if someone did the very unhelpful thing of translating it as "a deserted spot" (looking at you, N. T. Wright); or "a deserted place" (hey there, NRSV); or "a solitary place" (what's up, NIV?), but the story starts with Jesus and his disciples going, literally, to the "wilderness." As in the same word that was used to describe where God provided manna and quail for the newly freed Hebrews in Exodus. This is not an accident. Jesus is starting a new Exodus, and just as God provided for the needs of the people then, Jesus is going to do the same for the people now.

This was one of those times when Jesus was, indeed, going to perform a sign for the people. See if you can figure out what this sign points to.

Jesus asked one disciple, named Philip, "Where shall we buy bread for these people to eat?" and you can tell from his answer how this question made Philip feel: "Even if we could find a breadmaker, it would cost us half the **money** we make in a year to buy all the bread they had, which wouldn't be anywhere near enough. Everyone would get one bite." Philip was overwhelmed by how impossible the question was. Then Andrew, another disciple, jumped in and said, "Here's a boy with five little rolls of bread and two fish." Imagine the group looking at the small lunch. It wouldn't be enough to share with even one other person, let alone a huge group of thousands.

Then Jesus told the disciples, "Have the people sit down." People found spots on the **grassy** hillside overlooking the glittering lake. And Jesus took the

---

Key Word—Denarii
Jesus asks the disciples why they don't just give the people food to eat if the people are hungry. I like to imagine Jesus had a little twinkle in his eye when he was saying that. The response is quick: "What, are you kidding? It would take two hundred denarii to feed them all!" For those of you who aren't up on the current exchange rate, this is not exactly like saying two hundred dollars. In fact, a denarii at the time was the value of a day's labor for a workingman, so two hundred denarii would equal two hundred days' work. We're talking tens of thousands of dollars, not hundreds, which would check out with the reality of providing lunch for more than ten thousand people including women and children.

Historical Context—Grass
At one point in the story there's an interesting little detail. Jesus tells the people to sit down on the grass. Those of you who live in wetter climates might not think anything of that. But for those of you who live in a climate like Israel's (like I do here in Southern California), this actually tells you something: It's spring, because spring is the only time that grass grows wild in Israel. The scholar Craig Keener says this meant that food stores would have been at their lowest point of the year, with the autumn harvest long in the rearview, and the later spring harvest still to come (*Gospel of Matthew*, 404). In other words, there would not have been enough food in the wilderness even if the disciples had enough money to buy it, and the connection to manna in the wilderness is highlighted all the more. The scholar Joel Marcus connects this with the spring festival of Passover, and the connection to the Last Supper is highlighted all the more (*Mark 1–8*, 408). Either, or both, would add a layer of symbolic meaning to what Jesus was up to, all from one little detail we might otherwise miss.

loaves, gave thanks, and started passing out **bread** bits to the group. He took the fish, gave thanks, and started passing out fish chunks to the group. And the Bible says people could have as much as they wanted. They **ate** and ate until they were completely full.

Bread and fish are fine foods, of course, but let's imagine you were the boy, and you had picked your favorite lunch to bring along. What would you want to see Jesus multiply for this meal?

Back to the hillside. For people living when Jesus lived, food didn't come from stores full of choices. Food was grown and made by hand, and there wasn't always enough. So this meal would have been special for so many reasons: It was a surprise feast, it was all you can eat, and of course, it was made by a miracle.

But the people did not really understand what this sign of bread for all pointed to about who God is or what God was doing. The very next day, Jesus was in a new location, not too far from the one the day before, but somewhere far enough away that the people needed to look for him. And look they did, until they found him again.

They were back in hopes of more bread, more fish. Jesus said to them, "You came to find me not because you understood the sign but because you filled up on the bread I gave you. You just want more to eat!"

Connections—Last Supper
When it's time to pass out the food, Jesus looks up to heaven, blesses the bread, breaks it, and passes it out to his disciples. It's exactly the same as what he does at the Last Supper. Jesus is the bread of life, which is the deeper truth this miracle is pointing toward.

Connections—Water to Wine
One of the key connections between these two provision-of-food miracles is the abundance of it all. Jesus turned a ridiculous amount of water into wine, and now provides twelve baskets beyond what is needed here. These miracles are pointing not just to Jesus being powerful; they're pointing to what Jesus is up to. He's bringing God's kingdom into the present, and one of the features of that kingdom is an abundance of good things, all provided by our good God.

And as the people asked questions, and as Jesus kept talking with them, they remembered another time God had fed a huge group—long ago there was manna in the desert. "Moses gave us bread from heaven!" they said. "What will you give us?" But Jesus took the chance to make something clearer to them: "God gave you bread from heaven. And God gave you me. I'm bread from heaven."

This made the crowd think, "Um, Jesus, you're not bread and you're not from heaven. We know your mom and dad. You're from Nazareth. " But Jesus was hoping they'd see what the sign pointed to.

Do you have a guess?

Jesus was there to give the people life. Just like literal bread feeds us and gives us life, Jesus came to give us life. The people were hungry again, but Jesus was offering himself. They liked the food, but Jesus was offering friendship.

I wonder how long Jesus and the disciples talked about the problem of hungry people?

I wonder if you can think of another story with bread in it from the Bible?

I wonder what the people thought and felt as they returned home the night Jesus fed them?

JESUS MEETS ZACCHAEUS

LUKE 19:1–10

> **The Main Idea:** Jesus loves everyone, and he offers the abundant life of God's reign to everyone. In other words, Jesus wants us. The only requirement to experience this salvation is to accept the offer. While the poor and marginalized are often more ready to accept than the rich, Zacchaeus shows that Jesus responds the same to all people, no matter their social status, wealth, gender, or even moral status.

When Jesus was alive on earth, God's people were living in the land God had promised. Technically. It didn't feel the way they hoped, the way God described, the way it had in the past, and there was one reason for that:

Rome.

The Romans had occupied the land and were in charge of it. They were controlling and cruel in many ways, including collecting money, called taxes, from the Jewish people for the Roman leaders. Taxes are meant to work where everyone pays some and that money gets used to help all. It did not work that way in Rome. They mainly just kept the money.

Enter tax collectors. They would go out and get the taxes. Plus extra. Which *they'd* keep. And there was nothing you could do about it.

Most people in the community did not have a lot of money. Imagine someone from your community became a **tax collector**. It might feel like they chose Rome instead of their neighbors. This feeling is why people hated tax collectors, which must have included Zacchaeus. Here's his story.

Zacchaeus heard Jesus was walking through his town, Jericho, and went to the road hoping to see him. But everywhere Jesus went people came to see him, making the road crowded with people, so tall and deep that Zacchaeus, who was short, could see nothing at all.

So Zacchaeus ran ahead, farther down the road. He reached a sycamore tree and climbed up. As Jesus passed his perch, he stopped, looked up and said something surprising.

What could Jesus have said that you would find surprising?

Jesus said . . . Zacchaeus's name. Surprise one.

Then Jesus said he was coming to Zacchaeus's home to **eat**. Surprise two.

Historical Context—Chief Tax Collector
We talked about how tax collectors weren't exactly highly regarded in the story about Jesus calling the disciples. In this story, Zacchaeus is a chief tax collector. While this might seem to be a title that would bring some status with it, in reality Zacchaeus still would have been despised. For his fellow Jews, it would have meant he was even more of a collaborator with their Roman oppressors. For the Romans, wealth generally brought honor and status with it. But Joel Green points out that in their society, *how* one got their money made all the difference (*Gospel of Luke*, 668–69). In more modern terms, Zacchaeus was "new money," and the "old money" of the Romans would have held him just as much in contempt as if he had been poor.

Historical Context—Meals
The people are scandalized by Jesus' decision to eat with that sinner Zacchaeus. There are a couple reasons for this, one from a Roman and one from a Jewish perspective. In the very hierarchical social system of Rome, accepting hospitality from someone or eating in their home had implications that were similar to but beyond what we might think today. It put you in the debt of the host, and the expectation was that you would repay that debt in some way. It might almost have seemed that Jesus was being "bought" by this dishonest rich guy. From a Jewish perspective, eating with a "sinner"—meaning someone who was not faithfully following the Jewish law—would have contaminated a person in a moral sense. For the Pharisees, it would have been proof that Jesus could not possibly be God's representative. He was a liar who had to be stopped.

Did you know…

- Having company come over was a big deal? AND…
- If you were not very powerful in the community, you could not invite somebody powerful to your house?

If you were Zacchaeus in the tree, hearing Jesus' words, what would you be thinking or feeling?

When people heard Jesus' plans, they grumbled and said, "I can't believe he's going to have dinner with a sinner like that!"

But Zacchaeus? He felt excitement and joy. The Bible doesn't tell us what they talked about during that visit, what they ate together, or how long Jesus stayed. Instead, we hear how the visit ended.

That's surprise three.

Zacchaeus said to Jesus, "I am going to give half my **wealth** to those who are poor. The people I cheated on their taxes? I'm going to give back the extra I took times four."

Connections—Rich Young Ruler
One of the interesting things about the story of Zacchaeus is how it breaks a pattern that shows up especially in Luke. Many of Jesus' interactions have gone against the social grain, so to speak, showing care for the marginalized and vulnerable like children, women, the poor and disabled, while painting the elite in a bad light. A reader would be forgiven for thinking that Jesus cares about those lower on the social ladder *instead of* those high on the ladder, that Jesus is just picking a new group of favorites and excluding the rest. But the two stories that Luke puts back-to-back—the so-called "rich young ruler" (see, e.g., Luke 8:18–30) and Zacchaeus—give us a more nuanced picture. Both are rich; both are "rulers" in some sense; both come to see Jesus. But the similarities end there. The nameless young man keeps all the commandments; Zacchaeus is a sinner. When Jesus invites the young man to a life of generosity he goes away sad; Zacchaeus spontaneously gives away more than half his fortune. The story of the young man ends with Jesus saying how it's virtually impossible for a rich person to find salvation; Zacchaeus' story ends with Jesus proclaiming that "salvation has come to this house" (Luke 19:9 NASB). Together, we see the message more clearly: Salvation is available to all who respond by trusting Jesus, no matter what their identity or status.

"Today," said Jesus, "**salvation** has come to this house, because he too is a son of Abraham. You see, the son of man came to seek and to save the lost."

A "son of Abraham," you see, is part of the community, someone who picks their neighbor, not Rome. A true son of Abraham means Zacchaeus is part of God's family—he's acting how the family acts—showing the world God's love. Which is what God always hopes will happen when someone who was lost is found. So Jesus keeps seeking, even people who are hiding from God's love or ignoring it because they have money. Jesus wants them. He wants us, too.

Key Word—Salvation
The idea of salvation coming to Zacchaeus' house is central to the story, and this is one of those times when we get a glimpse of what that word actually means. Jesus is not saying that Zacchaeus will go to heaven. That would be to import a completely foreign idea to the story. Instead, Jesus proclaims salvation *today* in response to Zacchaeus' changed relationship with money. Zacchaeus had been a slave to the god Money, and it had corrupted his whole world: cutting him off from community, chaining his heart, destroying his reputation. Jesus has set him free to experience life, joy, generosity, and community again, or maybe for the first time. Salvation.

I wonder if the grumblers
ever changed their minds?

I wonder what Zacchaeus was thinking while
he and Jesus made their way
from the road to his home?

I wonder who, today in our world,
is like Zacchaeus was then?

YOUR KID SAYS

"I KNOW THIS ONE ALREADY!"

There's no getting around it: Repetition is part of our faith experience. We just have this one book, a series of poems and prophecies, songs and sayings, and of course, stories. So we revisit and retell the same stories over and over.

The repetition, at any age, can be beautiful. It can also be boring, which is why I find it amusing when an adult is scandalized by a child expressing the latter, as if they themselves *never* get tired of the same text on repeat.

But we can help kids practice revisiting stories and working through that "heard it all before" feeling. And one way we can do that is to think about pizza.

Pizza is awesome, delicious, and offers endless variety. It's practically foolproof... unless one of two things happens.

1. Pizza is awesome...
unless you only ever order cheese.

Look, I love me a cheese pizza. But if you made that my only topping for all of time, eventually I'd give up on the idea that this is an interesting food.

Sometimes kids get cheese-pizza Bible stories—the same simple version over and over.

No wonder kids struggle on the repetition front. Adults are off learning new things about old stories between live teaching, podcasts, social media clips, and books, while kids are often told the story in the same way every single time.

This is especially true in a "humans are heroes" approach.

Take this week's story, for instance: Zacchaeus was bad, met Jesus, and became good.

That *is* a boring story, and that's one of the reasons kids (rightfully) express that they know it already. They've heard *that* version a zillion times.

Two solutions come to mind here: One is to mix up **how** the story is told. Make it silly, move around, invite interruptions, or tell it wrong on purpose so they can correct you. Changing the *style* helps younger kids especially.

The other option is to mix up **what** from the story is included. Add a fun fact, reveal a bit of context, or tell it from a new point of view (like a person from the crowd, a religious leader, a disciple). But if you choose this option, be careful of the other thing that ruins pizza.

2. Pizza is awesome… unless you dump everything on it.

If one were to simply slide a disc of dough down the assembly line and douse it with every topping available, the result is likely to be enjoyed by only a scant few in this world. So, too, a story that is told with every possible insight and detail often fails to be a story at all.

It's counterintuitive, but one reason kids get bored with the Bible is that they're told too much. It may happen as a reaction, swinging the pendulum from too-simple or too-young styles. Or perhaps it happens as their grown-up realizes the complexity of the Bible themself and wishes they'd known sooner.

The sweet spot: Sprinkling on a new thing or two.

Imagine if the various details of a Bible passage—genre, context, key words and numbers, et cetera–were toppings on a menu. This time you might choose sausage and peppers, and next time you might go veggie. As you get more familiar with the layers and details in a story, you hang on to them and share them a bit at a time. They can make the story deeper and richer but don't have to be given all at once.

A colleague called this the "simple, next, complex" approach.

- SIMPLE—New story? Tell it simply: Who was there, what happened, what do we notice about who God is or what God's like?
- NEXT—Heard it before, but still into it? Or it's been a while? Add a new element to it, in either the style *or* the content.
- COMPLEX—Kid getting older or bored? Tell them a new fact or insight that adds interest or fresh meaning to the story.

So taking today's story of Zacchaeus, this might go like:

Simple
Zacchaeus wanted to see Jesus, climbed a tree, got invited over, changed, Jesus declared "salvation has come to this house." Jesus loves everyone! Jesus invites everyone!

Next
Tell the story from the point of view of a bystander on the road below Zacchaeus or a guest at his house that afternoon.

- "I couldn't believe it! He stopped. Stopped right where he was walking and looked...up. To Zacchaeus. Ugh, I can't stand that guy..."; or
- "I couldn't believe it! I was at a table for dinner...with Jesus. Me! I'd heard others say that he wasn't like the rest, that he didn't avoid people like me and Zacchaeus, but I wasn't sure I believed it."

Complex
- Explain how Zacchaeus' job didn't just bother people because of his stealing, but also because it made him an ally with Rome. Paradoxically, the Romans would have shunned him. He would seem to be rich and powerful on the outside (which our culture says makes you important and happy), but he would likely have felt rejected and lonely.
- Talk about who's "in" and "out" in their world, and why. What about for you? Is there anyone who's political allyships make you inclined to reject them? Can you share that in an age-appropriate way?
- Connect the dots to other stories of God engaging with so-called rejects, like the Samaritan woman at the well or the hemorrhaging woman.

Kids tend to stay more interested in stories when we mix up the toppings: Use a creative or fun style; add a new detail or layer (but not all of them!). When our kids say they know a story already, we can ask: Have they heard only the cheese-pizza version? Have they had every detail dumped on them? What could we try to address next?

JESUS WALKS ON WATER

MATTHEW 14:23–33; MARK 6:45–51; JOHN 6:16–21

The Main Idea: Jesus is Israel's God, Yahweh, in human form. And just like Yahweh set Israel free in the Exodus so they could be a community that lives in ways that show the world what God is like, Jesus is setting all people free so they can be a community that lives in ways that show the world what Jesus is like. God saves, again and again.

The disciples—Jesus' closest followers—were coming to the end of the day with tired bodies but full tummies, because Jesus had just provided food for a huge crowd. Then they got into a boat on the **Sea of Galilee**, which is a smaller lake—too big to swim across, but you can see the shore all the way around it.

Jesus didn't get into the boat, though; he went away on his own to pray—to talk with God.

Historical Context—Sea
Unlike some other ancient cultures, Israel was more "mountain people" than "beach people." The sea was unpredictable, fickle, powerful, dangerous, and chaotic. It was almost like some sort of evil monster with a mind of its own. If you've ever been caught in a rip current or tossed about by a particularly powerful wave, you might begin to understand. Which is why the Old Testament makes such a big deal of God's power over the sea. Yahweh forms the sea with a word in creation, splits it in the Exodus, controls it in Jonah, even *walks on it* in Job 9:8 and Habakkuk 3:15. All this is background to what this story is saying about who Jesus is.

The Bible tells us that when evening came, the boat, battered by the waves, was far from the shore, because the wind was against them. Remember, there weren't motors on boats at that time, so having the wind blow the wrong way could leave you stuck and waiting for it to change.

They were out there through the night, but then, early in the morning Jesus came **walking** toward them on the sea.

How do you think they responded to this?

When the disciples saw him walking on the sea, they were terrified. They said, "It is a ghost!" And they cried out in fear. But immediately Jesus spoke to them and said, "Take heart, **it is I**; do not be afraid."

Now there was another time, long ago, when God said something similar, back when Moses came to a bush that was on fire but didn't burn up. God spoke to Moses, saying it was time to go to Egypt and free God's people from enslavement. And Moses replied, "So, I go to Pharaoh, king of Egypt, and say the God of the Hebrews says to let the people go. Pharaoh is going to say 'Who sent you? What god?' What should I say?"

And God names Themself, saying, "I Am."

Remember, Jesus didn't speak English, so when Jesus says, "It is I," everyone in the boat (who certainly knew Moses' story forward and backward)

Historical Context—Walk on Water
There *were* Greek and Roman stories of gods or heroes doing something superficially similar to what Jesus does in this story. However, it was always because they were running so fast that they didn't sink. There is no story of someone calmly walking out in the middle of the sea like this, except, of course, when the Old Testament describes Yahweh doing exactly that—hovering over the waters at creation.

Key Word—It's Me
Jesus' words to the disciples may sound normal: "Hey guys, it's me," but they add one more layer to the bigger message of this story. The words could just as easily be translated "I Am," and they are the exact same words God uses in the story of the burning bush when Moses asks for God's name. Yahweh. I Am.

would have heard how that sounded a whole lot like "I am." It's a little clue: Jesus is God in a body, living among us.

This isn't the only story connection we'll find between these two, but for now, let's head back to **Jesus on the sea**.

Jesus says, "Take heart, it is I; do not be afraid." And Peter answered him, "Lord, if it is You, command me to come to You on the water."

So Jesus said, "Come." And Peter got out of the boat, started walking on the water, and came toward Jesus. But when he noticed the strong wind, he became frightened, and as he felt himself beginning to sink, he cried out, "Lord, save me!" Jesus immediately reached out his hand and caught him.

Jesus saved him. Which brings us to our second connection. After Moses met God at the burning bush, he went to Pharaoh. Moses said, "I Am, the God of the Hebrews, says to **let them go**," and… God saved them.

Salvation is kind of God's jam.

Genre—Miracle Stories
There are lots of stories about Jesus doing miracles, all of which show that Jesus is able to use God's power. But the key to really understanding a miracle story is to ask what it shows us about who Jesus is and what he is up to. In this case, the echoes of what God did in the Exodus are part of that broader meaning. As N. T. Wright puts it, this story is told not so much to show us that "Jesus can do whatever he wants but because this particular thing is so closely associated with what Israel's God does at a key moment in Israel's history" (*John for Everyone*, pt. 1, 76).

Connections—Exodus
This story is full of word choices that intentionally echo stories from the Exodus. The story begins with Jesus going up on a mountain to pray, just like Moses went up on a mountain to talk with Yahweh. Jesus is going to "pass by" the disciples just like God "passes by" Moses on the mountain in Exodus 33 when Moses asks to see God's face. Jesus' words to the disciples, "I am," echo God giving the name Yahweh at the burning bush. Jesus walking on the sea as if it were dry land makes us think of the Israelites walking through the Red Sea on dry land. Even the time that Jesus shows up—during the "fourth watch," which was between 3:00 a.m. and 6:00 a.m.—is exactly the timing of God saving Israel at the Red Sea (see Exod. 14:24). The gospel writers keep focusing our attention on the story of the Exodus to help us see what this story is saying about who Jesus is and what he is up to.

If you read this story in a Bible, there's one last part. Jesus says to Peter: "You of little faith, why did you doubt?"

We don't know what kind of voice Jesus used, but I imagine it was gentle. I think Jesus knows that walking on water, surrounded by waves, would be scary.

But I think Jesus also was saying "Hey, you can have faith. Put your trust in me, and even a little trust, if it's in me, is enough." We don't need big trust because of big waves. We just need to be sure our trust is in the person who made those waves in the first place, can walk on them if he wants to, and can calm them in an instant. Which is, by the way, where the story ends:

When they got into the boat, the wind went quiet. And those in the boat worshipped him, saying, "Truly you are the Son of God."

I wonder why Jesus decided to walk
to them on the water?

I wonder why Peter picked joining Jesus
on the water as the sign it was him?

I wonder if it took a little or a long time
to connect their time in the boat
to other stories from the past?

JESUS WELCOMES THE CHILDREN

MATTHEW 19:13–15; MARK 10:13–16; LUKE 18:15–17

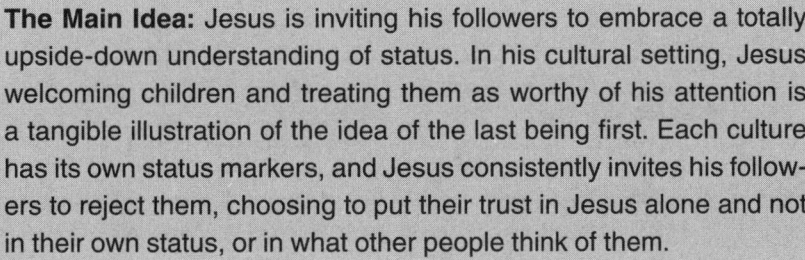

The Main Idea: Jesus is inviting his followers to embrace a totally upside-down understanding of status. In his cultural setting, Jesus welcoming children and treating them as worthy of his attention is a tangible illustration of the idea of the last being first. Each culture has its own status markers, and Jesus consistently invites his followers to reject them, choosing to put their trust in Jesus alone and not in their own status, or in what other people think of them.

One day as Jesus was out and about, parents began to bring their **children** to him. They wanted him to touch them and bless them. The disciples watched this happening and began to scold the parents.

 Historical Context—Children
One of the keys to understanding what's going on under the surface in this story is to understand just how different ancient Rome was from our world today in its perspective on kids. Children, according to the scholar Joel Green, "possessed little if any intrinsic value as human beings" (*Gospel of Luke*, 650). The reason for that? Kids are vulnerable, entirely dependent on others for their survival. In Roman culture, any dependence on another person lowered your social status below that person's, and so the complete vulnerability of a child put them at the very bottom of the social ladder. (There are some really horrific implications of this that we're not going to get into right now.) The disciples are trying to protect the honor of Jesus by keeping these worthless creatures away from him. But this dependence is exactly why Jesus sees children as a model for humanity. Children depend on their parents unselfconsciously in exactly the way humans are meant to depend on God completely, with no shame.

"You're bothering Jesus with these children."
"Could you keep hold of your kids? Don't let them run up!"
"Jesus doesn't have time for kids."

But when Jesus saw what was going on, he felt **angry**. Not at the parents. Not at the kids. At **the disciples**.

"No! Let the kids come here! Don't stop them from coming to me. Goodness! The **kingdom** of God belongs to kids and anyone who is willing to be like them!"

Key Word—Angry
This is one of those stories where Jesus gets mad (it happens far more often than some people think!). Even Jesus' words themselves in the original Greek have a sharp sound to them. When Jesus gets angry, we should pay attention to why, because that's showing us the sorts of things that make God angry. One of the most consistent reasons? Powerful people hurting vulnerable people, including keeping them away from God's presence in some way. In this case, the disciples keeping children away from Jesus' touch shows that they are completely missing the point of what Jesus is up to, who gets to be a part of it, and how they (as leaders) should conduct themselves. So, Jesus gives them a much needed telling-off.

Connections—Who is greatest?
The point Jesus is trying to get across to the disciples in this story is one they had a really hard time getting. All through the gospel stories we see them trying to position themselves for places of power; they all want to be the greatest. We need to remember that's because the perspective of the last being first, and leaders being servants, was completely foreign to everything they had been taught about what it meant to be human, especially for the male disciples. It wasn't until Jesus' death and resurrection that they finally started to get this key piece of Jesus' teaching.

Key Word—Kingdom
Jesus holds the children up as models for God's kingdom. This concept is central to Jesus' teaching—that in him the kingdom of God has come to earth and is becoming a reality here and now, not just in some future heaven. For kids, this sounds like: "Jesus talked about something called the kingdom of God. It's not a place on a map; it's a group that lives together like God really is King, and tries to show what God is like in the way they treat each other and the world." Or, "God dreams of a world that works in ways that match who God is, and the kingdom is where people say yes, that they want to make that dream come true as they follow Jesus together."

Jesus often talked about this kingdom. It's not a place on a map. It's any place where people live together like God really is king. They live together in ways that match who God is. And it's a place for kids.

After Jesus spoke, he took the children up in his arms. He placed his hands on their heads. He **blessed** each one of them. Child after child after child.

Historical Context—Blessing
Kids might be a little confused by what exactly is going on in this particular story. Why do the parents want Jesus to touch or bless their children? One helpful thing to remember is that in the ancient world, childhood was a dangerous thing, especially for very young children like the ones Jesus is touching. A much higher percentage of babies did not survive to adulthood when compared to today, and as any parent knows, even today that's a very anxiety-producing thing! For the parents who see who Jesus is, his touch would symbolize God's blessing and protection over the child. The scholar Joel Marcus also sees some similarities between this story and the blessings godparents would give to babies, meaning that Jesus is becoming a sort of godparent to these children, welcoming them into God's family (*Mark 8–16*, 717).

I wonder what the kids told Jesus?

I wonder what Jesus said to the kids?

I wonder how long they were together?

FOUR FRIENDS BRING A FIFTH FRIEND THROUGH THE ROOF

MARK 2:1–12; LUKE 5:17–26

> **The Main Idea:** Jesus' response to this man points to the holistic care God has for humanity: We are meant to live connected to God, ourselves, each other, and creation. Jesus doesn't just forgive; he doesn't just heal. We are all invited, for our part, to help others experience the same. So sometimes, like the friends, we get to be part of removing that barrier for others.

There were five friends living near the area where Jesus was, and one of them could not walk. The Bible doesn't tell us why that was—if he was born with a **disability** or something had happened to him during his life. What we do know is that being disabled at this time often meant life was difficult and lonely. Disabled people were often left out of community life.

Historical Context—Paralytic

The ancient world was not a friendly place for the disabled. Joel Green points out that they were banned from the priesthood, in certain places were excluded from fully participating in community gatherings, and were often alienated in a number of ways, big and small (*Gospel of Luke*, 239). Our culture has made some strides in this area, but we shouldn't lose sight of the fact that Jesus' healing went beyond the physical aspect of healing the man's legs. It included social and relational aspects as well, healing how the man was seen by his community.

Word got to these friends that Jesus was not only nearby, but he was healing people. They made up their minds: They were getting to Jesus. Four of the friends carried their fifth friend on a mat to the **house** where he was. There was no question if it was the right place; the huge crowd spilling out the doors and windows was a sure sign.

But that crowd was a problem. There were so many people stuffed shoulder to shoulder that a fly couldn't even buzz between them, let alone a group of five with a mat to carry. But they had made up their minds: They were getting to Jesus.

We don't know who had the idea first, or how long they talked about it before they agreed to it, but once they couldn't go through the crowd, they decided to go through the roof.

Imagine you are one of the people who had found room inside the house.

Jesus is speaking, when suddenly you hear scuffling, thumping, and indistinct voices. Then a thud. Then another. Thud. Thud. Thud. It seems to be coming from above your head! So you look up, and get a clod of **roof** right on the nose. Others have noticed it, too, of course, and the only thing to do about

---

**Fun Detail—At Home**
The story begins with a rumor that Jesus "is at home" (Mark 2:1), and so the crowds came to see him. Which means it might have been Jesus' own roof the four friends destroyed! Let's just say Jesus' response is quite a bit…um…more gracious than mine would have been in similar circumstances.

Fun Detail—Roof
Roofs in Jesus' day were flat, and could be accessed by an external ladder so that people could climb up and enjoy cool night breezes in the hot summertime. They would have been made out of wooden beams that then were covered with layers of reeds and several inches of clay. The issue of accessibility–which we likely see quickly, given our own culture's increasing awareness of its importance–isn't humorous. But the gumption and creativity of these five men who won't be stopped? Our narrator hopes we see some humor in how they righted this wrong. The friends up on a roof with shovels, the noise of their digging being heard by the people inside, the clumps of dirt and reeds showering down on top of Jesus as he teaches—it should make us smile to imagine.

it is to move out of the way of the falling roof clumps because they just keep coming. By now Jesus is also looking up, watching what is clearly becoming a hole in the roof.

Then there's a head, right in the hole, calling, "Right, you strong ones, ready now! Get right under here so you can take hold of him."

Him?

Him who?

But there's no time to ask because the head is gone and now, in the hole, are feet, then knees, then the legs of a man being held by the torso as he is lowered into the hole, into the house, into the presence of Jesus. Thank goodness the men inside do what they are told and take hold of him, because the man who has come down cannot walk on his own, you realize.

And now that he's there, it's silent. Everyone is staring at the man. And at Jesus.

And Jesus is staring between the man and the hole. What he saw, the Bible says, is "their faith." The faith of all these friends who had made up their minds to get to Jesus. They trusted him.

What Jesus said next had two effects at the same time. For some, it filled their hearts with hope like warm soup in a tummy on an ice-cold day. They felt covered by love like they'd sunk into a hot spring. For others, though, his words hit like a slap, stinging the part of them that felt sure they knew just what God did and did not allow. Because Jesus' words? Only God Themself, or an official priest on God's behalf, was allowed to say them.

"Dear child, your sins are forgiven."

Jesus didn't mean the man had been disabled because of sin, he just knew what's true about every person: We all have times when we don't reflect who God is in the ways we act or talk.

Those six words hung in the air, until the reactions of everyone else joined them. Grumbles. Murmurs. How dare he?

Historical Context—Forgiveness of Sins
Much of the argument between Jesus and the scribes hinges on whether he has the authority to forgive sins. In the Old Testament, forgiveness is something that is only available in the way God says it is, specifically through the system of sacrifices that allows *the priest* to declare someone's sins forgiven. The priest has the authority to forgive sins, in other words. The problem here, as N. T. Wright puts it, "isn't so much that Jesus is 'claiming to be God' (though Luke will soon make clear that when people met Jesus they were indeed meeting God); he is claiming to *speak for* God, in a way which undercuts the normal channels of authority" (*Luke for Everyone*, 60). Since the scribes in this story were very possibly priests as well, this makes sense of why the whole incident is personal for them. Jesus is saying that he can speak for God apart from the system of sacrifices and the priests who served at the temple.

Connections—Daniel: Son of Man
This story is one of several where Jesus refers to himself as "the Son of man." It's possible Jesus thought this was a cool way to say he's just a Normal Human Dude, like the *30 Rock* meme of Steve Buscemi saying, "How do you do, fellow kids?" More likely, Jesus is quoting the visions from the book of Daniel. Take it away, N. T. Wright: "There, 'one like a son of man' is the representative of God's true people. He is opposed by the forces of evil; but God vindicates him, rescues him, proves him to be in the right, and gives him *authority*" (*Mark for Everyone*, 17). In Jesus' day, this figure was often seen as one who would bring judgment on sinners, purifying God's people by getting rid of the bad people. What's fascinating here is that instead, Jesus is using his authority to offer *forgiveness*, purifying God's people in the completely opposite way.

Connections—Exodus
Jesus' words before healing the man are that the sign is "so you may know" that Jesus has authority. They are an interesting echo of the exodus story. Over and over, as Yahweh does signs and brings plagues, it is repeated that the whole process is "so you may know" who God is. The miracles are done so the Hebrew people would know (see Exod. 6:7); so all Egypt would know (see Exod. 7:5); so Pharaoh would know (see Exod. 9:29); so the whole world would know who Yahweh is. It's a reminder that miracles are never just magic tricks; they are meant to point us to who our God is, and what They are like.

But it was like Jesus could read their words in the air. So he spoke to those folks who were so upset, the ones who just knew that Jesus was not qualified to **forgive sins**. "Only God can do that!" they'd hissed to each other.

"Oh, your hearts!" Jesus said. "So quick to assume you know what God will or won't do. What's easier? To tell this man his sins are **forgiven** or to tell him he can get up and walk?"

Jesus could very well do both, and so he did. And if they wanted to, that would show them that Jesus had the same authority as God **to do the same things** God did—forgive and heal.

To the man, he said, "Get up, take your mat and go home."

Home. Forgiving sins and healing bodies, they both had the same goal: Bring him home. Jesus was making sure the man knew that his whole life mattered to Jesus. And Jesus wanted him to be whole. And for anyone there who was willing to see it, Jesus was making sure they knew this was why he was here. Home and wholeness, this was his goal.

I wonder how far they traveled to get to
the house where Jesus was?

I wonder how long it took to make
the hole in the roof?

I wonder how different people felt about
the day when they got home that night?

JESUS RAISES LAZARUS

JOHN 11:1–46

The Main Idea: Jesus is the bringer of life, even out of death. The day that has been long hoped for, the day when God would restore life to the dead, has come in the person of Jesus.

Jesus was friends with two sisters, Mary and Martha, and their brother, Lazarus, a wonderful name for nicknames, like Zee-Zee or Russ. The Bible tells us a story about them in a book called John, and it starts when the sisters send a message to Jesus: "Lord, your dear friend is very sick."

But when Jesus heard about it he said, "Lazarus's sickness will not end in death. No, it happened for the glory of God."

Jesus loved Martha, Mary, and Lazarus, but he stayed where he was for the next two days. Then he said, "Let's go back to Judea... Our friend Lazarus has fallen asleep, but now I will go and wake him up."

The disciples said, "Lord, sleeping will help him feel better—sleep will help him heal." See, they thought Jesus meant Lazarus was simply sleeping, but Jesus was using sleep as an expression—he meant Lazarus had died.

Jesus explained that to them: "Lazarus is dead." Then Jesus said something that sounds strange: "And for your sakes, I'm glad I wasn't there, because now you will really believe. Come, let's go see him."

When Jesus arrived at Bethany, he learned that Lazarus had already been in his grave for **four** days. Jewish burial traditions were very important—a body was first placed in a tomb, usually a cave, and later, when it was only bones, those were wrapped up specially and buried in a permanent spot. And then the whole community would come together to mourn—mourning is not just feeling sad about something, but also having the time and space to let that sadness out.

When Martha heard Jesus was coming, she went to meet him. Mary stayed in the house.

Martha said to Jesus, "Lord, **if only you had been here**, my brother would not have died. But even now I know that God will give you whatever you ask."

And Jesus replied to her, "Your brother will rise again."

"Yes," Martha said, "he will rise when everyone else rises, in the resurrection at the last day."

Key Number—Four
That Lazarus had been in the tomb for four days gives us a couple of important pieces of information. First, as we said above, it meant that Lazarus was probably already dead by the time Jesus got the message to come to Bethany. Second, in a world before modern medicine it wasn't always obvious when someone had died, and there were instances where someone was thought to be dead but then revived. Four days, though, would mean that possibility was ruled out. Jesus did not pull a Miracle Max and notice that Lazarus was "only mostly dead." He truly raised him from death back to life.

Your Kid Asks: Why Did Jesus wait?
It's a version of what Martha herself says: "If you'd been here, he wouldn't have died!" The story actually gives us a couple of clues. First, when Jesus got to Bethany, Lazarus had already been dead for four days. That means he was dead already, or nearly, when Jesus first got the news. He couldn't have made it there in time anyway. We also should notice the disciples' reaction to the news that they are going to Bethany, which is just outside Jerusalem: "But they're going to kill you!" Thomas then says, "Well, we might as well go die with him" (see John 11:16). Jesus knows that going so near Jerusalem will set in motion the events that will lead to his own death. It's inevitable. So should he go now? N. T. Wright guesses that Jesus spends the two days before setting out praying, in conversation with his Father about whether now is the time to go and die, and what he should do about Lazarus (*John for Everyone*, pt. 2, 3).

Again Jesus said something strange. He told her, "I am the **resurrection**
and the life. The one who believes in me will live, even though they die; and
whoever lives by believing in me will never die. Do you believe this?"

"Yes, Lord," she replied. "I believe that you are the Messiah, the Son of
God, who is to come into the world."

After they talked, Martha went back to Mary, pulled her aside, and said,
"Jesus is here. He wants to see you." Mary immediately went out to find Jesus,
who was outside the village a bit.

In Jesus' time, no one mourned alone. The community came to be with
them, so when they saw Mary get up, they thought she was going to Lazarus's
grave, and they got up and followed her.

Mary got to Jesus and fell at his feet. Through her tears, she said the same
thing as her sister: "Lord, if only you had been here, my brother would not
have died."

Jesus looked around, and everywhere he turned, there was sadness. Tears
were streaming down every face. It shook him to his very center.

"Where is the body now?" he asked. They started in that direction, and
then Jesus' troubled heart began to overflow into **tears**. He wept, the big kind
of crying where everything wrong on the inside finds its way up to the surface

---

Key Word—Resurrection

There is obvious foreshadowing here of Jesus' resurrection, even if Lazarus is not resurrected in quite the same way that Jesus is. Martha believes that God will resurrect those who trust in Yahweh, which is a vision that comes from Isaiah 65 and 66, but this was always a future hope. One of the things this story is doing is bringing that hope forward in time. Jesus is offering life now that will continue on into eternity.

Key Words—Jesus Loved and Jesus Wept

In this story we get two peeks into Jesus' emotional life. He is said to *love* Lazarus and his sisters, and then he *weeps* at Lazarus's tomb. Sometimes these things are talked about as examples of Jesus' humanity, because he experiences emotions. But Marianne Meye Thompson asks us to consider why those can't be just as much a part of Jesus' divinity. The God we meet in the Bible is consistently an emotional God, and in Jesus' love and sorrow, we see God's love for and sorrow over this broken world.

and seems to come to the outside, maybe through your tears, or the groany noises you make, or your snot.

All the while people had been watching Jesus' reactions and feelings, and they started to talk about him. Some of them said, "Look at how much he loved him!" But some said, "This man healed a blind man. Couldn't he have kept Lazarus from dying?" Maybe Jesus could have helped before, when it was just a matter of being sick. But now? When Lazarus is dead? There's nothing that can be done *now*.

Nothing is harder to fix, after all, than being dead.

The group all arrived at the grave, which, like many graves at the time, was a cave with a big stone in front of the opening.

"Take away the stone," Jesus told them.

Martha was the one to speak up and say what everyone was thinking: "Lord, he has been dead for four days. The smell will be terrible."

Jesus responded, "Didn't I tell you that if you trust me, you would see God's glory?" So they took away the stone. Then Jesus prayed out loud, so that the group could hear, and said, "Father, thank you for hearing me. You always hear me, but I said it out loud because of all these people standing here, so that they will believe you sent me."

Then Jesus shouted, "Lazarus, come out!"

And he did.

The dark, empty hole of the cave entrance was filled in by a whole living person. Though he was still in his burial cloths, this was not a mummy or a ghost. Everyone was seeing it with their own eyes: resurrection.

Genre—Miracle Stories

It's always important with miracle stories to remember that they are written to show more than just that Jesus has power. They are meant to point to something about who Jesus is. In this case, Jesus names it in his conversation with Mary and Martha. "I am the resurrection and the life," Jesus says (John 11:25). This miracle is showing us that not even death can get in the way of the life Jesus offers, and it is meant to encourage us that life is what God has in store for all of us one day.

I wonder why Jesus waited?

I wonder why Jesus cried?

I wonder why Jesus only spoke for Lazarus to come out?

JESUS HEALS A WOMAN AND A GIRL

MARK 5:21–43; LUKE 8:40–56

> **The Main Idea:** Jesus came so that all people could experience the life and wholeness of being a part of God's family. God's commitment to justice includes making sure that those who are excluded, like the woman, are placed on the same level as the powerful, like Jairus. The Old Testament had always pointed forward to a time when God would bring exactly this sort of renewal and joy, and Jesus is showing that the time is now. God's justice is about all people having life, joy, community, and abundance.

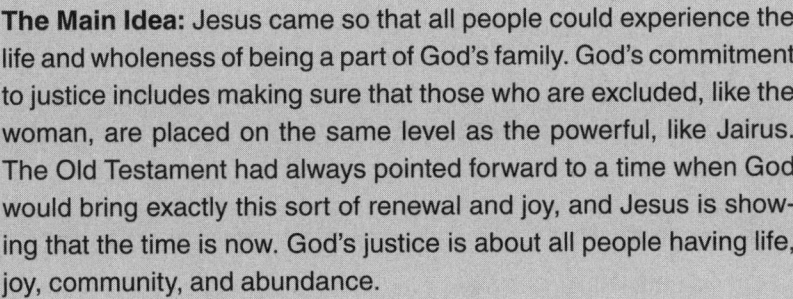

Get to Jesus. Get to Jesus. Get to Jesus.

He repeated the words again and again: A mission. A hope. The only hope.

His daughter was dying, and everything possible had been done. Except this. Except finding this man who had been healing people and asking him if he'd help.

Jairus knew Jesus, of course—every leader in the synagogues did by now. They didn't agree about what to make of him. But who cared what people thought about whether Jesus was allowed to do what he was doing right now? Allowed or not, he sometimes healed people.

Get to Jesus. Get to Jesus. Get to Jesus.

There! In that knot of people; there were always people.

"Please. Please can you come with me? Please can you come to my little daughter? **She's sick**—dying—please come. Lay your hands on her—rescue her and let her live!"

Jesus went off with Jairus.

Got to Jesus. Got to Jesus. Got to Jesus.

He tried to hurry but not be rude about it. He tried to keep them moving but not shove too much.

Get home. Get home. Get home.

"Who touched my clothes?"

They had stopped. Still.

Get home. Get home. Get home.

Genre—Healing Stories
Stories of healing show up in all the gospels as they tell the story of Jesus' work in the world. A key thing to remember is that in the ancient, pre-medicine world, sickness took on a much larger significance than many of us might think at first. The experiences of those with chronic illness are becoming more and more visible today, and those experiences give us an important glimpse of the full significance of what Jesus did for those he healed. Being sick often put limits on your ability to engage in society and relationships. Certain illnesses prevented you from being able to be in community or even worship in the temple or synagogue. Healing was about more than your body; in other words, it was for your whole self, your whole life, your family and community and relationships and religious life. Healing stories are about God bringing life in ALL of those areas, not just a healed physical body.

Literary Feature—Markan Sandwich
Mark sometimes has one story get interrupted by another before we go back to the first story, creating what scholars sometimes (humorously?) call a "Markan Sandwich." Oh, those witty academics. Mark does this to link the two stories together. Mark does this to show that the two stories are not unrelated, random events; they have something to say to each other. In this case, the stories are both about healing women: one young, one old; one rich, one poor; one part of the social elite, one an outcast. The woman and Jairus, in fact, are almost as opposite as two people could be in their time and place. And not only does Jesus heal both women, but he puts the healing of the elite one on hold to tend to the outcast. Mark puts these stories together so that we can't miss how God's commitment to justice played out in Jesus' ministry.

"This crowd is nearly crushing you," Jesus' disciples said to him. For it was Jesus who'd asked the question. "You're really asking, 'Who touched me?'"

Everyone. Everyone is touching you.

Jesus turned this way and that, looking.

Get home. Get home. Get home.

Then the crowd shifted and a woman came to stand in front of Jesus, shaking head to toe.

She had snuck into the crowd. *Get to Jesus. Get to Jesus. Get to Jesus.* She wasn't supposed to be there; she wasn't allowed based on their customs. For **twelve** years she'd had a chronic illness—she bled and it wouldn't stop. Doctors made it worse instead of better. And all the while the customs about purity and blood said she couldn't be in the community.

But on this day, she came determined. She snuck through, kept low, closed the gap bit by bit.

Get to Jesus. Get to Jesus. Get to Jesus.

"If I can just touch his clothes, I'll be saved." And she reached. Felt the fabric on her fingertips. Then she felt something else entirely.

She knew. It was done. Her bleeding had stopped.

But she hadn't planned to be caught. The only thing to do was tell him everything and see what he would say back. So she did.

And he said, "My daughter, your faith has rescued you. Go in peace. Be healed from your illness."

His daughter? Like family? Healed? Like whole? It was beyond, far beyond anything she'd imagined when she set her mind to find him.

Key Number—Twelve

The number twelve is a common symbol in the Bible because that is the number of tribes in ancient Israel. Twelve represents the whole of Israel, all of God's people. Like, all the tribes are included. In this story, the girl is twelve years old, and the woman has been bleeding for twelve years. Mark doesn't tell us these details by accident. He wants to highlight that Jesus' life and ministry mean that the whole of Israel will be raised to new life, that all of God's people will be healed. That Jesus is bringing God's justice and life to all people.

All the while Jairus stood by, watching and listening, until his attention was pulled away by a group approaching from the direction of his own home.

"Your daughter has died. Don't bother Jesus anymore."

Get to… Get to… The world felt like it had stopped and like it was swirling at the same time. Too late? How could they be too late?

It was Jesus who spoke next: "Don't be afraid. Trust me." And he began to walk with Jairus again.

To the house. Full of **wailing, crying people**. "Why all this fuss? The child isn't dead, just asleep."

They laughed at him for this.

Inside. But only Jairus and his wife, plus Peter, James, and John were allowed in.

To the bed. To her side. And Jesus **took the girl's hand** in his own and said, "Time to get up, little girl!" And she did. Up from bed. Up from death.

Fun Detail—Professional Mourners
In the ancient world, people would sometimes hire mourners to wail and cry outside the home of a family member who had died. Apparently they wanted to make sure there was enough grief being expressed. These are probably the people Jesus talks to when he gets to the house of the little girl. Unfortunately for them, Jesus is about to put them out of a job.

Historical Context—Clean and Unclean
To fully get what Mark is saying in these stories, we need to understand how the Old Testament Law talks about cleanliness. There's a ton that could be said on this topic, like whole books, but what's most relevant for this story is that two of the most unclean of all the unclean things were dead bodies and people who were bleeding. Especially a woman who was bleeding. Especially if that bleeding was the sort that happened monthly. The second relevant thing is that if someone was themself unclean, or if they came into contact with something or someone unclean, they would need to isolate themself from society and go through a process of becoming clean again.

In other words, this woman had been unclean, socially isolated, for *twelve years*. And she was taking a huge risk by being out in public at all, let alone approaching and then touching Jesus. The consequences of making a revered rabbi unclean by touching him would be unimaginable for her. But she doesn't make Jesus unclean, and neither does the little girl's body when Jesus touches it. By all the normal laws of society, Jesus should have been doubly unclean. But instead of uncleanliness attaching itself to Jesus, cleanliness goes out from him, restoring life and community to those who had been denied them.

Up for a **snack** (Really. The Bible tells us she was given something to eat first thing!)

That night, two families came together in ways they'd never have dreamed of that very morning. That's often how it was with Jesus—when he did things like heal, he wasn't just saying that **where God reigns** people are well, he was also bringing people back to the community, because where God reigns people belong.

Fun Detail—Snacks
The story ends not with Jesus making some grand pronouncement about how great and powerful he is, but with Jesus telling the family to give the little girl something to eat. This might be so we would know that she really was fully healed and was able to sit up and keep some food down, but it also shows Jesus' care for the girl. She isn't a prop in Jesus' story, but an actual human Jesus loved.

Connections—God Is Just
Also in the New Testament, Jesus driving out the money changers from the temple is meant to highlight his commitment to justice. That happens in Matthew 21. The Old Testament also talks about God's sense of justice in many places. The burning bush story in Exodus 3 highlights God's hearing of the cries of the oppressed slaves. Especially for older kids, you might try exploring this idea with one of the psalms of lament, like Psalm 6. These are prayers where the writer cries out to God to rescue them, often demanding that God do so because it's the right and just thing to do. These psalms acknowledge what is wrong in the world and, sometimes, demand that God do something about it.

Connections—God-Centered Storytelling
These stories also highlight Jesus' power and goodness, as well as his tender care for those who would have been far below him socially. Jesus consistently treats women with dignity and respect in ways that were distinctive and even shocking for his day. You could highlight how Jesus keeps the powerful man waiting in order to help the powerless woman. Especially for the woman, Jesus' healing doesn't just make her better; it makes her clean, meaning that she can be restored to relationship and community in a way that wasn't possible for her before.

I wonder what they gave the girl for a snack?

I wonder what the woman did or didn't know about Jesus before meeting him?

I wonder what it was like for Jairus to stop when Jesus stopped on the way to his house?

THE SAMARITAN WOMAN AT THE WELL

JOHN 4:1–42

The Main Idea: There are so many stories that want to help us see Jesus as a life-giver, including this one where water is life. But Jesus doesn't just say, "I'm water," to a crowd, or to his disciples. He says it to a supremely unlikely conversation partner: a Samaritan woman with a hard story. It's not just that Jesus gives life, it's that the life he gives is for anyone and everyone.

Once when Jesus was traveling, he went through Samaria. **Samaria** was a region by Israel, but even though they were close to each other, the people were not close. They had different understandings of what God had done and how best to follow God, but those differences had become fights, had become a divide, and had become "we are enemies."

Historical Context—Samaritans
The Samaritans were the people who lived in the land that used to be the Northern Kingdom of Israel. After the Assyrians conquered the northern tribes, they exiled large numbers of the people, and then imported other people from a different part of their empire. This was a favorite tactic of the Assyrians to prevent rebellions. The resulting population was mixed in terms of race, ethnicity, and culture. The problem from a Jewish perspective, though, was the mixed religious practices that resulted—mixing worship of Yahweh with worship of other gods. This caused the animosity between Jews and Samaritans that this story mentions. Among other things, a Jew would refuse to drink from the same vessel as a Samaritan, making it all the more striking that Jesus begins the whole interaction by asking the woman for a drink.

But Jesus stopped in Samaria even so. He was hot, tired, and thirsty, and so he went to the well in the **middle of the day**.

A Samaritan **woman** came to draw water, and Jesus said to her, "Give me a drink."

You gotta know that this is *not* what anyone would expect Jesus to do.

But Jesus asked her. And they got to talking—about water, about their shared stories of their ancestors, about who Jesus was—and then he said this weird thing: "I would give you **living water**."

Did he mean literal water? No, this was a metaphor for who Jesus was.

Historical Context—Midday
On the one hand, Jesus finding the woman at the well in the middle of the day may be an echo of the story of Jacob meeting Rachel in Genesis 29. On the other hand, many scholars argue it is a reflection of the woman's status in the community. Most would come to the well in the cooler hours of the morning or evening, and so her presence at the hottest time of day may show that she is trying to avoid the eyes, and words, of the village.

Historical Context—Women
The status of women in the ancient world was significantly different than it is in our own day. For one thing, women generally didn't own land, and so they were dependent on their male relatives until they were married. If a woman was sent away from her husband, or if her husband died, she lost her source of survival. The Samaritan woman, then, would have needed to take what she could get to survive. Jewish culture also had very strict rules about when a man could speak to a woman, and it was generally frowned upon. Speaking to a stranger of the opposite sex alone had…questionable…moral connotations, which explains the embarrassment and confusion of the disciples when they found Jesus doing it. All this makes it even more significant that this woman, of all people, is the first witness who acknowledges that Jesus is the Messiah.

Key Words—Living Water
"Living water" was the way people described water that flowed—like a spring or river—as opposed to water that sat still—like in a pond or a well. Living water is better than still water. It's less likely to make someone sick, and it basically never runs out. Jesus is building off the woman's pride in her ancestor Jacob for having provided a well by saying that he is even greater, since he's able to provide living water. Jesus is also building off the words of Jeremiah, who calls God a spring of living water (see Jer. 2:13); and the words of Psalm 42, which compares a heart longing for God to a deer longing for living water (Thompson, *John: A Commentary*, 100). Jesus offers the holistic life and well-being that God promises.

What might that mean? How is Jesus like water?

He told her, "Everyone who drinks this water gets thirsty again. I have water to give that makes it so you're never thirsty. It's water that keeps flowing forever, giving life."

Of course the woman wanted this special water, so she said to him, "Give me this water, so I won't be thirsty again and I won't have to keep coming back here to the well."

Jesus said to her, "Go, call your husband and come back."

I don't know if it's what the woman guessed Jesus would say, but now she was in a tough spot, because she had no husband and told Jesus so, to which Jesus said, "You are right. In fact, you have had **five** husbands, and the one you have now is not your husband."

What does this mean about this woman, then?

She's a Samaritan, a woman, and a person people thought poorly of. Like three strikes in a baseball game. But given the way her culture worked at the time, she's also a victim, someone with limited power in her situation. There's so much she cannot control or change. But maybe this water, or this man, can change things for her?

When Jesus' disciples came and found him, they could hardly believe their eyes. Jesus, talking one-on-one with a Samaritan woman? But whatever they

---

 Key Number—Five

The woman has had five husbands, although there is no indication in the story itself how this came to be, and—despite what some readers have done—Jesus doesn't pass any sort of judgment on her. Instead, he offers her the sort of holistic life (living water) she has been longing for.

One interesting thing you might layer on for older kids comes from the scholar Marianne Meye Thompson. She points out that legend says the Assyrians brought in five different groups of people and settled them in Samaria, each bringing their own gods. Since the Old Testament often uses the metaphor of going after other husbands to describe the people worshipping gods other than Yahweh, John might be using this detail to have the woman represent the Samaritans as a whole being invited back to worship Yahweh alone (Thompson, *John*, 102).

thought or felt, they kept their mouths shut and watched as she left her jar right there at the well and went back to the city.

"Come and see!" she told everyone she passed. "At the well there's a man who told me everything I have ever done! He cannot be the **Messiah**, can he?"

Can he? Several people believed her, and they asked Jesus to stay in town a while longer. For two more days Jesus was with them, and that was a very important part of how people came to realize that the things Jesus the Messiah—for he was—was saying and doing weren't just for Israel, but for everyone. Even... maybe especially?... the unlikely people.

Key Words—Savior of the World
After the woman tells her town about Jesus, these Samaritans are the first to proclaim that Jesus is the Savior of the world. "Savior" is a word the Old Testament applies to God, especially when looking forward to the day when God would bring salvation to the whole world. This phrase in the wider Roman world, however, was only ever applied to the Roman emperor. If any Romans were around to hear the townsfolk, they would have heard it as a direct challenge to the power of the emperor.

I wonder if Jesus picked this woman for any special reason?

I wonder what it's like to "not be thirsty" in the way Jesus means?

I wonder how the disciples felt or thought about Jesus' choices to talk with her and then stay in a Samaritan town?

PART V

EASTER STORIES

JESUS ENTERS JERUSALEM AS KING

MATTHEW 21:1–11; MARK 11:1–11;
LUKE 19:29–44; JOHN 12:9–19

The Main Idea: Jesus, the victorious King, is riding into town. God's kingdom is here.

One day near the end of Jesus' life, he was not far from Jerusalem when he gave a couple of his disciples an errand. "Run ahead to the village. When you get there you'll find a **donkey** no one has ever ridden before. Bring him to me, please. And if anyone asks, 'Hey, what are you doing with not-your-donkey,' say, 'The master needs it.'"

Do you think anyone did stop them? Do you think this answer worked? Why or why not?

Key Word—Donkey
As funny as it might seem to us today, in the ancient Near East the donkey was seen as a ride fit for a king. Specifically, it was what a king would ride after they had already won victory. It's the king saying they don't need their warhorse anymore, because there is no battle to fight. First Kings 1 has a similar situation when Solomon rides to his coronation on a donkey after David's death. Jesus riding on a donkey also brings to life Zechariah 9:9, where a humble but victorious king comes riding in after God won a victory to deliver Israel.

Well, Luke says that the **owners of the colt** did indeed ask what was going on, and the disciples gave Jesus' answer to them. And… that's all we hear about it! So it worked.

They brought the colt to Jesus and put their own cloaks—and a person only had one!—on its back for him. Then Jesus got up on the colt and began to ride toward Jerusalem, and as he did, others, too, took their **cloaks**—their only cloaks!—and spread them on the road for him. Then someone shouted, "Blessed is the king!"

King? Was this who Jesus really was? Not just a messenger filling their hearts with the hope of a kingdom of God's own on earth, but the king of it, too?

"Blessed is the king who comes in the name of the Lord!" The king. Here. So someone else shouted, "Peace in heaven, and glory in the highest heaven!"

And someone else cried, "**Hosanna!** Save us!"

Your Kid Asks: Did Jesus just steal a donkey?
Maybe? It's not clear. One way of interpreting what's going on is that Jesus is doing what a king has every right to do: take a donkey when he needs it. The owner of the donkey might not like it very much, but no one would question the king's right to take it. It's just part of being king. On the other hand, we know from the Gospel of John that Jesus had close friends like Mary, Martha, and Lazarus in the village of Bethany. The way the story is told sounds like maybe Jesus had prearranged things with a friend, "Hey, when I come back to town I'm going to need to borrow your donkey for a bit."

Historical Context—Palms and Coats
We obviously have different customs today for how to honor someone, but both of these details show us the specific type of honor the people are showing Jesus. These are things people would do to welcome kings to town. In fact, a couple hundred years before Jesus a guy named Judas Maccabeus defeated the Syrians and claimed the throne in Jerusalem, and he was welcomed in much the same way.

Key Word—Hosanna
The shout "Hosanna!" literally means "Save us!" It was used in Jesus' day like a combination of plea for deliverance and praise, looking forward to the deliverance God would surely bring. The crowd follows their hosannas with a quote from Psalm 118, a song of praise because Yahweh is a God who saves God's people from their enemies. The scholar Joel Green notes it was also used in Old Testament times each year at the anniversary of the king taking the throne, specifically during the part of the celebration when the king actually entered Jerusalem (*Gospel of Luke*, 686). The people combining hosannas with this particular psalm were sending a very clear signal of what they expected: Jesus is the King who will save Israel.

And as the shouts rang out, the group Jesus was with turned their travel party into just a plain old party. A party that felt just like the ones you'd throw for a king entering a city after winning a **victory**.

Imagine you were there, too, in a crowd acting just as if Jesus the King had won. What would you be hoping he'd beaten? The power of homework and pop quizzes! The bullies! What else?

Now, we know that Jesus would beat the power of death itself. But then? The people mostly hoped this meant that he planned to beat Rome. Ugh, Rome. This empire of violence and cruelty that seeped into their land, a toxic ooze. Would King Jesus raise an army now? Take them on? Drive them out? Some people desperately hoped he would. Others desperately feared he would.

See, Jesus had been talking about God, doing amazing and miraculous things, and spending his time inviting people to trust him for a few years, which had a few different effects: one, lots of people said yes; and two, some other people got worried. They worried about how popular he was. More popular than they were. They worried he was leading people away from God. After all, if they disagreed, it must be because Jesus was wrong. And they worried about Rome. This "kingdom of God" Jesus kept talking about certainly meant something to King Caesar. It meant trouble. And if it meant trouble to Rome, it meant trouble to the Jewish people.

So these worried leaders spoke up: "Tell your disciples to stop!" Pipe down before the soldiers catch on. Before you get us all in trouble.

But Jesus said, "Look, if they get quiet, then the rocks will get loud."

Historical Context—Passover and Hanukkah
Speaking of Judas Maccabeus, his victory was the beginning of the festival of Hanukkah (which John mentioned just a bit ago, in chapter 10). That festival celebrates God's miraculous deliverance of Israel from their Syrian oppressors, which this story echoes in some ways. This story doesn't happen at the time of Hanukkah, however, but rather at the time of Passover, which is the celebration of God's miraculous deliverance of Israel from a different oppressor: Egypt. The timing of Jesus' entrance to Jerusalem, combined with the symbolism of *how* he entered, would have called both of these great acts of deliverance to mind. They would have raised the expectation that Jesus was about to bring a new deliverance from oppression. Which he did, but not in the way many of the people had expected.

I wonder why people laid down their cloaks?

I wonder how different people felt about
this procession—like grown-ups, or kids,
or Jesus' friends, or leaders,
or people just watching?

I wonder if Jesus felt afraid to go
back to Jerusalem?

YOUR KID ASKS

IF JESUS ALREADY WON, THEN WHY DOESN'T IT SEEM LIKE IT?

This is a paradox that has confused Christians for thousands of years. The New Testament is pretty clear—the kingdom of God is here, present tense—and yet, when we look around it sure doesn't seem like it. About seventy years ago the theologian George Eldon Ladd used the phrase "already, but not yet" to describe the kingdom—that it is at the same time "already" here and "not yet" fully expressed in the way it will be one day.

Sure, your kid says, *but why?* One way to approach this with kids is to emphasize that God is not ever going to *force* someone to live in God's kingdom. It *has to be* freely chosen or else it's not God's kingdom at all, because that's not how our God does things. Jesus' announcement is not "The kingdom is here, so now you're all going to be forced to fall in line." That's not the sort of King Jesus is (unlike all the other kings/gods). Instead, the announcement is "The kingdom of God is here." What if you were to choose to live as if that were true? You'd find it's a much, much better place to live. We get to say yes to that invitation, but many people say no. Many people choose to keep on living the old way, as if the kingdom weren't here, and God lets them.

JESUS ANOINTED BY MARY AND THE LAST SUPPER

MATTHEW 26:26–29; MARK 14:3–25; LUKE 22:14–20

The Main Idea: Jesus' response to being anointed and some key reasons for repeating the ritual of communion overlap as they show his generous and loving ways.

Jesus was arrested and killed during a major holiday week, called **Passover**. Passover was a time for God's people to look back and celebrate how God freed the people from enslavement in Egypt. But this Passover, people were looking at Jesus and his followers, watching their every move. Everything Jesus did seemed to have extra meaning. (Although a lot of the time people knew it meant... *something*, but they weren't actually sure *what*.)

During this week Jesus also started saying things that had his friends and followers thinking, "I hope he *doesn't* mean *that*." Like that he wasn't going to

Connections—Passover
Jesus is taking the ceremonial meal that remembered the Passover and reimagining it. Each year, the Jewish people remember the night God freed them from slavery in Egypt, creating them as God's people in the process. It was a way of proclaiming who God is, and who they were in light of who God is. Jesus, then, is saying that his own body and blood—his crucifixion—were going to be a key piece of a new Exodus. Just as God had set the Hebrews free from slavery in Egypt, now God is doing a new work of deliverance for the whole world. God, through Jesus, is setting people free once more, re-creating them as God's people in the process.

Historical Context—Perfume

Bodies are smelly things. Today we've got ways of covering up that reality, indoor plumbing chief among them. In the ancient world, where both water and plumbing were much harder to come by, most people just dealt with the smell most of the time. Perfume was a luxury not many could afford for regular use, and primarily showed up in two contexts for anyone other than the very rich. First, prostitution, which explains in part why the woman's actions were shocking to those watching (although this might not be a detail you'd choose to share with your kids). Second, burial, as a way of covering up the smell of death. This is the interpretation Jesus gives for her behavior. Instead of the reckless action of a loose woman, this is the prophetic action of a devoted disciple who has paid attention to Jesus' words (unlike the male disciples), and knows that his death is coming soon.

Historical Context—Three Hundred Denarii

When you read the story in the Bible, the disciples say the perfume could have been sold for three hundred denarii. That is not the same as three hundred *dollars*. A denarius was roughly the payment a laborer might expect for a full day's work, say, one hundred to two hundred dollars today, meaning this is around a *full year's* income for a typical worker at the time. The woman is showing just how extravagantly valuable Jesus is to her, and Jesus is affirming her for it. Adding to the extravagance is the way she pours it. The alabaster jar would usually have a narrow neck so the perfume could be poured slowly and in small amounts, but she breaks the neck so that it can pour out quickly and completely. Not only is the perfume irresponsibly expensive, but she also uses way too much of it, in fact, the whole bottle.

Literary Feature—Juxtaposition

If you read this from the book of John, Judas is highlighted as the one who speaks up about the wasted money, because he wants more money in the shared purse that he can help himself to. In fact, the gospel writers set the characters of the woman and Judas in contrast in interesting ways. As the scholar Joel Marcus says, "Whereas the woman gives freely of her [perfume] to do Jesus good, [Judas] takes money to betray him; whereas she will be remembered [for what she has done], it would be better for him if he had never been born" (*Mark 8–16*, 942).

live much longer. That he was headed for arrest and death. Jesus was well aware that the Romans and the religious leaders both saw him as a threat. They wanted him gone.

For instance, that week Jesus had dinner with a man named Simon, and the Bible makes sure to include that he was also known as Simon the Leper, because they want us to remember Jesus' habit of eating with people who had been left out. As Jesus sat at the table, a woman came in with a jar of **expensive perfume**.  Was it a gift for Jesus? Or for Simon the host? She approached the table with it, and just when they expected her to give the jar away, she…pulled out the stopper. Tipped it over. Poured it out on Jesus' head. Every precious, costly drop.

People were stunned. **Angry, even.** What a waste!

Jesus knew what they were thinking and spoke up. "This was a lovely thing to do for me. She was getting my body ready to be buried. Just ahead of time. You wait, when people tell my story, they'll tell hers, too."

And we do, because it was generous and full of love, and that is precisely what Jesus likes best.

Later that week, it was time for Passover meals to be eaten. Just like every other Jewish person, Jesus planned to celebrate Passover with a traditional meal, one that generation after generation ate as they told the story of what God had done for them. So he sent Peter and John into the city to find a room for the group and set up the meal.

That evening, an upstairs room was filled with the smells of this story—herbs and bread, lamb and wine. Jesus sat at the table with them all, and then he took this special meal and gave it extra meaning. He took the **bread**,

---

 Key Image—Bread
Bread, when it shows up in the Bible, is usually a symbol of God providing. It shows up as manna in the post-Exodus wilderness, the miracles of Elijah, Jesus feeding the crowds, and more. In the Passover meal—the bread that Jesus is repurposing at the last supper—the bread is a reminder of God's deliverance of the Hebrews from slavery in Egypt. It's the bread that they couldn't even allow time to rise because they had to get up and flee so quickly. Jesus is bringing those meanings of bread together, saying that through his own broken body the disciples (and the whole world) will discover God's provision and deliverance once again.

thanked God for it, broke it into pieces to share, and said, "Take it, for this is my body." And he took the cup of **wine**, thanked God for it, and passed it around for them to share and said, "This is my blood of the **covenant**, poured out for many."

"This is the last time I'll eat or drink until the kingdom is totally, completely here."

We still eat and drink together to remember Jesus' body and blood, even now. We remember that he came, lived, died, and rose, because he was generous and full of love, precisely what our God is like.

Key Image—Wine
Wine was a key part of the Passover meal. The various cups of wine were shared among the family eating together and provided structure to the ceremony; they were like the cues for what came next. Jesus referring to the wine as blood, however, is unique. Obviously there's some physical resemblance between wine and blood, but this was not part of the Passover ceremony in any way. In fact, drinking blood is shocking from a Jewish perspective, where draining the blood out of an animal before eating it was a key part of kosher food laws. Blood was seen as the life force of a creature, and some pagan religious rituals would include drinking the blood of an animal as a way of absorbing its vitality or spirit into yourself. This is both why Jews avoided it and why Jesus is using it. God's people aren't supposed to look to bulls or other animals for power and life, but Jesus' own life and power is exactly what is being offered here. The wine, then, becomes a symbol for Jesus' continued presence with and empowerment of his followers.

Key Word—Covenant
Jesus refers to a covenant, or new covenant, depending on which gospel you're reading. A covenant in the Bible was like a super promise made between God and God's people. The people would promise to faithfully put their trust in God, and God would promise to protect and be present with the people. Usually the blood of animals was a part of the ritual associated with making a covenant. Jesus is saying that now, all those who participate in this meal—remembering Jesus' death on their behalf—would be included in the covenant promises of God. Instead of ethnicity, faithfulness to Jesus is the only criterion necessary to be a part of God's family.

I wonder how she decided to pour her perfume on Jesus?

I wonder if Jesus' friends ever felt upset at him about saying he was going to die?

I wonder what smelled best at the Passover dinner?

JESUS WASHES THE DISCIPLES' FEET

JOHN 13:1–20

> **The Main Idea:** Jesus does not use power the way the rest of the world uses power. Jesus chooses to lay aside pride and position and honor in order to serve and sacrifice. If we are Jesus' followers, then we should allow that example to inform who we are and how we relate to others.

Near the end of Jesus' life, he did some very unexpected things, like return to Jerusalem, even though the leaders wanted him gone. While he and his disciples were in Jerusalem, they met together to eat the Passover meal, and again, Jesus went for the unexpected.

He went for the feet.

See, people wore sandals and walked on dirt roads (which would have been, shall we say, messy, given that there was no modern plumbing). Feet, then, would be somewhere between dusty and disgusting, and so you would never **lie down to eat** without being sure to have them washed. A servant, a low-ranking servant, would wash everyone's feet for them.

It was time for Jesus and his disciples to eat together, but instead of a servant, Jesus was the one who got up from the table, took off his main clothes and laid them carefully down, then picked up a towel. He wrapped it around

Key Word—Laid Down
John gives hints in the story that Jesus' washing of the disciples' feet is a symbol of what he is about to do in dying for them on the cross. For example, the words John uses to describe Jesus laying down his clothes before washing and then taking them back up again are the same as the words for Jesus laying down his life and then taking it back up again in the resurrection. Then, Jesus tells the disciples that they are to imitate him in their own lives of service to one another. We imitate Jesus when we disregard our own rights and humbly serve others in mundane, everyday ways, like washing feet.

Historical Context—Reclined Eating
At fancy meals in Roman times, the people wouldn't eat sitting up at the table. Instead, they'd be given couches to recline on, leaning on their elbows with their faces toward the table and their feet away from it. That meant, among other things, that everyone's feet were on full display, which is why washing them was an important part of making the meal enjoyable for all.

Historical Context—Humility, Honor, and Shame
In Jesus' day, humility was not a prized virtue. This was a culture where your social status and value were determined by how much honor you had. Doing the job of a servant, like Jesus does, would not be a good thing because it would be like giving away your honor. It would be the equivalent of admitting that you were way down the social ladder.

On top of this, ancient culture was far less individualistic than ours. Your own honor didn't just depend on your own actions, but also on those of the people you associated with, your friends and family. Peter would have seen Jesus' lowering of himself as also lowering the disciples in the process. If their leader is like that, what does it say about the people who would choose to follow him?! Jesus was shaming them all! It isn't a coincidence that at the end of this story Judas leaves to betray Jesus. This life of shame wasn't at all what he thought he had signed up for.

Your Kid Asks: Why would Judas betray Jesus?
We didn't include details about Judas in the paraphrase, mainly because it's your call when your child is ready for the story, given that Judas dies by suicide. However, given that they might know this piece from another context, I wanted to address it in brief.

As far as why Judas did it, the fact is that the Bible doesn't tell us a whole lot about Judas and his motivations. We know he was helping himself to money that was supposed to be shared among them all, and that he demanded a monetary reward for turning Jesus over, so it's safe to say he was a "What's in it for me?" sort. It's also possible (but not known for sure) that his last name, Iscariot, indicates he was part of a movement that wanted to violently revolt against Roman power.

The timing of when he betrays Jesus also gives us a clue. In John's Gospel, Jesus rides triumphantly into Jerusalem and says some confusing things in chapter 12, and

Jesus Washes the Disciples' Feet

his waist, poured water into a large bowl, and did what no teacher, no leader, **no important person** ever did.

He went to each disciple, one by one, and washed their feet.

He did it for Peter, who would later say he didn't even know him. He did it for **Judas**, who would lead the Romans to arrest him. Each person sat as their Teacher, their Leader, the one they believed God had sent to save all people, did the job of the lowest servant. For them.

This was a big deal. **Peter** even tried to get out of it, but Jesus explained that this experience was important. It meant a lot now, and it would mean even more to them in the future. He didn't understand that now, but he would in the future. So Peter changed his mind.

When Jesus was finished and all twelve disciples had been washed, he rejoined the group and said, "Do you understand what I have done? You call me Teacher and Lord. You're right, I am. So if that is who I am, and I wash your feet, let my example lead the way. I did what a servant does. I want you to also serve each other in love."

---

then the foot-washing story follows immediately after in chapter 13, at which point Judas leaves. Reading between the lines, we can imagine that Judas followed Jesus into Jerusalem expecting the triumphal entry to be followed by the good stuff—Jesus seizing power and leading the violent uprising that would kick Rome out once and for all, with Jesus' followers (like Judas, of course) given positions of power and prestige in the new government. Instead, Jesus does pretty much the opposite—takes on the role of a slave and shamefully washes his disciples' feet, then tells his followers to do the same. It was the confirmation of what Judas must have feared—that Jesus wasn't going to be the sort of king Judas had imagined at all. He was a fraud who needed to be stopped.

Your Kid Asks: What is Peter talking about?
If you read the story in John, you'll see that Peter and Jesus have an extended back-and-forth about bathing practices. At first Peter refuses to allow Jesus to wash his feet (see note on shame), but when Jesus says he needs to, Peter then asks Jesus to wash all of him, which Jesus says he *doesn't* need. It's all a bit confusing, really. In a nutshell, what Jesus is getting at is that Peter has already had his whole self metaphorically washed when he decided to follow Jesus (which the later church would symbolize with baptism). Now, he just needs to have his feet washed, since they're what's gotten dirty. It's a metaphor for the ongoing forgiveness Jesus offers his followers when they've made mistakes.

I wonder whose feet were the dirtiest?

I wonder if any of the disciples had ticklish feet?

I wonder how others felt when they heard
a disciple tell them this story later on?

JESUS' ARREST, TRIAL, AND PETER'S DENIAL

MATTHEW 26:47–75; MARK 14:43–72; LUKE 22:54–62

The Main Idea: The last days of Jesus' life are difficult, but focusing on the plot and not the overt violence of Jesus' experience helps kids understand some of why Jesus died. Peter's denial also helps shed light on the fear and shame that accompanied this part of Jesus' and his disciples' experience.

Jesus and his disciples had just finished their Passover dinner, which was sure to be a holiday meal to remember, given what Jesus had done and said. But if anyone was thinking they'd sit back, rest, and let the evening pass by, they were clearly not paying attention. Things were tense, like a bow pulled back, arrow ready to fly.

The group **sang a psalm** together and got up, one by one, to follow Jesus to the Gethsemane garden, where he wanted to spend time praying.

That's where they found him, the angry crowd carrying torches and weapons, armed like they were coming for a seriously dangerous person. But Jesus

Fun Detail—Hymn
According to the scholar Joel Marcus, the Passover in Jerusalem would have ended with the singing of a section of the Psalms known as the "Hallel," which means "praise" and comprises Psalms 113–118. That's a good guess as to which "hymn" Jesus and the disciples sang at the end of the Last Supper (*Mark 8–16*, 968). I have no idea what the tune was, so if you decide to give this song a shot, you'll have to make up your own.

made a choice about how to react: He chose not to fight back. In fact, Peter grabbed a sword and took a swipe at a guy's ear. Malchus was his name, and he was a slave of the high priest's; he likely had no choice about coming that night. Jesus wasn't having any of it. His last miracle before he died was to heal Malchus's ear.

Then they arrested him.

And all of Jesus' **disciples ran** for their lives. Away from that place. Away from Jesus.

You may know that after someone's arrested, they often have a trial. This was true then as well, and Jesus appeared before both government and religious leaders, who questioned him, challenged him, and accused him.

"You're a threat to the empire—you don't honor Caesar and you claim to be leading a different kingdom!"

"You're a threat to our safety—Rome will come for all of us because of you!"

"You're a threat to our faith—you act like you've got God's authority in you, and that's for only God alone!"

"You're a threat! A threat! A threat!"

Your Kid Asks: Why did the disciples scatter?
The thing about shame in the ancient world was that it was contagious. Associating in any way with a shameful person would mark you as being of similar character, and would have serious negative consequences in every aspect of your life. Death on a cross was the most shameful of deaths, and that meant the family, friends, and followers of someone who was crucified had a crucial choice to make. Should they stay loyal to the crucified person, and mark themselves as shameful, too, or should they disown them entirely in order to save their own honor and status? The disciples would have been terrified that they were going to be next, hung up on a cross just like Jesus was. But they would have been equally scared that even if their lives were spared, those lives would never be the same. They would be shunned by former friends, disowned by family, cut off from their hometowns and communities. Why risk all that for a dead guy who obviously wasn't the Messiah they had hoped for? I mean, there's no such thing as a dead Messiah, right?

And so Jesus had to go, **they claimed**. And it had to happen in a way that made it clear that no one else should dare threaten them as he had.

So Jesus was brought to a hill outside of town and killed the way criminals were—on a **cross**. There was a sign above his head that read "King of the Jews."

Throughout this whole horrible day, Jesus' followers tried to both lie low and stay near. What was happening to Jesus? What if they came for them, too?

Historical Context—Intra-Jewish Debate

One tricky part of talking about Jesus' arrest and crucifixion today is the long history of antisemitism that has grown up around these stories. Centuries of hate toward Jews as "Christ killers"—and worse—need to be approached sensitively. It's a historical fact that the Jewish leaders in particular, and the crowds in Jerusalem to some extent, were key characters in the death of Jesus. It's also a fact that the execution itself was carried out by the Romans. It's also a fact that all of Jesus' first followers, including most of those who wrote down the gospel stories we're talking about, were Jewish, too.

These stories are not antisemitic or anti-Jewish. They have been used that way, but that's an abuse of the stories themselves, a twisting of the words of Scripture to achieve some outside agenda. The reality is there is a long tradition within Jewish writings of an intra-Jewish debate about what faithfully following Yahweh looks like. You see this in Jesus' day from groups like the Pharisees or the Essenes, who each considered themselves the "true" Jews based on their understanding of God and what God required of people. More importantly for us, you see the debate all through the Old Testament, especially in the Prophets. The gospel writers would have seen themselves in the tradition of Isaiah or Jeremiah, criticizing the leadership that had led the people away from God and calling the Jewish people back to Yahweh, now with the added wrinkle of Jesus thrown in.

Historical Context—The Cross

The cross is such a common symbol today—standing on the roofs of churches, used in art that has nothing to do with Jesus, hanging around necks—that it can be hard for us to really wrap our minds around what it meant in Jesus' day. The cross was not just a means of execution; it was a statement. Execution on a cross was reserved for the ones Rome wanted to make an example of—rebels and traitors, those who posed the greatest threat to Rome's authority and power. It was public and humiliating, an obvious sign for anyone with eyes that Rome, and only Rome, held the actual power here.

Sometimes people today focus on the pain of crucifixion, the violence and horror of it all, but in Jesus' day the far more important thing about dying on a cross was the shame. In a culture where vulnerability and weakness were avoided at all costs, the cross was the ultimate punishment. Hung outside, naked, for all to see, at the complete mercy of the weather, scavengers, and insults from passersby. There was no better way for Rome to send a message to those who might have been thinking rebellious thoughts. Look at this guy. You want to be next?

Like Peter, hovering outside the house where Jesus' trial was held. He was spotted and a man said, "Weren't you with him, too?"

"Oh, no. No, I wasn't. You must be confused."

Another person recognized him: "Hey, you were part of Jesus' followers!"

"I wasn't. You are mistaken."

A third person later on said, "I'm sure you were with Jesus."

"No! Stop saying that. I don't even know the man!"

And after Peter had said for the third time that he was not with Jesus, an ordinary, horrible thing happened. It was nearly morning, so a rooster crowed. Ordinary. But Jesus had said, just a half day earlier, on the heels of Peter's own promises of everlasting loyalty, "You'll betray me, Peter, not just once, but three times, and not just someday, but today, before the rooster crows for morning."

Peter had sworn that was impossible. And yet here he was, alone, afraid, ashamed, and so, so sad. His friend, his Teacher, his Leader was going to die, and he hadn't been able to be there for him at all.

But even though we'll stop the story here, it isn't the end of the story. Jesus, after all, kept promising life. Life. Life. Life. So if everything is dead, clearly we aren't done yet.

I wonder where the disciples went when they ran from Gethsemane?

I wonder what happened to Malchus after this?

I wonder if Peter realized what was happening before his third denial of Jesus?

THE WOMEN VISIT JESUS' TOMB

MATTHEW 28:1–10; MARK 16:1–8; LUKE 24:1–12

The Main Idea: Jesus is alive! This is the simple but seemingly impossible claim—Jesus died but was raised to life again. And if that's true, it changes everything.

How do you keep going when your whole world has fallen apart? One thing at a time, maybe. Grab each spice, roll the cloth up slowly. One step at a time, maybe. Left, right. Side by side with other people who are maybe as wrecked as you are.

So the **women** disciples of Jesus kept going to the tomb that Joseph and Nicodemus had gotten for Jesus' body. They'd made it just in time for Sabbath

Historical Context—Women

One of the really surprising things about the story of the empty tomb is who it's about: a group of women. Women, you see, weren't considered reliable witnesses in the ancient world (*you know how emotional and irrational they are, they probably just made the whole thing up!*). A legal case that was based on the testimony of a woman would be thrown out of court, or maybe laughed out. In fact, this is exactly what many of the male disciples do when the women come with their ridiculous story of an empty tomb, thinking it was "stupid, useless talk" in Luke's words (imagine the mansplaining going on in that room: "Look, Mary, sweetheart, dead people stay dead, hon. Why don't you go get some rest?").

Any sort of storyteller who had any interest in *being believed* would have...left this part out, found some way around it, or had a man or two go with them. But if we've been paying attention to the story of Jesus (or even the whole Bible) so far, maybe it isn't so surprising. It's exactly in line with how Jesus treated women, completely expected from a God who shows no partiality. The women showing up first and being the first witnesses to the good

Friday evening, and all day yesterday they'd had nothing to do but be sad. It was a Sabbath of utter sorrow. And now, Sunday dawn, they would try to keep going, and **prepare his body** more properly.

Morning dew kissed the tips of their toes as they got close to the cave's entrance. Light danced off the droplets, but they didn't have time to gaze at it because, as suddenly as a lightning strike, they were surrounded by an even brighter light. Then they saw a **young man** at Jesus' tomb.

news that Jesus is alive lines up perfectly with the reality that these were the same women who stayed loyal to Jesus to the end, standing at the foot of the cross long after the men had run for their lives. The only conclusion we can draw is that it's true, because no one would ever make something like this up.

Historical Context—Burial
Jesus died on a Friday night, the beginning of the Sabbath. This meant that whatever burial he was given after his death would have been the bare minimum to take care of the body until after the Sabbath. That's why the women are coming on Sunday morning, not because they have any inkling that he might have returned to life. The women, N. T. Wright tells us, would have been carrying out the primary burial, where the body was wrapped in spices in order to lessen the smell. Tombs in those days were used repeatedly for a whole extended family, and more bodies would be expected to be added while the previous bodies were still decomposing. Once that was finished, a second burial took place with just the bones put into a container called an ossuary (*Mark for Everyone*, 222). These jobs were always done by family members of the deceased. The fact that these women are unrelated to Jesus is a clue that perhaps Jesus' blood family had disowned him in order to separate from the shame of this crucified criminal. We can't know for sure, since that's not what the resurrection story is focused on. But, as Ben Witherington III points out, Jesus' brothers are consistently skeptical of him in the gospel stories, and even his mother appears at the cross only in the Gospel of John when Jesus puts her in the care of one of the other disciples, more or less transferring her into a new family (*Matthew*, 525).

Your Kid Asks: Who was the young man?
Mark tells us that the women saw a young man at the tomb. Luke says it was two men in shining clothes. Matthew says they met an angel. A curious kid might wonder what's going on! First of all, the fact that the gospels don't try to smooth everything into one official version of the story makes it *more* reliable, not less. This is how eyewitness accounts of dramatic events work (and what's more dramatic than meeting an angel who tells you Jesus has been raised from the dead!). People notice different details, think different bits are important, and so they tell the same story in slightly different ways. Second, angels in the ancient world were often portrayed as young men in shining or bright white clothes, so the young man would have been recognized as an angel by anyone hearing the story.

"You're at a place for the dead, but you'll only find the dead here. You're looking for the living, so he won't be here. He's risen. Risen, just like he said. Go tell the disciples—be sure you find **Peter**, too. Tell them he'll meet them soon."

You may know this story, but imagine you don't. How likely would you be to believe this is real—from 1, a total trick; to 5, no doubt about it?

The women felt—well, what do you imagine they felt? How many feelings can a person feel at one time, do you think? They may have maxed out that number.

Then **they ran.**

They ran like Olympic sprinters, in robes that whipped about their legs until they just grabbed them and yanked them out of the way, sandals slapping, dust flying, hair sailing behind them.

They ran like life depended on getting this news to the others.

To the town. To the house. Through the door with a BAM!

Connections—Peter
In Mark's version of the story, the young man tells the women to go tell the disciples the good news, "including Peter" (16:7). Peter, whom Jesus once called "Satan" (Matt. 16:23), and who was last seen denying he had ever even known the Messiah he had sworn to stay with to the death. That may be why he's separated from the rest—tell the disciples… *including* Peter. They all need to hear the news, but especially Peter does. God has always been gracious and compassionate. The resurrection only confirms that God specializes in new beginnings, even for the Peters of the world.

Fun Detail—Mark's Ending (or is it?)
If you were to read this story in Mark's Gospel, you would find a strange thing. The story just kind of…ends. The women run away from the tomb because they are frightened, and then they don't tell anyone about it. And that's it. Most scholars believe the ending of Mark's Gospel was lost early on, maybe even in the first century. So, if you have a Bible that goes beyond Mark 16:8, then you're reading what most think were tacked-on endings that got added much later. Most Bibles include a note about this, and you might notice the tacked-on endings sound a bit weird compared to what's come before. None of this is a problem; it just reflects the realities of copying manuscripts in a world before printers and computers—a page gets lost, some ink gets spilled, your dog eats your scroll, and you can't just hit "undo." The consistency and reliability of the vast majority of the early biblical manuscripts are really remarkable compared to most ancient documents, and the few exceptions like this one just highlight that fact.

And the men jumped and stared while the women heaved and gasped. Finally they managed the word. The one glorious impossible word.

"**Alive!**"

Phhhhuuuuh, hhhhhuhhhh, phhhuuuuh.

"He's alive!"

Phhhhuuuuh, hhhhhuhhhh, phhhuuuuh.

"Jesus—an angel at the tomb—not dead—going to meet you—he's ALIVE."

One scanned until she saw him. Peter. They locked eyes.

"The angel said to tell you—Jesus is alive."

Historical Context—Resurrection

In the Jewish community of Jesus' day, the word "resurrection" had a very particular meaning. It was a future hope for the time when God's kingdom would come to earth in all its fullness, and Yahweh, the *living* God, would raise up those who had been faithful and had died. God would give them new life and new physical bodies to live in an earth made new. The expectation was for this to be a future, all-at-once event.

In the New Testament, we see the authors wrestling with what happened to Jesus in light of this expectation. He had been resurrected, and they make sure to tell us that he is *not* a ghost, *not* a vision, *not* a disembodied soul, *not* a warm fuzzy feeling in the disciples' tummies—he could stand among them, eat fish, and be touched and felt. He was really dead and hadn't just woken up after a particularly rough Friday night. This was something new, something entirely unexpected. It meant that Jesus really was God's representative, and that what he had said was true—the kingdom of God was here.

I wonder why God had these women hear
the news first without the others?

I wonder why the angel said "and Peter"
and not just "the disciples"?

I wonder how hard or easy it was to
run in their kind of sandals?

YOUR KID ASKS

UM, DID THIS STORY ACTUALLY HAPPEN?

This is a tough question! So let's talk about several options for responding to it and you can choose which seems to fit best with your kid and your situation.

One reason the question is challenging is that it highlights just how *wide* the gulf is between us and the original readers of the Bible. Thousands of years and huge cultural differences are a lot to bridge, and the reality is we just don't know exactly how every specific story might have sounded to ancient ears.

So here are four categories of Bible stories, from definitely happened to definitely didn't, and how you might talk about each with your kids. (And don't worry, we'll close with an idea for what to say if you don't know which category the story falls in.)

Under the heading of "true historical event," you find two categories:

CATEGORY ONE: This story literally happened, and it kind of matters a lot.

I'd put Jesus' resurrection here, but not many others in this category.

The main clue that the story is one where it matters that it actually happened is how the rest of the Bible talks about it. The whole rest of the New Testament refers back to Jesus having actually died and actually risen bodily from the dead. Paul builds his entire theology on it.

Similarly, that God actually set the Hebrews free from slavery in Egypt is a foundational story for the people of Israel. If God is a God who sets us free, then it kind of matters that the freedom part happens in real life. But the exodus story is a great example of category two.

CATEGORY TWO: Real historical event, but told with style.

Most of the stories in the Bible fit here, I think. And there's some overlap and fuzziness in these categories. Going back to the story of the Exodus, I think it's important that the core events of that story really happened, that God set the Hebrews free from slavery. But that doesn't mean the author can't tell the story with style!

And so there are exaggerations, symbols, and literary flourishes. And when we deal with Scripture as literature, that isn't the same as declaring it fictional.

These stylistic elements are there not to deceive us, but to entertain and engage us—to more effectively communicate what *actually matters*.

What actually matters is not the exact number of Hebrews who were freed; what matters is that it was a large group, made up of enough families and clans to become the people of God. What actually matters is not the exact number of years they wandered in the wilderness, but that it was a long time, a whole generation. And so on.

In this case you might say: **"I think this story did happen, and I also think the author might have had some fun telling the story in an exciting way. What's your favorite part of this story?"**

Now for the stories that likely didn't happen:

CATEGORY THREE: This is clearly fiction, but it's true fiction.

The clearest examples of this are Jesus' parables, which are helpfully labeled for us. But Jesus' parables highlight how throughout the Bible fictional stories are used to communicate some of the most profound and deeply true things about who God is.

I can't think of a more effective way to communicate the truth that God is like a father who runs to meet his lost son who has returned, and then throws a big party to celebrate. It's True, even if it never really happened.

Other examples of this sort of story are a little trickier, but many scholars think the stories of Esther, Job, and Jonah, among others, would fit here. In each there are clear exaggerations, stock characters, fantastical happenings, and other literary features that point toward the story being meant to be read as fiction. But, again, this wouldn't make it any less true.

So you might say: **"No, I don't think this story really happened. I think this was someone telling a made-up story to help us learn important things about God."**

CATEGORY FOUR: Maybe, maybe not.

I'm cheating a bit here, because this is less of a separate category than a blending together of the others.

Again, for the Bible to be *true*, it does not follow that every element *literally happened in exactly the way it's written on the page*. There are many ways of communicating important true things, from historical stories, to fables, to poems, to songs.

This actually means something really important as we engage with these stories with our kids: **We don't have to get it right all the time.**

Reading the Bible well is about hearing the good news of who God is and what God is up to, not about being 100 percent sure whether a story happened. In other words, "Maybe it happened, maybe it didn't, but here's what it tells us about God" is a perfectly fine answer to your kid's question.

And so you might say: **"I'm not sure if this story happened exactly like it's written or not, but I do think we can trust what the Bible tells us about who God is. Even if this story didn't actually happen exactly like this, what would it tell us about God?"**

Or perhaps you say: **"Wow, that's a tough question! What do you think? What parts of the story seem like they did happen, and what parts seem like they couldn't have?"**

BREAKFAST ON THE BEACH

JOHN 21

The Main Idea: How did Peter go from betraying Jesus to leading the church? Jesus found him and forgave him, then gave him a job to do. It's also important for us to see the kind of grace Jesus offers to even those who betray him.

It was too much. How could he be alive? He'd died. Not just peacefully, but brutally. Publicly. They all knew he was dead. And they all knew dead people stayed dead.

Well, okay, there was that one time with the little girl. And Lazarus.

But still.

And yeah, sure, they'd all seen him—twice now. How likely is it that a whole group has the same vision of a man who isn't really there?

Alive. He must be alive. But what did that mean? Would they see him again? What now?

With all the thoughts and feelings swirling inside him, Peter decided to get out on the water and fish. Some others came along, too.

Night passed. **Morning** came. The nets stayed empty.

As the sun began to rise, a man appeared on the shore and called out to them, "Haven't you caught anything?"

"Nothing at all."

"Hm. Throw the net to the other side of the boat, then."

As they did, Peter felt the **familiarity of the scene**. And as the fish began to practically jump into the net, he knew it was true. This was Jesus.

So, naturally, Peter jumped out of the boat.

They all made their way to the shore, where a campfire was already going, with fish roasting on it. And after they'd brought in the massive haul—**153 fish in all!**—they joined Jesus for breakfast on the beach, where he took bread, broke it into pieces, and **gave it to them**. He did that with the fish, too.

Peter ate, but he was also very aware that he and Jesus hadn't talked together since before his arrest. And after his arrest, well, Peter had denied

---

Fun Detail—Dawn
Jesus appears on the beach at dawn, with the disciples having come from a long, useless night of fishing. It's an interesting little detail that several of the resurrection stories happen at dawn, right as the new day is breaking, a symbol of new life.

Connections—Catch of Fish
In Luke 5:1–11 we get a similar story of a miraculous catch of fish. In Luke's Gospel, it's part of the story of how Jesus calls several of the disciples, including Peter in particular. Peter's story with Jesus began with a stranger telling him to let down his nets, only to find they were so heavy with fish he could hardly get them ashore. And now, on the other side of Peter's betrayal, his story with Jesus re-begins in just the same way.

Fun Detail—Fish
There's two fun little fish-related details in this story. First, the absurdly specific number: 153. Okay, so not 152, then? Second, Jesus was already cooking fish when the boat finally got to shore. But even so, he tells them to bring some of their fish. It might be a little clue that while Jesus doesn't *need* their contribution, he welcomes it all the same.

Connections—Feeding the Crowd
Jesus taking bread and giving it to the disciples sounds kind of like the Last Supper, but the way John writes this story makes it seem like the story he actually has in mind is the feeding of the five thousand. In both, there is bread and fish, and even the specific words for Jesus taking both and giving it to the disciples are the same. Why is the feeding of the crowd the connection John sees? Because the point in both stories is to reveal something about who Jesus is. In feeding the crowd, Jesus was showing he was the Bread of Life who would provide abundantly for his people. John wants to highlight that this provision continues on after the resurrection as well.

him. **Three times, even**. Maybe this was a goodbye meal and Jesus was done with him.

But Jesus is never done with anyone.

"Simon, do you love me?"

"Yes, you know I'm your friend."

"Then feed my sheep," Jesus said.

Jesus asked again, "Simon, do you love me?"

Again he said, "Yes, you know I'm your friend."

And Jesus said, "Then take care of my **sheep**."

Then Jesus asked a third time, on this third appearance to Peter, "Simon, do you love me?"

And Peter felt hurt. Yes, he'd been wrong to betray Jesus, but it didn't change his love for him. Why ask **three** times? Except perhaps, that three is

---

Connections—Peter's Denial

There's an obvious connection between Jesus' conversation with Peter and Peter's earlier denial that he even knew Jesus. There are three questions to match the three denials. There's even an interesting little parallel in that Peter denied Jesus while sitting by a charcoal fire. Here, Jesus has a charcoal fire going to cook fish. His restoration by Jesus is an important part of Peter's own narrative arc, since he would go on to be an important leader in the early church. In that sense, it closes some gaps for the first readers of this gospel.

Key Word—Sheep

Jesus is referred to earlier in John as "the good shepherd" (10:11). The shepherd is an image for what the leader of God's people is supposed to be that goes all the way back to Moses tending sheep in Midian when he suddenly sees the strange sight of a bush burning but not burning up; carries on through the boy David being called in from watching his father's flocks in order to be anointed king; and culminates with Jesus. Except, as this story shows us, it doesn't end with Jesus. Jesus passes the job of caring for his flocks on to Peter. Jesus is here sharing his own work and responsibility, just as God has always done from the very beginning.

Key Number—Three

The number three is a common element in storytelling, one people still use today in stories and jokes. Jesus asking Peter three times if Peter loves him is an example of this, but it's more, too. It's a reminder to Peter (and us) that Peter had denied Jesus three times as well. However much Peter failed, Jesus' grace matches it and more (and the same goes for us).

sometimes a special story number. New life often happens after three—like that time Jesus fed the crowd who'd been with him three days, and of course that time, just recently, when Jesus died. I wonder if Jesus asked three times to help Peter see: There was new life for him, too.

And Peter answered, "Yes, I do love you." To which Jesus said, "Feed my sheep." Then Jesus told Peter that this new life ahead would be hard, and said, "Follow me."

They were back at the beginning. Follow me. Peter could decide: Yes? Or no? And Peter knew, with Jesus alive, everything was different now. And he said yes.

I wonder where Jesus got his fish from?

I wonder why the Bible tells us this story—Peter messing up so bad and then Jesus and Peter mending it—when it makes Peter, a big-time leader, look so bad? I wonder why they didn't skip it? Leave it out?

I wonder how Peter would tell others the story of this day?

ON THE ROAD TO EMMAUS

LUKE 24:13–35

The Main Idea: Jesus' resurrection appearances remind us that the disciples needed time to process what was happening—as any of us would in their shoes. They had questions and doubts, and Jesus himself came to help with them.

On the same day the women found the tomb empty, two of Jesus' followers were making their way from Jerusalem to the village of Emmaus, which was about seven miles off. They walked along together, talking about everything that had happened, when suddenly they were joined by **someone they didn't recognize**.

"You all are in deep conversation, but would you share what you're talking about?" Jesus asked. And even though they looked right at him, their eyes couldn't recognize him.

And what a question! "You must be literally the only person in this whole area who doesn't know what's been happening."

"Happening with what?"

"Not with what, with who. Jesus. The man from Nazareth. He was a prophet who spoke with power and acted with power in front of God and everyone else. But the leaders handed him over to Rome to be killed on the

cross. We had hoped…we had hoped he was the one God promised to send to save us, to **redeem** Israel, but it's been three days now.

"But on the other hand, some women from our group went to his tomb this morning and came back with this wild report that he was actually alive. They say they saw an angel, and when some of our men went to check everything out it was true that the tomb was empty."

This is when Jesus jumped in and said, "Why is this so unbelievable? It's not like the prophets didn't talk about this stuff, how the Messiah would **suffer**, die, and be raised up again." And then Jesus went on, telling them the stories they all knew from Scripture, but that they hadn't fully realized were about Jesus. How could they be about Jesus? At least, they couldn't be if it was true that he was dead. On the other hand, if the women were right, if he was actually alive, well then, that changed things.

Your Kid Asks: Why don't they recognize Jesus?
We don't totally know the answer to this one. Maybe they just couldn't believe their eyes because *of course* Jesus was dead, so this person standing in front of them obviously couldn't be him. It might be as simple as that, but it's also clear from the resurrection stories that two things were true. First, Jesus' new, resurrection body was recognizably his own. He was the same person, with nail marks still in his hands. Second, his resurrection body was different in some way that made it hard for his friends to recognize him, especially at first. This might be related to the seeming paradox that Jesus could be touched and could eat food but also could walk through walls (another piece kids often ask about!). It's certainly related to the fact that this new body is no longer subject to the usual decay and death that our bodies are now. So maybe the effect of that is to look different in some way.

My favorite way to describe some of this comes from C. S. Lewis's *Perelandra*. He uses the analogy of how something more solid, like a rock, can pass through something less solid, like water. And, then, water can pass through air. So maybe Jesus' resurrected body is actually *more* solid in some sense than our current physical world, and can therefore pass through what we think of as solid things.

Connections—Exodus
The disciples communicate their disappointment by saying they had hoped Jesus was the one who would redeem Israel. "Redeem" is the word used in Exodus to describe what Yahweh did in freeing the Hebrews from slavery in Egypt. A key expectation for the Messiah was that he would be the one through whom God would once again free Israel from pagan oppression, and they expected it to look similar to what God did back then to Egypt. Their disappointment came from the reality that Jesus was supposed to be killing pagans, but instead, had been killed by them.

By this time they had walked to a fork in the road, and Jesus made as if he was going to keep on going, but the men insisted he turn with them to the home where they planned to stay so that he could eat with them. When they all sat down at the table, Jesus was the one who gave thanks to God for the food, then he took **bread** and broke it and passed it to them. And that was the moment their eyes could see: It was Jesus. But no sooner did they recognize him than he disappeared.

Key Word—Suffer
Jesus' response to their disappointment at this lack of redemption is to explain the Bible to them, from Moses all the way through the prophets. The main thing he needs to set straight is their understanding of the relationship of the Messiah and suffering: that the Messiah *had to suffer*. As N. T. Wright puts it, "They had been seeing [the Bible] as the long story of how God would redeem Israel *from* suffering, but it was instead the story of how God would redeem Israel *through* suffering" (*Luke for Everyone*, 294). This has been a theme Jesus often touched on in his teaching, that when you really look at the stories in the Old Testament *all* the prophets suffer, so why would the Messiah be any different? This is a key truth about following Jesus that Christians forget again and again: We are supposed to model our own lives after a God who suffers, not one who smites his enemies.

Key Word—Fulfilled
Jesus says that his suffering was necessary for the Scriptures to be fulfilled. Joel Green points out that Jesus is not saying some particular verses or predictions have been proved true. Instead, he is talking about the entire story of Scripture, the point of it all. When the Old Testament is read correctly, you'll see that Jesus' death and resurrection fit perfectly in with the story of how God has always interacted with the world and with Israel. The purposes and character of God throughout are fulfilled in the person and actions of Jesus, especially his willing suffering and death that bring life to the world (Green, *Gospel of Luke*, 857).

Key Word—Bread
The disciples recognize Jesus when he breaks bread and gives it to them. I had always thought this was a reference to the Last Supper, but the scholar Joel Green argues that the closer connection is with the story of Jesus feeding the crowd. Luke actually uses language that is closer to what Jesus does in that story, and, as Green points out, a key point of both stories is revealing who Jesus is. The miraculous feeding revealed Jesus to be the God who provides bread for his people, just like back in Exodus. This story reveals the stranger to be the same Jesus who broke bread and handed it to the disciples back at the feeding of the five thousand. In the gospels, in fact, meals are often places where revelation happens, where people discover more of who Jesus is and what Jesus is like (*Gospel of Luke*, 843, 849).

Turning to each other they said, "Wasn't it like our hearts were on fire inside of our bodies as he explained scripture to us?"

"We have to go tell the others!"

They got up and made their way back to Jerusalem again as fast as they could. They must have been tired, but they also might have been full of the energy that came from realizing the impossible had happened. Jesus was alive!

They found the others and burst into the room with the news: "We've seen him! we've seen Jesus! He was with us on the road, he broke bread, and then we realized it was him. The women are right. He's alive."

The words had just spilled out of their mouths when over their shoulders they heard four of the sweetest words they could ever dream of, because of who was speaking them.

"Peace be with you."

One problem, though. When the words are coming from someone you **were sure was dead**, they don't feel sweet. Peace doesn't seem real. So naturally, they all freaked out and assumed they were seeing a ghost. And so Jesus offered them his hands, still scarred from the cross, but real. Right there, to touch. He asked if they had any fish, and then ate it all up. And they all found that their disbelief was being pushed aside bit by bit by new feelings: Hope. Joy.

Historical Context—Resurrection

As we've seen in previous resurrection stories, Luke is very clear about what has happened to Jesus. He is not a revived corpse, and he is not a spirit or vision. Those were the normal "life after death" options in the ancient world, and Jesus does *not* fit into those categories. The word for what has happened to Jesus is "resurrection," a new body made to live forever in God's restored creation. If you wanted to do a super-deep dive into this topic, N. T. Wright's book *The Resurrection of the Son of God* gives hundreds and hundreds of dense pages on what Jews and Gentiles each thought about the afterlife and how Jesus' resurrection stories fit (and don't fit) into those expectations. It's a really great book, but written at a pretty scholarly level and definitely not a fit for everyone.

I wonder how much the men believed versus didn't believe that Jesus was alive at first? Like, what percent of each?

I wonder why they couldn't recognize Jesus?

I wonder how Jesus could disappear at dinner?

PART VI

THE CHURCH CARRIES ON

THE HOLY SPIRIT COMES AT PENTECOST

ACTS 2

The Main Idea: God is doing a new thing, and the promises that were made in the Old Testament are coming true. The Spirit has come and good news and blessing are available to all people, no matter who they are or where they are from, all because of Jesus.

Jesus' **followers** had been waiting together. Waiting, as best they could tell, for God to come to them in some way that would help them know what happened next.

See, Jesus had been raised to life, spent time among them all, and then returned to heaven. But before he'd gone, he'd told them things like, "You'll receive power from God's holy Spirit, who will come to you. And then you'll tell others, near, far, to the ends of the earth, even! You'll tell them about me and the life God invites them to have."

Key Word—Apostle
This word means several different things among different flavors of Christians today. When it starts showing up in the Bible, though, it specifically is referring to people who saw the risen Jesus and then went off to tell others what they had seen. They are eyewitnesses to the truth that Jesus is alive, and are sent out to spread the good news.

So they were waiting when the holiday of **Pentecost** began, in the same upper room where they'd had dinner together before Jesus died. It wasn't all that long before this, and it also felt like ages ago. So much had happened.

More was going to happen, they trusted. Maybe they weren't surprised, then, when the room filled with a sound like whipping wind, and what looked like little **fires** floated up above their heads, and they opened their mouths to speak and other languages—ones they hadn't spoken before—came out.

Or maybe they were. It's pretty surprising, after all.

The Pentecost holiday brought even more of the **Jewish community together** in Jerusalem, so there were people from in town and what felt like

---

Historical Context—Pentecost
The festival of Pentecost was one of three feasts each year when any Jews who were able would come gather in Jerusalem. The name comes from it occurring fifty days after Passover, and it was intended to correspond with two things. First, it was roughly when the spring wheat harvest began each year, so it was an opportunity to celebrate God's goodness and provision with the literal "first fruits" of the harvest. Second, it looked back to the giving of the Torah at Mount Sinai, which happened (you guessed it) fifty days after the original Passover.

The coming of the Spirit at *Pentecost*, in other words, doesn't happen by accident. The time is meant to point to at least three things. First, the good news about Jesus is available to every tribe and language and nation, just like the Old Testament had always promised. Second, the coming of the Spirit to the disciples is the "firstfruits" of a much larger harvest yet to come. And third, this new message from God as spoken by Peter is a continuation and expansion of the message given to Moses on Mount Sinai.

Key Image—Fire
Fire in the Bible is usually a symbol of God's presence, and this story is no exception. The image of tongues of fire is meant to express God's Spirit coming upon the disciples so that the message they then bring and the work they then do is recognized as coming from God.

**Literary Feature—Exaggeration for Effect**
Luke gives us a little hyperbole when he says that Peter speaks to Jews from "every nation under heaven," but the nations listed as examples do cover most of the known world at the time from the far east of Elam to the far west of Rome. The point is not to give the exact geographical roots of the listeners, but to capture the truly global nature of this new movement of God.

every town there. They spoke many languages, but then, suddenly, so did the disciples! All of these people were hearing their own language spoken by people they knew didn't know their **language**.

They were amazed. They were confused.

"What does this mean?" they asked.

"It means they're drunk. That's what it means," said some.

Then the twelve got up and stepped forward together, and Peter spoke to the crowd.

"Everyone listen! We're not drunk. It's 9:00 a.m. for goodness' sake! No! Remember God's message through the prophet **Joel**? It's happening!

"God said, I'll pour out my Spirit on all people. Men and women, young and old, slaves, even—they'll have messages from God to share. You'll see signs

---

Connections—Babel
In Genesis 11, we have a little parable about all the people in the world trying to build a tower, but then God coming down and scattering them across the whole earth and confusing their languages so they can't understand one another. The very next story is about God promising a man named Abram that his descendants will bless "all the nations of the earth." In Acts 2, we get the fulfillment of the promise to Abram, and the reversing of the story of Babel. With "all the nations of the earth" present, the good news is proclaimed so that everyone can understand and be blessed by it.

Historical Context—Joel
Peter's message begins (well, after clarifying that they are NOT, in fact, drunk at 9:00 a.m., thank you very much!) with a long quotation from the prophet Joel. Joel looks forward to the last days, when God would pour out the Spirit not on a select few, but on everyone—all genders, ages, and social classes. Peter's point is, "Look! It's happening right in front of you!" In the paraphrase we skip over the part in Joel about signs and portents and the sun being turned to darkness and the moon to blood and such, but let me say a couple of words real quick here in case your kid reads it.

This is what is sometimes called "apocalyptic" language. The Old Testament Prophets and Revelation are full of it (in fact, "Revelation" is the English translation of the Greek "Apocalypse") and Jesus speaks this way in Mark 13 and elsewhere. This language is NOT meant to be taken literally. It's the equivalent of what we mean when we say something was "an earthshaking event." We don't mean there was an actual earthquake; we mean the event was incredibly, world-changingly important. In this case, God is doing a new thing that will turn the world upside down (there's that apocalyptic language again!).

all over that a new time has begun. And everyone who calls on the name of the Lord will be saved.

"People of Jerusalem! Jesus came to begin this new time, and God gave him power to prove it. You saw yourselves the mighty works Jesus did! The religious and Roman leaders had him killed. But God was working all along, and raised Jesus back to life. Death was squeezing Jesus tight, but God opened death's grip. Death can't hold on when God wants life!"

And Peter went on, telling the people how Jesus fit in with the stories and messages God had given even very long before.

"God has made Jesus Lord and Messiah!" Peter said.

Then it was the people's turn to respond. What did they make of this message? Was God bringing a new time? Had it begun with Jesus? Was this another sign of it right inside their ears?

Yes, some thought, it sure seemed like this was true. So they asked Peter, "What now? What do we do from here?"

Peter told them to be baptized as a symbol of turning toward God's work in Jesus. So they were, lots of them.

They joined together to become a group who would live together in this new time that had started with Jesus—a time marked by God's love, generosity, kindness, and care.

I wonder why Peter talked about prophets from the past, like Joel, to help people trust that God was working now?

I wonder what it was like to instantly speak a new language?

I wonder what they saw and heard and felt when the Holy Spirit first filled the room? If it was a movie we could watch now, what would we see and hear?

YOUR KID ASKS

IS ETERNAL LIFE JUST LIVING UP IN HEAVEN?

Every "Top 5 Most Used Christian Phrases" list includes "eternal life." It's how John 3:16 is translated and therefore we use it: "Everyone who believes in him will not perish but have eternal life." If you have ever believed the phrase "eternal life" refers to the afterlife, a life that begins after death, in heaven, not on earth, forever (as I have), then you, like me, have some familiarity with the Greek influence on New Testament scholarship.

All Greek to Me

Centuries of New Testament scholarship have treated it as if it were written by Greek philosophers. Greek philosophy was the foundation of Western education for much of the past two thousand years, so scholars were trained to read things through that lens.

And Greek philosophers, when they used the Greek word "*aeon*," were often referring to eternity, and to abstract principles like souls and such. But literally the word "*aeon*" means "the age," so the eternity concept would be like when we use the expression "Oh, this is taking ages!"

But when Jews, who *actually* wrote the New Testament, used the words "the age," they weren't usually talking about eternity, they were referring to the common Jewish belief that beyond this present age there is an age to come, sometimes referred to as the kingdom of God, when God would put things right again.

Other parts of the Bible regularly talk about eras or ages as well. They are a squishy combination of the ***time***—when things are happening, and the ***culture***—what the culture is like.

The ***present age*** is the one where empires rule, oppression is rampant, and inequity keeps people from life. The present age seems to be all around us, but according to Paul, with the death and resurrection of Jesus, the *age to come* is here.

The ***age to come*** is when the world really is in harmony with and reflective of God's own character. A world that works in a way that matches who God is.

John 3:16:
A Case Study

I use N. T. Wright's translation, and one reason for that is how he renders phrases in particular ways to help us as contemporary readers hold on to a sensibility that would have been inherent to original readers and hearers; "eternal life" being one of them.

John 3:16 in Wright's *New Testament for Everyone* reads: "This, you see, is how much God loved the world: enough to give his only, special son, so that everyone who believes in him should not be lost but should share in the life of ***God's new age***."

"God's new age," "God's coming age," or "the age to come" all show up in the space that my memory-verse-shaped brain expects to see "eternal life." But even though the new age is, indeed eternal, it's more than just a disembodied, post-death experience.

In "the age," life would be characterized by God's character, and the life that God had promised for God's people would be reality. Importantly, this was not some disembodied heaven, but was a tangible, this-world reality. The expectation was that in the age to come, God would make this world right.

It's the life that God has promised to bring into reality, here on earth, one day.

The reason this is so important to grasp is that it's exactly the concept of eternal life that often leads Christians today to think that life in this world doesn't really matter compared to the eternal life, the future heaven, that they are looking forward to.

The life of God's coming age *is now* when properly understood. It continues forever, too, but it matters that we live as if we were a part of that coming age. As we live like the age to come is here now, we will experience Life with a capital *L, and* we will help others experience that Life.

Acts and Onward: It's Our Life Era

The claim the apostles make again and again in Acts, the claim Paul makes throughout his various letters, the claim the writer of 1–3 John makes is this: The age to come is overlapping with the present age, and anyone who trusts Jesus will live like it.

The book of Acts, then, is often about whether or not the apostles are correct that age has actually arrived in Jesus (lots of conflict on that) and the books of Romans through Revelation are often about how Jesus' people should live in this world since that age has arrived.

These first Christians are practicing living "age to come" lives in the midst of the "present age," living beautifully ordinary lives together that align with God's character here and now. And especially in Acts, they are often facing challenges from those who say the age to come has not arrived, Jesus has not brought a new era, and you all are leading everyone away from God.

Most of the New Testament is about how it's our Life Era, so let's get to living it.

PETER HEALS, THEN PREACHES, THEN GETS IN TROUBLE

ACTS 3–4

> **The Main Idea:** As the Church carries on, they don't just talk about Jesus; they do the things Jesus did. In this case, Peter heals a man by the power of "the name of Jesus." It's not like Jesus' name is a magic word, but it is like the community empowered by God's Spirit will, in very real ways, keep bringing life and wholeness to the places they exist.

The afternoon sunbeams made the road to the temple nearly golden-colored as Peter and John, along with so many other Jewish people, made their way to the temple for prayer. Near the gate—the one called Beautiful—a man was being gently set down by some others, because he could not walk on his own. Since he was also not able to work, he would sit by the Beautiful Gate and ask others for the money he needed. As Peter and John walked by, the man asked them to give him some money.

Instead, Peter stopped and said, "Look at me," and the man looked up expectantly. But he was likely not expecting what Peter said and did next. "I don't have silver or gold, but what I do have I'll give to you. In the name of the Messiah, Jesus of Nazareth, get up and walk!" Peter's hand extended through the golden sunshine to the man's and grabbed on, and the man felt his feet and ankles become strong, and he stood. Not just stood—jumped! And he kept at it—walking, then jumping, and all the time praising God. The people were amazed at the beautiful thing happening at the Beautiful Gate. Then Peter, John, and man went inside the temple together, where Peter spoke to the group gathered there.

"Why are you so amazed? You've got to remember and start seeing that this, and everything like it, is happening because Jesus of Nazareth, **who you rejected**, is actually risen. And that means so many of the messages God gave to **our prophets from the past** pointed forward to Jesus. And that means what's left for you to do is turn toward Jesus so you can start enjoying refreshment from God and the life God's offering you all."

Connections—Prophetic Critique

I played it down in this paraphrase, but the speech Peter gives is one of many in the New Testament that highlight the conflict between Jesus or his followers and "the Jews." Since we live on the other side of thousands of years of often violent antisemitism, these passages rightfully bring up some sensitive issues.

On the one hand, we should remember that Jesus, Peter, and most of the writers of the New Testament were themselves Jewish. They would have understood what they were doing in speeches like this as being in the same tradition as the Old Testament prophets. In other words, their message was part of an ongoing, intra-Jewish debate about what God was up to. This is not anti-Jewish, but part of a debate *among* Jewish people about what it means to be Jewish.

On the other hand, we *do* unfortunately live in a time when this passage and ones like it have been weaponized against Jewish people in horrifying ways. We need to be mindful of this when telling stories like this one, being careful about how the words Peter speaks in his particular context might need to be adjusted somewhat to ours, not to change the message, but to communicate it more clearly and sensitively.

Connections—Old Testament

Peter's speech is absolutely full of quotations from and references to the Old Testament. He is working very hard to make sure his listeners understand that Jesus is not some new god who has shown up on the scene, but is rather one and the same with *the* God, Yahweh, who they already know. These events are part of the same story about Israel's God they find in the Old Testament. N. T. Wright puts it like this: "[Peter] is understanding the Old Testament as a single great story which was constantly pointing forwards to something God was going to do through Abraham and his family, something that Moses, Samuel, Isaiah, and the rest were pointing on towards as well. This great Something was the restoration of all things, the time when everything would be put right at last. And now, he says, it's happened! It's happened in Jesus! *And you can be a part of it*" (*Acts for Everyone*, pt. 1, 59, italics in original).

No sooner did Peter finish than the temple leaders came upon the group, and they were completely annoyed by Peter's speech, by the disciples as a group, and by the fact that they just would not shut up about the idea that life was available through Jesus.

So they locked them up for a night, and the next day they brought them back out to be questioned. "How did you do this?" they asked them. "What power did you use? **What name** did you invoke?"

"Whose name, you ask? Whose name gave us power to do this good thing that brought this man wholeness? This man is well because of the Messiah Jesus of Nazareth!"

But the leaders did not want to hear Peter's response. They wanted him to stop talking about Jesus, to stop telling other people about Jesus, and certainly to stop doing anything out of the ordinary, like healing, in the name of Jesus. So they tried the only thing they could think of to make them stop: **threats**.

Key Word—Whose Name?
Peter and John are asked how they healed the man: "What power did you use? What name did you invoke?" (see Acts 4:7). Peter responds that it was done in the name of Jesus, the Messiah.

In the ancient world, the name of a powerful person was thought to carry with it some of that person's power. The name of a god might be able to do what we would call magic, for example, or a representative of the emperor might use his name to show they have the power and authority of the emperor on their side.

We might see things a bit differently today, but we can still get the gist of what's going on. The Jewish leaders know that Peter and John have shown great power; now, they want to know where that power came from. Who gave these nobodies the right to do something so amazing and so disruptive? Whose power and authority do they have on their side?

Your Kid Asks: Why are the priests so mad?
It's a good question: Why are these people so upset about someone being healed? What kind of meanies are these guys? The simplest way to think about this is that Peter and John are directly challenging the power and authority of the religious leaders, and people with power really, really don't like to be challenged. Like, ever. Being able to heal a man that the priests apparently couldn't heal. Telling them the healing was done by the name of Jesus…you know, that guy you all killed a little while back. It's not a good look for the priests. And they know it.

And those threats did nothing. The rest of the community? Many of them—thousands—believed Peter, and John, and the others. They believed that God was doing a new thing because of Jesus, and they joined in. It wasn't just that they changed their minds; they did these wild things, like selling stuff sometimes so that there'd be extra money for others who needed it. They cared for each other, and began to enjoy the life God was bringing right then and there, together.

I wonder how the man would tell the
story of his day in his own words?

I wonder if Peter, or John, or any
of the others following Jesus felt
afraid of the temple leaders?

I wonder how people now could care for
each other like they did then?

PERSECUTION COMES

ACTS 6–12

The Main Idea: Acts includes a series of stories about Jesus-followers being persecuted, which opens up a great space for questions like: What would make them want to keep going? What had they experienced of God to give them strength? and How and why do people keep trusting Jesus when circumstances are really bad?

It wasn't a surprise. The trouble had been on the way for a while. Plus, Jesus had said it was coming. Still, when it came, it was hard.

No matter how much Jesus' followers said they were sticking to what God had always said in the Bible, there were leaders who said they were disrespecting God's words and stories from the past. No matter how much they explained that Jesus fit right in with God's promises—he must be messiah, others said **they were stirring up trouble**. No matter how much they said,

Historical Context—Messianic Movements
Jesus was neither the first nor the last person to claim to be the Messiah the Jewish people had been waiting for. For all the rest, the person at the heart of it was killed by Rome and that was the end of it.

For the Jewish Leaders…
their perspective, then, the Church was confusing. Didn't they get it? It was over. Their guy was dead, not leading a victorious fight against Rome. Anyone with eyes could see that he was clearly not the Messiah. Just shut up and go home already!

For the Church…
they were convinced that Jesus was the true Messiah. The resurrection had resulted in them rethinking who the Messiah was supposed to be, what he was supposed to do. They had reoriented their expectations around Jesus.

"We know it sounds wild, but **if Jesus was raised**, it must be true," some leaders said, "You're spreading lies." No matter how much they loved each other, took care of people who were poor, helped people who were sick, the leaders still claimed, "Your message is dangerous for us all."

So the **leaders** set out to stop it. They told them to stop talking about Jesus. But they wouldn't stop.

Some of them—Peter and John, for instance—hit them and hurt them. They didn't stop.

Connections—The Resurrection
Perhaps the main reason for the split between the Jewish leaders and the Church is rooted in Jesus' resurrection. The Church knows it happened and acts accordingly. The leaders know it didn't happen—I mean, who ever heard of such a thing?!—and act accordingly.

For the Leaders…
If Jesus wasn't raised from the dead, as the Jewish leaders believe, then the early Church are dangerous liars. They are deceiving the people and leading them away from the true God to follow this crucified Jesus charlatan. And they're potentially going to provoke Roman violence on the whole Jewish people. If we assume that Jesus stayed dead, then the response of the Jewish leadership is entirely reasonable.

For the Church…
However, if Jesus was raised, all that changes. That would mean his words really were from God, and that following him was the way to life. The early Church was able to continue proclaiming the good news, enduring the persecution that came as a result, because of the strength they were able to draw from the reality of the resurrection.

Key Word—Authority
One of the key themes of the stories in Acts is authority: Who speaks and acts for God?

For the Jewish Leaders…
believed they had rightful authority. It says right there in the Torah that the priests in the temple are the ones who can do things like lead the people in worship, bring them before God, speak on behalf of God, and forgive sins. Anyone who denied that, as the Church did, was denying the clear meaning of the Scriptures. (And in addition to these seemingly righteous motivations, the religious leaders kinda liked their power and didn't want to give it up.)

For the Church…
though, sees a different source of authority: Jesus. If Jesus really is God's son, who has been given all authority on heaven and earth and has given that authority to his followers, as he said in his final words before ascending to heaven, then that changes everything. The priests and religious leaders aren't speaking on behalf of God, and Jesus' followers have no obligation to listen to them. They must, as Acts puts it, obey God rather than men.

They put them in prison. They didn't stop. They'd just carry on talking about Jesus in the jail, or singing songs to God. A couple of times an angel from God met them in the jails and helped them escape again. This did not go over well.

Was there any stopping this group? Any shutting them up?

Maybe it was time to just get rid of them.

Whatever **challenges and hardships** Jesus' followers had faced before, they were worse now, as those who disagreed with them got organized to stop them, no matter what.

Historical Context—The Jewish People as Persecuted Minority

Sometimes stories like this one are told in a way that divides the characters into almost cartoonish "good guys" and "bad guys" with very little nuance. While this sort of approach does make the stories simple, it also has the negative effect of making them seem fundamentally unreal. Cartoonish figures, after all, are inevitably outside of the reality we face day-to-day.

The more unreal the story gets, the easier it is to safely put it "back then," in a kind of mythical past that prevents us from engaging with the real-life choices and motivations of the characters in the story, which might actually have something to say to our own choices and motivations in our real lives today. So that we can better engage with the reality of this story, here are some things to keep in mind about the religious leaders on one hand and the Church on the other:

The Jewish people in the first century had endured centuries of oppression as religious minorities in various empires. This history and identity—having been slaves for hundreds of years in Egypt, then exiled in Babylon and Assyria and Persia, and now under the thumb of Rome—shaped both how the Jewish leaders responded to the Church and vice versa.

For the Leaders…
this history had made them afraid. They knew the power of empires like Rome, and how much pain Rome could inflict if it wanted to. And so, they're trying to keep the peace, prevent any offense that might cause a violent response. These Christian troublemakers who keep stirring people up with stories about that Jesus guy Rome crucified, they needed to be shut up for the good of everyone. If not, who knows what Rome might do. This wasn't an irrational fear either. About a generation after the stories in Acts, a Jewish rebellion resulted in Roman legions marching on Jerusalem and destroying the temple.

For the Church…
is also drawing from this history and identity, but in a different way. They see themselves as being in line with the Old Testament prophets, who are bringing a true message from God to a religious leadership who doesn't want to hear it. They are the faithful remnant.

Stephen and James were killed. Hundreds, like Philip, had to move far away to places like Phoenicia, Cyprus, and Antioch.

As they did, they carried in their minds and hearts the memory of Jesus' own words: "This is how it'll be in the world. There will be trouble. Take heart. I've overcome the world."

It didn't feel like it, in those days. It didn't feel at all like a new time had begun, full of all these God-matched things like joy and justice, life and love. That new time hardly felt real at all. It felt like the old time of sadness, hurt, and death was all that was real.

But again, they remembered Jesus. They told their story to whoever wanted to hear it, and many heard about Jesus and felt amazed about him, and about these people who loved him so much that they held on to him even now. And those who were new to the group joined those who'd known Jesus a long time to eat meals together—eating always reminds you that God gives life, after all—and as they broke the bread and drank the wine, they'd say: "We remember Jesus. We hope in Jesus. We live in Jesus."

I wonder how they felt about God while this was happening?

I wonder who helped Jesus' followers.

I wonder if anyone felt too mad to think about loving enemies like Jesus said?

YOUR KID ASKS

IF THERE'S A GOOD AND POWERFUL GOD, WHY DO BAD THINGS HAPPEN, ESPECIALLY TO PEOPLE WHO ARE TRYING TO FOLLOW GOD?

Kids notice the ways the world falls short of the goodness and justice of God, and they ask the very fair question: What's up with that?

When the young Church encounters organized, violent persecution for the first time, we have an opportunity to touch on one possible way of addressing this question. As has been the case in previous times we've tackled this topic, what follows is *not comprehensive*. With something this big and weighty, it's best to come at it from different angles at different times, each time saying something true in a way your kid can understand without overwhelming them with everything at once.

So here is *an* answer, not *the* answer.

In the story told in Acts, the young Church encounters opposition from the religious leaders of the day, who are angry that these Christians keep talking about this Jesus guy. Between the lines of the story, you can see the Church wrestling with the question of why this is happening to them, as well as why God isn't doing more to protect them from it. They are facing pain, sometimes violence, precisely *because* they are following Jesus.

Let's set this alongside two other stories from the Bible (I could pick out more, but for the sake of the word count, I'll limit to these two). The first is Jesus' crucifixion. The second is the story of Joseph in Genesis.

In all three cases, we have people who trust God and are following God as best they can. In all three cases painful, sometimes violent, things happen. How should we think about that? Let's look at some common features:

First, in all three stories, God is not *causing* the pain. The bad things that happen are the result of outside forces, whether you want to describe those as individual people doing bad things (lowercase sin) or societal structures that bring about injustice and violence (uppercase Sin). Some large chunk of the blame for the ways this world falls short of the goodness and justice of God should be laid at the feet of humans and sin/Sin.

God has given humans real responsibility and real choice, and when humans choose poorly that has real-life consequences for them and for the world around them. When bad things happen where this is clearly a factor, talk about that with your kid: *"I know it's hard that this has happened. God chooses to give people the ability to make choices, and sometimes they make bad choices that hurt other people. I think God wishes things like this didn't happen, too, but God isn't going to control us and force us to make good choices."*

Second, God is not sitting back and allowing these things to happen because God doesn't care. The Bible shows us that God cares deeply about injustice, and is just as sad about it as we are.

What we see in all three stories is that one way God responds to bad things happening is by being with us through them. The Bible never promises that God will stop bad things from happening; it does promise that God will be *with us* in the midst of them.

That's a refrain in the story of Joseph: God was with him. It's something emphasized in Acts as well: the presence of God with the Church through it all. If we look for and lean into God's presence in the midst of trouble, we will find that the same is true for us. It doesn't make the bad less bad, but it does give us strength to endure it. Whenever something painful is happening, we can encourage our kids to look for God's presence with them in the middle of it.

And then finally: **In each of these stories we see the good news of the resurrection: that our God is a God who consistently brings life out of death.** In Jesus' story, this is literal, of course. But we see it in Joseph saying to his brothers that they had meant to do evil to him, but God had used it for good. We see it in the ways the persecution of the church is the catalyst that pushes the gospel out of Jerusalem, in the process bringing life to the wider world.

It's crucial here to remember, ***this doesn't make the bad things into good things***. The things that happened were still bad. Throwing your brother Joseph into a pit and selling him into slavery? Bad. Crucifying Jesus? Bad. Throwing the early Christians into jail, beating them, and sometimes killing them because of their faith in Jesus? Bad. No good that God brings out of those situations changes that.

The amazing power of our God is shown not in pretending that bad things are actually good if you squint hard enough. The power is in God's ability to take even the darkest of situations and bring life *even there*. Our God is a God of resurrection life, and we can therefore expect the same in our times of trouble. This expectation sometimes requires patience, because the good that God will bring out of whatever situation sometimes takes a long time to manifest. When appropriate, we can use stories of how God has done this in our own lives to help our kids trust that God will do the same for them.

PHILIP AND THE ETHIOPIAN EUNUCH

ACTS 8:26–40

The Main Idea: God's delightfully diverse family is for everyone. Always has been. But we see this in many of the stories at the start of Acts. It's as if Luke—yep, the same guy who wrote the book with his name—really wants us to notice: It's actually happening! To God, the more unique and varied kinds of people joining the family, the more beautiful the whole group becomes.

One of Jesus' followers was a man named Philip, who found himself in Samaria telling people about Jesus, because it wasn't safe to stay in Jerusalem any longer. Until one day, a messenger from God said to him, "Go out to that road in the desert—the one that goes from Jerusalem to Gaza." That was it, the whole message. There's a lot the Bible does not tell us: What did the messenger look like? Sound like? Was this all he said, or just all that got included in Luke's version of the story?

And in case you hoped for more details from Philip's side, prepare yourself for disappointment. Because all the Bible says next is, "So he got up and went." We don't know if he took time and thought about it, or if he grabbed a quick snack for the road first. We don't know if he thought this was normal or strange. We just know he did it.

On the road Philip saw a man in a chariot, riding away from Jerusalem. The man was Ethiopian, the head of the finances for all of the queen's money, and a member of her royal court.

Even though he worked for someone that powerful, he himself would actually have been left out in a lot of ways based on his role. Because he worked for the queen, he was also what was called a "**eunuch**." These were men who had a procedure to remove their testicles. It was thought to keep the royal women safer, but it also made them "less manly" based on what the culture valued.

While he rode along, the man was reading from **Isaiah** the prophet's words. God's Spirit said to Philip, "Get up close to the chariot." So Philip ran up to it and heard him reading.

"Do you understand what you're reading about?" Philip asked him.

"Of course not—I'd need someone to make it make sense for me." And he urged Philip to join him in the chariot as he read on.

Connections—Jesus on Eunuchs
This story isn't the first time eunuchs show up in the New Testament. In Matthew 19, Jesus mentions them as positive models of those who are a part of the kingdom of God.

In its cultural context Jesus' choice of role model is genuinely shocking. Eunuchs were looked down on for not being "manly" enough and for not being able to fulfill their duty of having children. They were not allowed to be full members of the worshipping community of Israel (see "Historical Context" above). But Jesus responds to the men's question about divorce, not with the encouragement to "be a better *man*," but to "be more like the eunuchs; they're part of God's kingdom" (see Matt. 19:12).

Connections—Isaiah
The passage the Ethiopian quotes to Philip comes from Isaiah 53, a part of Isaiah that is looking forward to the future salvation that God will bring, and it's no accident this is where he is reading. Just a few chapters earlier, Isaiah 45 talks about Ethiopians experiencing the blessing of God. Just a few chapters later, Isaiah 56 says that "eunuchs and foreigners" coming to worship Yahweh will be a key feature of the hoped-for age to come (see vv. 3–8). Central to it all was the Servant Isaiah foresaw who would somehow bring all these things into reality through his own suffering. That person, Philip explains to the Ethiopian, is Jesus. Because of Jesus, those who used to be excluded would now be included.

The exact section the Ethiopian had come to was comparing…someone…to a sheep about to be killed, but didn't fight it or make any noise. That…someone…was killed unfairly, and they died too young to even have children to live after them, but many people didn't even care.

And if that feels a little confusing to you, then you feel just like the Ethiopian felt.

"Okay, is he talking about himself? Someone else?" he asked.

Thankfully, Philip felt clear—this little section pointed to Jesus, and it was part of a bigger section that said even more about Jesus, and that was part of a bigger story of God bringing life and saving the world through Jesus. And Philip could tell that whole story from any starting point, even starting in the **middle** like this. So he did.

They rode on together and eventually came to some water. A river? A puddle? We don't know. It was wet, which was enough for the Ethiopian's idea: "Baptize me here! We have water; there's no reason not to! Stop the chariot!"

No reason not to? Was that true? Was he right?

Some might say a reason not to was that he wasn't Jewish; he was Ethiopian. But God has always dreamt that the entire world, with all its different and unique people, would be included. The Spirit *did* just give them all language skills for many nations, after all.

Literary Feature—Chiasm

A chiasm is a common literary feature in the Bible used to highlight what was most important. Today, when we want to emphasize the point we are making, we might put it at the beginning to catch someone's attention, or maybe at the end to make it the last thing said. In the Bible, the writers would often put it right in the middle and then would build the rest of the section out from the middle so that what led up to and followed the main point would be mirror images of each other. In this story, verse 34 is the center of the chiasm: the eunuch's question of who the prophet Isaiah is talking about. Philip's answer, of course, is Jesus, and the truth that Jesus is the answer to this central Old Testament hope is the core of Philip's message.

What about this reason: He's a eunuch. The temple has rules about where someone like him can go. But Jesus did say that *he's* the temple now, and the Spirit *did* just send Philip here, to this man specifically.

Maybe there were reasons, but the reasons weren't right. The Ethiopian eunuch was right: There was no reason not to.

So Philip and the Ethiopian eunuch climbed down from the chariot to the pond/river/stream/puddle, and Philip baptized him. As they came up, God's Spirit swooped Philip away—poof! (If you wonder if the story tells us any details about what this was like, and you guess… probably not, you're right!)

While the two never saw each other again, the eunuch went on from there delighted with God and full of God's joy.

Connections—Rahab
An interesting parallel to this story is the story of Rahab, the Canaanite prostitute who helps the spies escape from Jericho, but not before she decides she wants to trust in Yahweh and become a part of God's family. Openness to anyone who trusts God, no matter what, is not a Jesus thing; it's a God thing. God's people consistently find ways to build walls and close gates, but all through the Bible we get stories that tear them down (if we're willing to listen).

I wonder what Philip thought and felt
when the Ethiopian said,
"There's no reason not to baptize me"?

I wonder what about the conversation,
or about Jesus, made the Ethiopian
decide he wanted to be baptized?

I wonder if the Ethiopian eunuch would be
surprised or not about how important this day
would be for everyone trying to
follow where God's Spirit led?

PAUL MEETS JESUS

ACTS 9:1–19

The Main Idea: God picks unlikely people. Often this is applied to stories where the person God chooses is marginalized or powerless, because that's the most common version in the Bible. What this story shows us, though, is that God's tendency to pick the unexpected extends also to enemies, even powerful ones. It really is true, as Paul himself will say later in his own story, that God shows *no* partiality.

S aul has spent his whole life following God. **Everything that included—** learning about the Bible, being in groups that also followed God, even leading them!—he did. He knew God well.

Historical Context—Saul's Background
Other places in the New Testament give us some information about who Saul was. He was a highly educated member of the Pharisees who had trained under one of the more prominent rabbis of the day. He was wholeheartedly committed to Yahweh, and went above and beyond when it came to following the Old Testament Law. His persecution of the Church, therefore, did not come about because he was a "bad guy." It came because the *very first* of the Ten Commandments (to say nothing of the whole rest of the Scriptures) made it perfectly clear that there was one and only one God: Yahweh. Anyone worshipping someone else (like Jesus) needed to be stopped; they were leading the people astray after false gods. It's only when Saul has his vision that he comes to realize the truth—that Jesus and Yahweh are one and the same—which turned his response to Jesus around 180 degrees.

Key Word—The Way
This is one of the words the early Church would use to describe itself. Followers of Jesus were those who "belonged to the way" (see Acts 9:2). It's a word that highlights how following Jesus is not primarily about a set of beliefs that you either agree or disagree with. It's a way of life; something you do. It's living in ways that follow in the footsteps of Jesus—his character, his love, and his justice.

Fun Detail—Tied Up
Paul is twice described in the story as having set out to tie up, or bind, the Christians and lead them away to Jerusalem. Instead, Paul is the one who is tied up (metaphorically, at least) and who needs to be led by the hand into Damascus.

Key Word—Lord
Kids sometimes ask, "How do we know Jesus is God?" This story offers a helpful little detail with the word "Lord." As a Jew who knew his Torah backward and forward, Saul would have had some idea of what was happening when a sudden bright light was accompanied by a voice from the sky—this was God speaking. Paul's question "Who are you, Lord?" combines two things (Acts 9:5). On the one hand, Paul uses the word Jews would use to address God, "Lord." On the other, he's confused about what exactly is going on. Jesus' response, "I am Jesus," echoes God's response to Moses at the burning bush, "I am Yahweh," and would have been the beginning of Paul connecting the dots between Jesus and Yahweh in his own mind (v. 5).

So, one of our answers to kids might sound like: "People were discovering that Jesus was God along the way, and we have stories in the Bible that help us discover it with them, like Saul!" (Another would be Jesus walking on the water, saying, "It's me," in a way that sounds like "I am"—see page 212.)

Fun Detail—Saul/Paul
In this story, the main character is a man named Saul. Later, in chapter 13, we're told that he is also named Paul. Saul is a Hebrew name, one that we see in the Old Testament. Paul is a Greek name. It's true today also that people who live across language and cultural barriers often have different names or versions of their name depending on the cultural location they find themselves in. Up until this story, he spent most of his time in Hebrew-speaking Jewish contexts, using the name Saul. The work God is going to give him to do, though, will take him more and more into the Greek-speaking Gentile world, where he will use the name Paul.

Key Word—Suffering
Ananias hears that God has great plans for Saul, but also that God is in the process of teaching Saul how it is necessary for him to suffer. This is an echo of the necessary suffering of Jesus himself, and a foreshadowing of the suffering that is still to come for many of Jesus' followers later in Acts. It may seem a paradox that the good news of Jesus also includes suffering, but it's a consistent theme in Scripture. Jesus never promises us an easy, safe, carefree life; he does promise to be with us through suffering. Saul's story is a good reminder of that.

Which is why when he got wind of this group called **the Way**, and their message that God was saving the world through Jesus, he was very concerned. Jesus was that troublemaker, killed by Rome, who had made incredible claims about being sent from God and bringing life through himself. But anyone who actually followed God would know that only God can bring life.

No, this Way was not a way to life; it was a way to trouble, to chaos, to death. And it needed to be stopped.

So Saul got permission to go after these people himself. And now it was off to Damascus. The synagogue leaders had given him the okay to find and **tie up** any of these people and bring them back to Jerusalem.

He wasn't too far off when the trip was brought to a sudden stop by a light so intense, that instead of lighting things up, it was impossible to see at all! Saul fell right down to the ground. Then he heard a voice. "Saul, Saul, why are you coming after me to harm me?"

"Harm you, **Lord**? Who even *are* you?"

"I'm Jesus of Nazareth, the one you are seeking out, hurting, attacking. Instead, get up and go to the city and wait there. You'll be told what to do next."

Saul hadn't been traveling alone, and everyone with him had heard the voice as well, but no one had seen a speaker. And it was a good thing he traveled in a group, because when he stood back up from the ground, he opened his eyes and saw…nothing. So the men with him helped guide him the rest of the way.

For three days Saul waited in Damascus.

Meanwhile, in a different part of town, a man named Ananias heard God's Spirit say, "Go find a man named Saul. He's already seen a vision of you coming to put your hands on him and make him see again."

"**Saul**, like Saul, Saul? Like, the man who hurt so many of your people in Jerusalem and came here entirely so that he could tie us up, too?"

"Just go. I've picked him to help others know me far and wide. I've even **shown him how hard** saying yes to me will be."

Ananias set off for the house where Saul was.

When he arrived, he placed his hands on him. "Brother Saul," he said, "Jesus has sent me—yes, Jesus, who appeared to you on the road—so that you may be able to see again, and receive God's Spirit."

Something like scales fell off of Saul's eyes, and he could see again. And he got up, found water, and was baptized.

I wonder what Saul thought about during his three days waiting in Damascus?

I wonder if it was easy or hard for Ananias to go to Saul?

I wonder what the scales that fell off Saul's eyes were like?

PETER'S VISION AND CORNELIUS'S INVITATION

ACTS 10

The Main Idea: God's family is for everyone. Despite the Jews being the "chosen people," God had always planned for them to be the community who would show the whole world what God is like, inviting everyone to join in. For Peter, the time for that to become reality had come.

Jesus had a friend and disciple named Peter. After Jesus left earth to go back to heaven, Peter had a big part to play in helping Jesus' followers carry on. They knew some things: Jesus was alive. That meant the kingdom he talked about—the place that's not on a map, but where people live together like God is really king—that kingdom had come to earth. It was anywhere, everywhere that people practiced loving God, loving each other, and even loving their enemies. No one had to get that perfect, because God is so full of grace and kindness that trying to be perfect is just silliness. But they were going to carry on together living like this kingdom was really truly home, wherever they were.

They also didn't know some things. They didn't know exactly how it would work for the people who joined in to be a mix of Jewish and not-Jewish people. Peter was Jewish. Jesus was Jewish. At first, all the disciples were Jewish. But that was changing, which wasn't really too surprising, when they remembered that God's dream was always for the whole world to know what God was like, how loved they were, and to enjoy living from those truths.

But even if it wasn't surprising, it was tricky. See, the way the Jewish people as a group lived together was unique. They wore particular clothes and did not wear others. They set up their week to work on particular days, but not at all on one of them. And importantly for our story today, they ate particular foods and did not eat others. They also did not **eat** with people who didn't do the same. Like non-Jewish people.

One day Peter went up to the roof to pray. (Roofs were flat.) While he was praying, the Bible says he went into a trance and saw a vision.

What do you think that was like?

In the vision, he saw something like a sheet, and it was unfolding down to reveal that inside were all sorts of animals. Then a voice told Peter, "Get up and **eat what you'd like.**"

 Key Image—Table
Who you sat down to eat with was a really big deal in the ancient world. For Jews, dietary restrictions were one of the most important markers of their identity and faith. Eating with people who didn't share those restrictions could open you up to accusations of not taking your identity seriously. For Romans, the people you ate with also showed what sort of person you were. You ate with those who were of similar status to you. Eating with just anyone might result in losing honor in the eyes of others, and honor was all-important for a Roman. And so Jesus sets a table and tells his followers to keep eating together in memory of Jesus, and over time made sure they understood that the table was supposed to get wider and wider and wider, open to *anyone* who wanted to take a seat.

 Historical Context—Clean and Unclean
The vision Peter has is of unclean animals, meaning animals the people were forbidden from eating in the Old Testament. These food laws were one of the most important markers of Jewish identity. They were part of what made Jews who they were—holy, or set apart, different from all the other people groups.

The vision, though, is using unclean animals to broaden Peter's understanding of a major theme that shows up throughout the Old Testament stories. The Jewish people *are* supposed to be set apart, but that isn't the end. Their being set apart has a purpose beyond themselves. It is meant to be an example to the world of the life that is possible for those who put their trust in God instead of idols. Holiness was always supposed to be an invitation to the broader world so that all who chose to do so could join the family of God.

Um. No. Nopity nope nope nope. Because those animals? They are *not* on the menu of foods Jewish people eat.

So the voice repeated the words. Do you think it was a command? A direction? Or more like permission? An invitation? Both?

The voice said something else. "What God has made clean," said the voice, coming now for a second time, "you must not regard as common." And this all happened **three** times.

Peter's vision ended, and just then, down below at the front door, there was a knock. "We are here from Cornelius's house," said a servant. "He would like for Peter to come to his home to eat with him. He wants to hear more about this Jesus."

Ooh! A dinner invite!

One problem. Do you have a guess what it is?

Cornelius is not Jewish. He's a Roman military officer called a **centurion**, actually. And here's a big moment for Peter. For always, he's known that God is special and unique, and he's lived in ways that were special and unique, too. That was how he showed his love and trust for God. Cornelius's house, the

---

Key Number—Three
Important events seem to come in threes in stories about Peter. When he betrays Jesus, the rooster crows three times. When Jesus restores Peter he asks Peter three times whether Peter loves him. Here, the vision happens three times. There are lots of guesses as to why this might be, but my favorite is that maybe Peter just took a while for new ideas to sink in, and this was Jesus' way of saying, "No, seriously, Peter, this is important, so pay attention!"

Key Word—Centurion
Cornelius is a centurion, which meant he was a Roman military officer who would have had command over around one hundred men (that's the "century" part of centurion). N. T. Wright points out that his being posted in Caesarea, which was one of the more important military outposts of the day, tells us "he must have been a good and trusted soldier" (*Acts for Everyone Part One*, 158). What makes Cornelius unique, though, is that he is also a "devout" man who has put his trust in Yahweh (10:22). He was apparently already done with the pantheon of Roman gods, and convinced that Yahweh was the true God who was the source of life. This is why he is a perfect candidate to teach Peter that God's family is for everyone who wants to join.

food from his kitchen, would not be "clean" in the way Jewish customs would need it to be.

But something's happening here: The vision. The invitation.

If you are Peter, what are you thinking or feeling right now?

Well, the Bible says God's **Spirit** tells Peter: Three men are looking for you. Peter lets what he's seeing about God and hearing from God lead the way, like taking him by the hand and holding on tight while he walks into something new and risky and unknown. It's just dinner. But it's not. It's the beginning of something totally new for Jesus' followers. It changes their whole idea of what it means to carry on living together, loving God and each other in their regular lives. (Because it's always our regular lives, of course.)

We are always getting to know God more and more, which means sometimes what we thought about God changes. It was true for Peter, it's true for grown-ups, and it will be true for you.

Peter went with them, and met Cornelius and a bunch of other people who he'd invited to his home. He talked about Jesus, about what God was doing now that Jesus was alive, and about what God had shown him just that day.

"It's become clear to me," he said, "that God really does show no favoritism."

Even in the middle of Peter talking, God was not done. God's Spirit filled the room in a special way. The Bible says it "fell upon" the people—the Gentile people—who had come to dinner. God was clearly bringing them into the family; it was time to mark the occasion. They were baptized, and the story of God's ever-growing family spread.

Key Word—Spirit
We might pass right over the details in the story that the Holy Spirit came upon Cornelius and his household and they began speaking in tongues just like the disciples had at Pentecost (see 10:44–46), but it's actually really important. It's the fact that shows without a shadow of a doubt that God has fully accepted these uncircumcised Gentiles as part of the family. If God's spirit has filled them, then who are Peter and his friends to exclude them? It's kinda hard to argue with God.

I wonder if Peter's vision
made him hungry?

I wonder what the sheet looked like?

I wonder if Cornelius worried
Peter wouldn't come?

PAUL KNOWS THE UNKNOWN GOD

ACTS 17:16–34

The Main Idea: God really wants to be known, and not just by the "in crowd," whether that be Israel in the Old Testament, or the Church in the New Testament. God wants to be known by everyone—all sorts of people—and so God makes Themself known to all sorts of people in all sorts of ways, speaking to them in language and symbols and ideas that they can understand.

Have you ever read something or seen a movie set in ancient Greece or Rome? Cartoon people are usually wearing togas or robes, and buildings have lots of big columns. Well, that's one of the features we should picture in our story today, which is set in the city of Athens, Greece. And there was another big feature in the city of Athens—**idols**. So many idols. Gold ones, silver ones, wood ones, stone ones. Everywhere you looked—indeed,

Connections—Idolatry
The story in Acts has Paul being struck by the sheer number of idols in Athens, and he uses that fact as his on-ramp to talking about Jesus. It's an interesting connection to what is the core message of the Old Testament—trust Yahweh, not idols. Again and again in the Old Testament the Israelites are encouraged to turn away from idols and toward Yahweh alone. Now, Paul is taking that same core message to the Gentiles.

everywhere Paul looked—there was a new idol honoring one god or another. Zeus, Apollo, Athena, and so many more. There was even one "for the god we don't know," just in case.

Paul had met Jesus, and as someone who had always loved and served God, he realized: Jesus was the messiah God had promised. His resurrection proved it. And Jesus was ready to give life to everyone who wanted it. Might these Greeks want it?

Maybe so. Some of them had said they wanted to hear about his teaching. Then again, they called it **newfangled** and strange, and they really preferred the old traditions. Some were very suspicious that Paul was talking about **foreign** gods and leading people away from the good old Greek gods and goddesses. If they didn't like what they heard, Paul might be in trouble.

But **Paul felt clear and ready**: He could tell nearly anyone from anywhere about the God he knew, the God he loved with all his heart. Right in the

---

Fun Detail—New
Our culture values newness, the "latest and greatest," in a way that was most definitely not the case in the ancient world. In fact, the people Paul was talking to were the exact opposite. New was suspicious. Old was best. That Paul's ideas were "new" was very much not a mark in his favor.

Key Word—Foreign
The philosophers want to have Paul come speak to them so they can see if he is preaching about "foreign gods" (Acts 17:18). That might sound neutral to our ears, but it's actually a hidden threat. N. T. Wright notes that "preaching foreign divinities" was the charge that resulted in the philosopher Socrates being sentenced to death. It might be an odd perspective for us, but in the ancient world religion and politics were so closely entwined that the difference between a "preacher of foreign gods" and an "enemy of the state" was practically nothing (*Acts for Everyone*, pt. 2, 84–85).

Genre—Speeches
This is one of many speeches that appear in Acts and, like all the others, we should assume that it's a summary of what Paul actually said, not the word-for-word transcript. The realities of writing in the ancient world meant you had to sum up long speeches if you wanted to write them down at all. The words in Acts 10 would take only a few minutes to say out loud; it's safe to assume that Paul, of all people, would have been just a bit more long-winded than that.

middle of a crowd of **important thinkers**, Paul stood, cleared his throat, and raised his voice to be heard. "You all are obviously a religious group! So many shrines, so many idols, so many altars where you can worship those idols—even that one that says, 'To an Unknown God.'

"**I know that God**. The one you worship but don't even know it, is the God who not only made the whole world, but who rules over the whole world. This is not a god stuck in a shrine, sitting in just one city, limited to one place, tied to one temple. This God's temple? It's the entire world.

"And people don't have to scurry about, trying really, really hard to keep this God comfortable and happy. God doesn't need to take and take from

Historical Context—Philosophy
Up until this story, Jesus has been talked about mostly within the Jewish community, so the message has had a Jewish sort of flavor. Peter's speeches, for example, have basically summed up the whole Old Testament, just now with Jesus as the focal point. Here, Paul is talking to people who could not care less about the Old Testament or what the prophets had to say about Yahweh. N. T. Wright points out that in the same way the Old Testament shaped the perspective of Jewish people, philosophy like what Paul is interacting with here would have shaped the worldview of millions of regular Gentile folk who lived throughout the Roman Empire. Philosophy like this is what shaped how people thought and lived, and interacting with it would have been central to Paul's mission to the Gentiles (*Acts for Everyone*, pt. 2, 81).

Literary Feature—Organizing His Case
The two main schools of philosophy in Paul's day were Epicureanism and Stoicism, and in Paul's message we see him agreeing and disagreeing with some elements of both.

Paul agreed with the Epicurean perspective that God is not to be found *in* the world in the sense that pagan idolatry would have said. God is not in animals, in metal statues, or in trees. But he would have sharply disagreed with *why* that is the case. For the Epicurean, the gods are far away and have no interest in this world, and we humans should imitate them. But Paul paints a picture of a God who created and loves the world, and who wants so much to be in relationship with us that God became human in Jesus. Paul's God invites us to care deeply about the world as well, and to shape it to look more and more like Jesus.

As for the Stoics, Paul agreed with them that God is inside us and that we are God's children, but didn't go as far as the Stoics in believing that God and the world are basically the same thing. For Paul, we are God's children in the sense of being made in the image of God and being God's partners and representatives, not because we possess divine characteristics ourselves (for the Stoics, that characteristic would have been divine *logos* or "reasoning power").

people. In fact, this God gives! God gives life and breath to everything, God gives everything what *it* needs.

"God has always been this way and hoped that people might notice, go looking, and find God. But honestly? God is never far from any of us anyway—we live in God, we move in God, we exist in God. So even if you've never noticed it before, you can now. Everyone, everywhere can turn to this God."

Things seemed to be going well as the Greek thinkers heard Paul make his case. But then, Paul added something they really weren't ready for. You see, this was a group who agreed about something: There was no resurrection. No life after this life. And Paul—who knew they thought this way—said, "God's proving that all this is true, and the first sign? God resurrected Jesus."

At this point, some of them just laughed. "Oh! Ha! Never mind. I thought he was *serious* for a moment there." "Wow! **Resurrection!** That's.... one way to think about it."

But not everyone laughed. Some wanted to hear more: "Could you share again later?" "Would you tell us more about this next time?" The discussion was over, but the effect was not. Some Greeks—despite their idols and shrines and certainty that resurrection wasn't real—joined Paul and the other Jesus followers. The good news, the message about what God was doing for the whole world through Jesus, was spreading.

Key Word—Resurrection
Turning to N. T. Wright once again, he points out that one of the stories about the founding of the Areopagus in Athens—where Paul is speaking in this story—includes the God Apollo saying, "When a man dies…there is no resurrection." "No Resurrection Allowed" is like part of the founding documents of the place, but Paul makes Jesus' resurrection the core of his message (*Acts for Everyone*, pt. 2, 93).

I wonder how Paul learned all these things about God?

I wonder if Paul ever counted the idols as he walked along... one, two, three, four...?

I wonder what helps you trust God or what makes it hard for you to trust God?

COMMUNION GONE WRONG

1 CORINTHIANS 11:17–34

The Main Idea: Communion is an expression of the unity of all types of people in Jesus. The community remembers Jesus and recommits itself to a life together shaped around the person and character of Jesus. To eat the Last Supper together without living like Jesus together would miss the whole point and show that we didn't actually remember Jesus at all.

Remember how, near the end of Jesus' life, he and his friends got together to celebrate the Passover holiday? They ate and drank together, and Jesus transformed the holiday meal and gave it an extra meaning. It became a **remembering meal**, and the bread and wine were his body and blood. It became a new-promise meal, and the bread and wine were reminders that God had promised, because of Jesus, to take this world God loves and bring it back to its most wonderful way of being.

Connections—Last Supper
Paul himself draws a direct connection to the Last Supper to talk about how the Corinthian Church is interacting with one another in meals. He wants them to remember not just the part he quotes to them—Jesus breaking bread and sharing wine to represent his death. He wants them also to remember what happened right before those words—Jesus willingly taking on the humiliation of washing his disciples' feet, completely turning the status and power dynamics upside down with no concern for his own comfort. That is what he wants the rich in Corinth to imitate, which is something they would never have been asked to do before.

And before that meal began, when everyone was waiting on a servant to come wash their grody feet, Jesus got up from the table. He took off his clothes and wrapped himself in a towel. He filled a bowl with water and moved, person by person, washing their feet himself.

So when it was time for Jesus' followers to carry on the tradition of this meal, it was important to do it in a way that reflected Jesus. Even the way they ate together was supposed to be like Jesus, and this changed a lot from how **every other meal** worked.

At every *other* meal, it mattered who was most important, but for Jesus' people, **status and fanciness** shouldn't matter at all. At every *other* meal, the host and their favorite guests get the best and the most to eat. But for Jesus' people, if Jesus gave everyone the same food, they should all keep getting the same food. At every *other* meal, the honored guests would get the best seats where everyone could see how important they were. But Jesus' table was long

---

Historical Context—Meals
In ancient Roman culture, meals did not usually take place across social classes, and if they did, they were highly segregated events. Those with higher status would receive more and better food than those with lower status, and would have received that food in a different, probably more private, setting. The riffraff could eat their scraps in a crowd outside. This is what we should imagine happening in church gatherings in Corinth, and explains why Paul reacts as strongly as he does. This way of eating is the opposite of who Jesus was, and so it needs to stop.

Historical Context—Patrons
In ancient Rome there was an established role that the rich were expected to play in their cities: patron. Taxation in Rome was almost entirely for the purpose of feeding, equipping, and paying the army, so any other social services relied upon gifts from the wealthy. In return, the rich were honored and given the highest status in the community. It seems what is happening in the Corinthian Church is that the rich who are financing the community, including hosting gatherings in their homes, have just assumed that they will be given the same high status in the church that they would receive for similar generosity outside of the Church. It makes sense from that perspective, but Paul is having none of it. That's the world's way of doing things, but Jesus shows an entirely different way.

and wide, and everyone who sat down was an honored guest of his, and there was no such thing as a "best" seat. This was still true after he had returned to heaven.

But doing things so differently was really hard for the important, fancy people. They were just so used to being important and fancy. They were used to the best food and the best seats. They thought that was how things were supposed to be. So they kept coming to Jesus' table in the way they were used to—taking the best for themselves without even thinking about it!

Until Paul got wind of the way things were going. He had feelings. And opinions. Strong ones! So he wrote a strongly worded letter.

What do you think Paul's feelings and opinions were? What would you say in a strongly worded letter?

Paul wrote them to say, "I've heard you come together to remember Jesus, but clearly–you've forgotten! You've forgotten that *he makes us all equal!* You've forgotten that he served us so much, so we serve each other, no matter how fancy! You've forgotten that he gave and gave, so we don't stash up the best and the most for ourselves!

Literary Feature—Hyperbole
Paul, like any other good speaker or writer, often uses rhetorical flourishes like exaggeration to make his points. When he says that some members of the community are going hungry while others are getting drunk, he may or may not be speaking literally. It's very likely that the rich are not *actually* getting drunk, but Paul is using hyperbole to highlight the *far more serious mistake* of eating their fill while their siblings get nothing.

Key Word—"Test Yourself"
Some of us may have grown up in churches where Paul's instructions to the Corinthians were turned into a hyper-individualistic, self-centered introspection-and-confession time before taking communion. This is…kinda the exact opposite of what Paul is saying. Not that we shouldn't consider our own attitudes and hearts as part of taking communion, but the attitudes Paul is concerned with in this story are our attitudes toward one another. Paul cares about the individuals, too, of course, but this story is about the state of the Church community as a whole, not the state of our individual hearts.

"So from now on, when you all come together, **everyone is an honored guest** at one shared table. Jesus hosts us all, so we act like him, loving each other and sharing with each other. MmmmK?

"By the way, I'll be coming around for a little visit, so if you need a little… help… sorting this out, we can do that then."

We don't have any story to tell us what happened in this group after the letter arrived. So using your best guess, what do you imagine?

God's family shares, loves, and serves, because we are all one, thanks to Jesus.

Key Word—Unity
There's a verb that shows up over and over in this little story that means, literally, "to come together." It can mean to physically gather in one place, but also to be united together in a more metaphorical sense. The scholar Richard Hays notes that Paul is playing off these two meanings. Both should be true of the Church, but in Corinth they are gathering without the unity part, which defeats the purpose of the gathering (Hays, *First Corinthians*, 194).

I wonder what kinds of foods
they ate together?

I wonder what happened after
this group got Paul's letter?

I wonder what you like best
about communion now?

PHILEMON

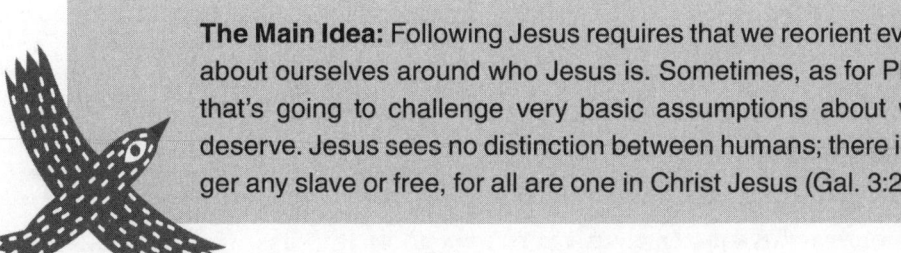

The Main Idea: Following Jesus requires that we reorient everything about ourselves around who Jesus is. Sometimes, as for Philemon, that's going to challenge very basic assumptions about what we deserve. Jesus sees no distinction between humans; there is no longer any slave or free, for all are one in Christ Jesus (Gal. 3:28).

There is this little letter near the end of the Bible called Philemon, and it's called that because it's a letter to a man named Philemon. Paul wrote it to him, later in Paul's life. By then Paul had been put in prison because he wouldn't stop talking about Jesus. That might seem like a strange reason to go to prison, except that if you keep claiming that Jesus is king, when everyone is quite sure that Caesar is king, well, you're just stirring up trouble. You might even be planning to lead a rebellion. Paul had no plan for a rebellion or a battle, but he did very much believe that Jesus was king, and that in Jesus' kingdom, love was the most important law of the land.

Now, somehow or another while in prison, Paul met a man named **Onesimus**. This might not have been the man's name at birth, but because the

Fun Detail—Onesimus
Onesimus's name literally means "useful," and was likely a name given to him by his slave master as a not-so-subtle message about his purpose in life. Paul, though, uses that in several ways to make plays on words. He says in verse 20 that he wants to "have some benefit" from Philemon, a phrase that uses the same root word as Onesimus. That is, he wants Philemon to send Onesimus back to Paul as a free man. After naming Onesimus in verse 10, in verse 11 Paul uses a different word for "useless" and "useful," *a-chrestos* and *eu-chrestos*, which would have sounded identical to *Christos*, that is, "Christ." Onesimus is now in Christ, and that should change everything for Philemon.

man was enslaved, it had become his name. **Slaves** don't always get to choose their names. Sometimes they are just given new ones. The name Onesimus meant "useful one."

Onesimus, for his part, was done with being a slave and had run away. And the reason I'm telling you about Onesimus, when I started this story talking about Philemon, is that the master Onesimus had run away from was Philemon. But somehow Onesimus had found Paul, and when Onesimus met Paul, Paul introduced him to Jesus.

This changed things. Because even though Onesimus was a runaway slave and Philemon was his master, that was not the most important thing about either one of those men's identities. Onesimus was part of the family of God; Philemon, too, was part of the family of God. This meant that they were brothers to each other, family, and equals. So now there was a question Paul needed to answer. How should he, as a leader in the Church, advise Philemon about what to do next?

 This **letter** is a clue about the answer. Paul sent Onesimus back to Philemon with a note. Philemon could read it and make his own decision about

---

 Historical Context—Slavery
Books and books have been written on slavery in ancient Rome, but we're going with a brief account here. It was in some important ways different from slavery in the most recent couple of centuries. Slavery tended to be based not on race, but on being a prisoner of war, for example, and it was somewhat more common for slaves to become free one way or another. But in the most important ways, slavery was then what it's always been. Slaves were property and their master could do to them whatever they wanted. Slaves were at the bottom of the social hierarchy, seen as almost subhuman. Helping a runaway slave, as Paul is here, was a serious crime. Paul's strong hints in this letter would have been a radical departure from what was normal in Roman culture.

 **Genre—Letter**
The letter to Philemon is not really just a letter to Philemon. Paul's introduction and conclusion make it clear that this letter is just like the others that are included in the New Testament: It's meant to be read out loud in front of the whole Church community. This is surely part of Paul's strategy of putting pressure on Philemon to make the right decision without actually commanding him or forcing him to do anything. He's putting Philemon's reputation in front of the Church at play.

what to do, which makes sense when you think about it. People in the family of God do not control one another, even if one of them knows they are right and the other is wrong. Just like God doesn't control us.

What did the letter say? It said Paul loved Philemon. It said that Philemon gave him great joy. It said Paul also loved Onesimus, and was so grateful to have met him while in prison. It said that, however useful Onesimus might've been as a slave, wasn't it wonderful that now he was so much more, part of the family, a **brother**?

Paul also had a few **tricks** up his sleeve when he wrote this letter. You see, the only reason Philemon knew Jesus was because of Paul. Philemon owed Paul his whole self. And Paul decided to sneak that little reminder in along the way. At one point, he told Philemon: If Onesimus owes you anything, just charge it to me. The funny thing is that whatever Onesimus owed Philemon, Philemon owed Paul so much more.

Key Word—Brother
Some readers of Philemon have seen Paul's use of the word "brother" and have assumed that Onesimus is not really a slave, but is Philemon's prodigal younger brother. This is not right. Paul is using the word "brother" rhetorically to highlight the new family that is created among followers of Jesus. He also, in the process, telegraphs exactly what he expects Philemon's response to be. After all, who would enslave their own brother?

Literary Feature—Rhetoric
This letter is an absolute marvel of rhetoric. Paul manages to make his meaning perfectly clear with hints and suggestions and wordplay without ever coming out directly and commanding Philemon to do anything specific. At the same time, he makes sure Philemon has no choice but to do the right thing. He basically builds an elaborate trap, walks Philemon right into place, and then springs it. Just a couple of my favorite examples:

Greeting Philemon as "beloved" would have carried the cultural need for Philemon to reciprocate that love by doing something for Paul, a fact Paul builds on when he emphasizes how Philemon owes Paul his whole life. But by all means, charge Onesimus's debts to my account! Unsaid is "…but you'd still be heavily in my debt even after that!"

Paul doesn't mention the purpose of the letter until he's already established: (1) Philemon's good work on behalf of the Church ("which of course you're going to continue, right?"); (2) Paul's authority to "be bold" and command Philemon to obey ("but I'd rather leave it up to you instead"); and (3) Onesimus's new status as Paul's spiritual child. Only then is the runaway slave mentioned, when Philemon already has no choice but to go along with what Paul wants.

And so Paul hoped that love would lead Philemon to do something that never happened in that time or culture: to let Onesimus go. After all, Paul's whole message was that Jesus made it possible for those who were far apart to be brought back together, whether it was people far from God, people far from their own selves, or people far from each other. If you are reading the Bible for yourself, the word for it is "reconciliation." God is, in Jesus, reconciling everything, bringing it all back together. Could God do it for these two?

We know Onesimus brought the letter to Philemon. We don't know what happened next. Having the letter for so long, in time for it to be included in the Bible, might be a clue, though, that Philemon listened, and the letter remained special to him, a reminder of the power of Jesus' love in real life. It's a wonderful story of the everyday ways that knowing Jesus matter.

And ever since, those of us who read it are invited to think: How might God's big love for us and in us lead us to treat each other?

Key Word—Koinonia
Paul's idea of the way the community of Jesus' followers ought to relate to one another is summed up in the Greek word "koinonia." It's often translated as "fellowship," but doesn't have a great English equivalent that captures the full meaning. Scot McKnight writes that its "core idea is active association, mutual participation, identification with one another, relational interchange and exchange, and partnership" (*Letter to Philemon*, 70). The breadth and depth of what followers of Jesus are supposed to be for one another completely rules out one Christian enslaving another, to say the least. Paul's point is clear.

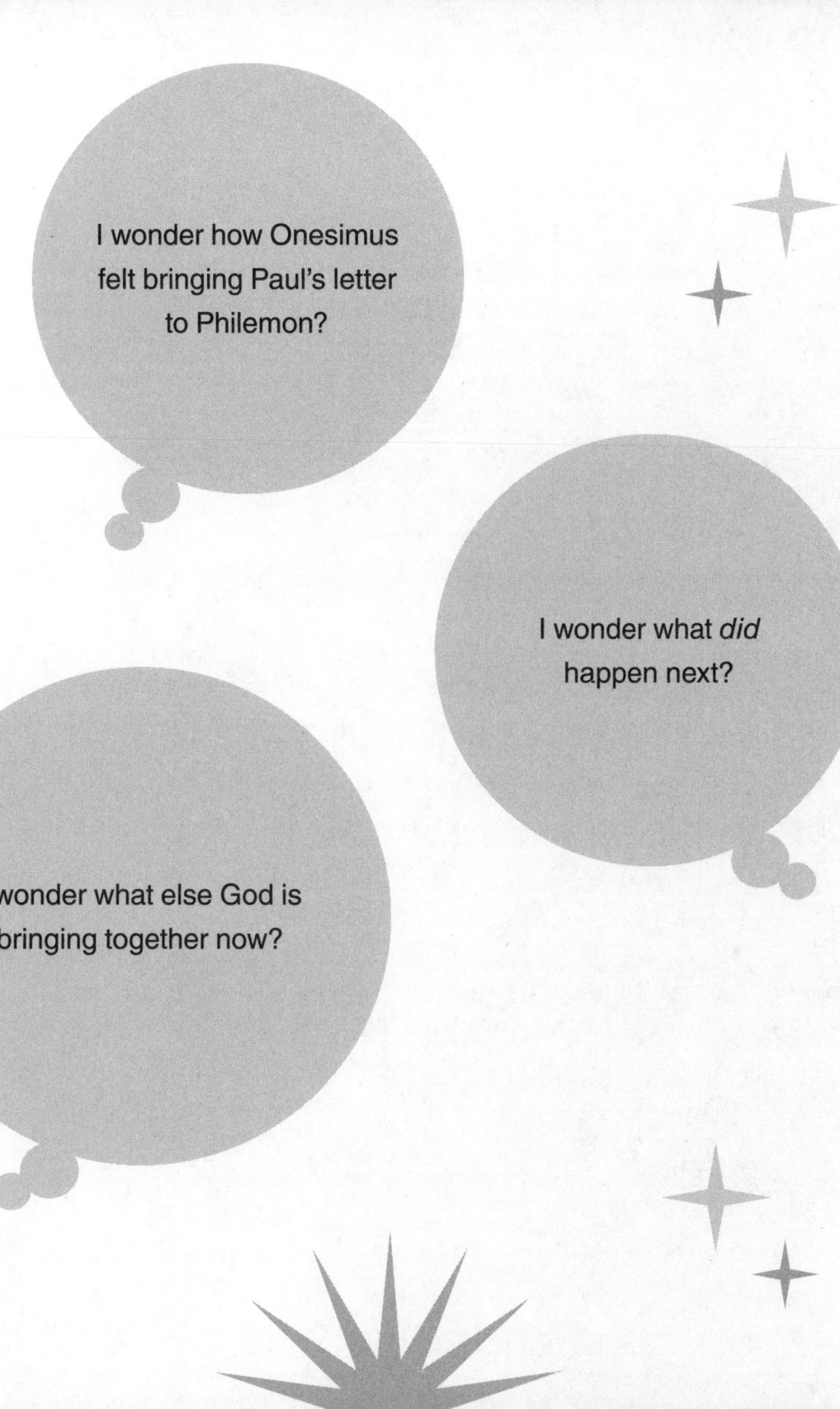

REVELATION

The Main Idea: This is a letter written to encourage a group of Christians to hold tight to Jesus in the face of opposition, even harm. It's written in a style called "apocalyptic," which is not about the end of the world. It's also written in "codes" because of censorship. But the style is just a tool for the message: It seems like the empire is all-powerful and Sin is winning. Hold tight to Jesus. He will make all well one day and you'll see: You were not a fool. Life and joy will be yours.

There was once a group of Jesus followers living in a land ruled by an evil emperor. He was controlling and cruel, demanding and violent. It was a dangerous time for them, because the **emperor** also expected people to worship him as if he were god.

But these people who loved Jesus also believed this: There's just one God, and the emperor ain't it. If we worship the emperor, what would that say about our love for Jesus? If we don't, what will happen to us?

Connections—Empire

The empire that was opposing the Church when Revelation was written was Rome. But all through the letter Rome is never mentioned, Babylon is—the empire that was the bogeyman of the Old Testament (except for the parts before that when Egypt was that empire). One of John's points in Revelation is that there is *always* an empire opposing God's purposes. Opposition to God is like a cyclical force, showing up again and again. The empire might take on different names, but they all share certain characteristics—they are oppressive and unjust, they seem all-powerful, they gobble up everything in their path, they are animated by Evil, but they will ultimately fall. In the face of empire, each generation is confronted with the choice to go along with its demands or to stick close to Jesus no matter what. One day God will put things right, and the people who stuck with Jesus will experience life and the vindication that they weren't foolish.

Far away from these Jesus followers, on an island where he'd been sent as punishment, lived a man named John. John also loved Jesus, more than anything. That's what got him punished in the first place.

John's heart broke for these Jesus followers as they faced such a difficult time. But he also knew that difficult times come with following Jesus, and we can get through them with Jesus.

Being stuck on an island does have the effect of limiting what a person can do to help. So John did what he could. **He wrote them a letter**, a letter he hoped would help them better understand what they were going through.

"It's like **beasts** are stomping through the land, eating everything up as they go!"

"It's like a dragon is loose and tearing the world apart!"

Genre—Apocalyptic
Revelation is the longest example of a genre of writing that was very common in its time. It's called "apocalyptic," from the Greek word that means... "revelation." "Apocalypse" has come to mean something like "the end of the world," but its original meaning is "a revelation of hidden truths," and that's important for our understanding of the genre.

Apocalyptic writing was highly symbolic, often coded, usually included heavenly messengers, and used exaggerated language about stars falling from the sky and mountains shaking and such things. That's why people started thinking it was about the end of the world, but that's a misreading of the symbols. Someone reading at the time would have seen those as symbols of important, world-changing events, God "turning things upside down."

Apocalyptic writing was used to communicate what God was up to behind the scenes when the world all around looked like God was nowhere to be found. It might include messages about what God would do in the future, but the main goal was to encourage people to be faithful in the present, when it looked like the empire was winning. The hidden truth that apocalyptic writing revealed was that God was still faithful.

Historical Context—Beasts
Lions and tigers and bears, oh my! Well, dragons and weird beasty things and such, but still. This is actually a fairly typical feature of apocalyptic writing, where one of the common symbols was representing powerful figures or empires with beasts. You see the same thing in the book of Daniel, where there is a vision of a series of empires that are represented by different mythical-ish creatures. Everyone would have understood these figures to represent Rome or the emperor or Satan, and no one would have been expecting an actual dragon to be traipsing around the earth.

Why beasts and dragons? Because the letter would certainly be read by the emperor's officials, and if they spotted anything they didn't like, they wouldn't pass it along. So John used symbols, almost **like a secret code**, to get the message through. Everyone who heard the letter read out loud would know the beast was the emperor, after all.

It wasn't just a letter to share that he understood their difficulty. John wanted to encourage them. "Hold tight to Jesus. I know it seems like evil is so strong. I know it seems like it's winning. But the story is not over yet. In fact," John said, "I had a vision from God about the end of the story.

"The evil empires end like an angel throwing a massive boulder right into the sea.

"It's like the dragon is caught, tied up, thrown in a pit, then the pit gets sealed up!"

And not only do the bad things end, good things—the best things—come, and they last forever.

"It's like Jesus sits on a beautiful throne, and it shines glory and goodness out for the whole world to enjoy."

"I heard a loud voice from the throne, and this is what it said: 'Look! **God has come to dwell with humans!** God will dwell with them, and they will be God's people, and God Themself will be with them and will be their God. God will wipe away every tear from their eyes. There will be no more death, or mourning or weeping or pain."

Literary Feature—Coded Messages
One of the uses of apocalyptic writing was to say the unsayable. The weird codes and symbols and numbers and such were used to communicate true things in a way that wouldn't be quite so obviously rebellious as saying them outright. It made it less likely that a person possessing this letter would find themselves imprisoned or worse.

Key Image—New Heaven and New Earth
The letter ends with the ultimate note of encouragement: a vision of the secure future God is preparing on the other side of all the suffering. There will come a day when God will remake the world into what it was always meant to be.

Throughout the letter, full of all these images, symbols, and **numbers**, the message John had for these Christians was this: Don't worship the emperor. Hold tight to Jesus. He's holding tight to you. I know it will be hard. You may even get hurt. But you aren't silly or stupid for holding tight to Jesus. You'll see. Someday you'll see, not just that you were right about who God is, but you'll enjoy the whole world made whole. It'll be all happy, no sad, all good, no bad. Forever.

"So come, Lord Jesus," wrote John at the close. "And may Jesus' grace be with you all."

Key Number—All of Them
Pretty much all the numbers in apocalyptic writing are symbolic, and should be read that way. Twelve represents the twelve tribes of Israel. Forty represents a long time. Seven represents completion or perfection. Six represents falling short of perfection. And so on. The main thing to know is that if there is a number, we shouldn't take it literally but should be curious about what it might represent symbolically.

Key (non) Word—Rapture
Like, this isn't a word that shows up in Revelation. Really, it's kind of the opposite of the core message of Revelation, which is meant as an encouragement for followers of Jesus to stay faithful *through* suffering. So, to sum up about the "Rapture": (a) It ain't a thing; (b) Revelation is an encouragement to go through the suffering, not escape it; and (c) the book ends with heaven coming down to earth, not people getting beamed up to heaven.

Key (non) Image—Battle
To anyone who has read the *Left Behind* books, this might come as a major surprise, but in Revelation itself, um…*whisper voice*…no one actually fights, y'all. No, seriously. In chapter 19, Jesus comes riding out armed with a sword coming out of his mouth (so, symbolically speaking he's armed with just his word), and the armies are all arrayed for battle, and then the opposing army is killed by the sword (so, like in Genesis 1, Jesus speaks and it happens). Then in chapter 20, an army comes against God's people again and fire from heaven consumes them. Any "fighting" (I'm putting that in quotes because even the fighting is symbolic) is entirely done by God, and even then it's just *snap* over.

I wonder what kinds of weird images
John would pick if he was writing now?

I wonder how the readers and hearers
of the letter felt after?

I wonder if you ever feel silly
for trusting Jesus?

WORKS CONSULTED

Alter, Robert. *The Hebrew Bible: A Translation with Commentary*. Vols. 1–3. W. W. Norton, 2019.

Birch, Bruce. "1 and 2 Samuel." In *The New Interpreter's Bible Commentary*. Vol. 2. Abingdon Press, 2015.

Blount, Brian. *Revelation: A Commentary*. Westminster John Knox Press, 2009.

Brueggemann, Walter. "Exodus." In *The New Interpreter's Bible Commentary*. Vol. 1. Abingdon Press, 2015.

———. *First and Second Samuel*. Westminster John Knox Press, 1990.

Chapman, Stephen B. *1 Samuel as Christian Scripture: A Theological Commentary*. Eerdmans, 2016.

Childs, Brevard. *The Book of Exodus: A Critical and Theological Commentary*. Westminster John Knox Press, 1974.

Coote, Robert B. "Joshua." In *The New Interpreter's Bible Commentary*. Vol. 2. Abingdon Press, 2015.

Evans, Craig. *Matthew*. Cambridge University Press, 2012.

Fox, Bethany McKinney. *Disability and the Way of Jesus: Holistic Healing in the Gospels and the Church*. InterVarsity Press Academic, 2019.

Fretheim, Terence. *Exodus*. Westminster John Knox Press, 1991.

———. "Genesis." In *The New Interpreter's Bible Commentary*. Vol. 1. Abingdon Press, 2015.

Goldingay, John. *Exodus and Leviticus for Everyone*. Westminster John Knox Press, 2010.

———. *Genesis for Everyone*. Westminster John Knox Press, 2010.

———. *1 & 2 Kings for Everyone*. Westminster John Knox Press, 2011.

———. *1 & 2 Samuel for Everyone*. Westminster John Knox Press, 2011.

———. *Joshua, Judges, and Ruth for Everyone*. Westminster John Knox Press, 2011.

———. *Old Testament Theology*. Vols. 1–2. InterVarsity Press, 2006.

Green, Joel B. *The Gospel of Luke*. Eerdmans, 1997.

Green, Michael. *The Message of Matthew*. InterVarsity Press Academic, 2001.

Hauerwas, Stanley. *Matthew*. Brazos Press, 2006.

Hays, Richard. *First Corinthians*. Westminster John Knox Press, 1997.

Keener, Craig. *The Gospel of Matthew: A Socio-Rhetorical Commentary*. Eerdmans, 2009.

Koester, Craig. *Revelation: A New Translation with Introduction and Commentary*. Yale University Press, 2015.

Longman, Tremper, III. *The NIV Application Commentary: Daniel*. Zondervan, 1999.

Longman, Tremper, III, and John H. Walton. *The Lost World of the Flood: Mythology, Theology, and the Deluge Debate*. InterVarsity Press Academic, 2018.

Marcus, Joel. *Mark 1–8*. Yale University Press, 2011.

———. *Mark 8–16*. Yale University Press, 2011.

McKnight, Scot. *The Letter to Philemon*. Eerdmans, 2017.

Olsen, Dennis. "Judges." In *The New Interpreter's Bible Commentary*. Vol. 2. Abingdon Press, 2015.

Seow, Choon-Leong. "1 & 2 Kings." In *The New Interpreter's Bible Commentary*. Vol. 2. Abingdon Press, 2015.

Thompson, Marianne Meye. *Colossians and Philemon*. Grand Rapids: Eerdmans, 2005.

———. *John: A Commentary*. Westminster John Knox Press, 2015.

Walton, John H. *The Lost World of Genesis One: Ancient Cosmology and the Origins Debate*. InterVarsity Press, 2009.

———. *The Lost World of Adam and Eve: Genesis 2–3 and the Human Origins Debate*. InterVarsity Press, 2015.

Walton, John H., and J. Harvey Walton. *The Lost World of the Israelite Conquest: Covenant, Retribution, and the Fate of the Canaanites*. InterVarsity Press, 2017.

Witherington, Ben, III. *Matthew*. Smyth & Helwys, 2006.

———. *Revelation*. Cambridge University Press, 2003.

Wright, Christopher J. H. *The Story of God Bible Commentary: Exodus*. Zondervan Academic, 2021.

———. *The Mission of God*. InterVarsity Press, 2006.

Wright, N. T. *Acts for Everyone*. Pts. 1–2. Westminster John Knox Press, 2008.

———. *Colossians and Philemon*. InterVarsity Press, 1996.

———. *Jesus and the Victory of God*. Fortress Press, 1996.

———. *John for Everyone*. Pts. 1–2. Westminster John Knox Press, 2004.

———. *Justification: God's Plan and Paul's Vision*. InterVarsity Press, 2009.

———. *Luke for Everyone*. Westminster John Knox Press, 2004.
———. *Mark for Everyone*. SPCK, 2014.
———. *Matthew for Everyone*. Pts. 1–2. Westminster John Knox Press, 2004.
———. *Paul for Everyone: The Prison Letters*. Westminster John Knox Press, 2004.
———. *Revelation for Everyone*. Westminster John Knox Press, 2011.
———. *The Day the Revolution Began: Reconsidering the Meaning of Jesus's Crucifixion*. HarperOne, 2016.

SPIRAL THE STORIES IN *WONDER*

Spiral learning is an educational approach where complex topics are broken into small pieces and introduced bit by bit. Rather than treating a topic (or, for our purposes, a Bible story) as "one and done," including every bit of information you could that one time you talk about it, you make it smaller on purpose, and then go around that same topic or story again and again, each time looking at something new or adding complexity.

Spiral learning approaches can take different shapes when applied to the Bible. For instance, with Bible stories, a spiral learning approach means we tell them repeatedly, but focus on one main attribute of God's each time. Then, we pick a new trait to highlight the next time. Alternatively, we could pick one of God's attributes, like goodness, and look for multiple stories where that trait comes out.

To help with this, I've taken the collection of stories in *Wonder* and grouped them by attribute.

Stories that show that God is good: 1. Creation (Genesis 1); 4. Waiting for Baby Isaac (Genesis 17; 18; 21:1–7); 8. God Provides Manna and Water in the Wilderness (Exodus 16); 10. The Law—Festivals and Jubilee (Exodus 20; 23; 31; Leviticus 23); 16. Elijah, the Widow, and the Last Cup of Flour (1 Kings 17); 31. Jesus Welcomes the Children (Matthew 19:13–15; Mark 10:13–16; Luke 18:15–17); 34. Jesus Heals a Woman and Girl (Mark 5:21–43; Luke 8:40–56); 49. Paul Knows the Unknown God (Acts 17:16–34); 52. Revelation (Revelation).

Stories that show that God is creative: 1. Creation (Genesis 1); 3. Babel (Genesis 11); 8. God Provides Manna and Water in the Wilderness (Exodus 16); 25. Wise Men Visit Jesus (Matthew 2); 26. Jesus Extends a Wedding Party (John 2:1–12); 32. Four Friends Bring a Fifth Friend Through a Roof (Mark 2:1–12; Luke 5:17–26).

Stories that show that God is a life-giver: 1. Creation (Genesis 1); 4. Waiting for Baby Isaac (Genesis 17; 18; 21:1–7); 5. Joseph (Genesis 37–45); 7. God Splits the Red Sea (Exodus 5–15); 8. God Provides Manna and Water in the Wilderness (Exodus 16); 9. The Law—Love God; Love Thy Neighbor (Deuteronomy 6:5); 10. The Law—Festivals and Jubilee (Exodus 20; 23; 31; Leviticus 23); 16. Elijah, the Widow, and the Last Cup of Flour (1 Kings 17); 17. God's Still, Small Voice (1 Kings 19); 19. Daniel and the Veggies (Daniel 1); 28. Jesus Feeds a Crowd (Matthew 14:13–21; Mark 6:31–44; Luke 9:12–17; John 6:1–14); 32. Four Friends Bring a Fifth Friend Through a Roof (Mark 2:1–12; Luke 5:17–26); 33. Jesus Raises Lazarus (John 11:1–46); 34. Jesus Heals a Woman and Girl (Mark 5:21–43; Luke 8:40–56); 40. The Women Visit Jesus' Tomb (Matthew 28:1–10; Mark 16:1–8; Luke 24:1–12); 41. Breakfast on the Beach (John 21); 42. Emmaus (Luke 24:13–35); 49. Paul Knows the Unknown God (Acts 17:16–34); 52. Revelation (Revelation).

Stories that show that God values diversity: 1. Creation (Genesis 1); 3. Babel (Genesis 11); 11. Rahab (Joshua 2): 25. Wise Men Visit Jesus (Matthew 2); 27. Jesus Calls the Twelve (Matthew 4:18–25; Mark 1:16–20; Luke 5:27–30; John 1:35–51); 35. The Samaritan Woman at the Well (John 4:1–42); 46. Philip and the Ethiopian Eunuch (Acts 8:26–40); 48. Peter's Vision and Cornelius's Invitation (Acts 10); 51. Philemon (Philemon).

Stories that show that God is a power sharer: 1. Creation (Genesis 1); 6. A Conversation with a Burning Bush (Exodus 3); 9. The Law: Love God; Love Thy Neighbor (Deuteronomy 6:5); 10. The Law—Festivals and Jubilee (Exodus 20; 23; 31; Leviticus 23); 12. The No-Fight Battle (Judges 6); 14. The People Want a King (1 Samuel 8–13); 15. Anointing David to Become King (1 Samuel 16); 21. An Angel Visits Mary (Luke 1:26–56); 27. Jesus Calls the Twelve (Matthew 4:18–25; Mark 1:16–20; Luke 5:27–30; John 1:35–51); 28. Jesus Feeds a Crowd (Matthew 14:13-21; Mark 6:31–44; Luke 9:12–17; John 6:1–14); 35. The Samaritan Woman at the Well (John 4:1–42); 38. Jesus Washes the Disciples' Feet (John 13:1–20); 43. The Holy Spirit Comes at Pentecost (Acts 2); 44. Peter Heals, Then Preaches, Then Gets in Trouble (Acts 3–4).

Stories that show that God is compassionate: 2. The Dream Is Disrupted (Genesis 3); 8. God Provides Manna and Water in the Wilderness (Exodus 16); 16. Elijah, the Widow, and the Last Cup of Flour (1 Kings 17); 17. God's Still, Small Voice (1 Kings 19); 20. The Prophets (Yep, All of 'Em); 28. Jesus Feeds a Crowd (Matthew 14:13–21; Mark 6:31–44; Luke 9:12–17; John 6:1–14); 29. Jesus Meets Zacchaeus (Luke 19:1–10); 31. Jesus Welcomes the Children (Matthew 19:13–15; Mark 10:13–16; Luke 18:15–17); 32. Four Friends Bring a Fifth Friend Through a Roof (Mark 2:1–12; Luke 5:17–26); 33. Jesus Raises Lazarus (John 11:1–46); 34. Jesus Heals a Woman and a Girl (Mark 5:21–43; Luke 8:40–56); 37. Jesus Is Anointed by Mary; and the Last Supper (Matthew 26:26–29; Mark 14:3–25; Luke 22:14–20); 42. Emmaus (Luke 24:13–35).

Stories that show that God is gracious: 2. The Dream Is Disrupted (Genesis 3); 4. Waiting for Baby Isaac (Genesis 17; 18; 21:1–7); 14. The People Want a King (1 Samuel 8–13); 18. Josiah and the Law (2 Kings 22–23); 20. The Prophets (Yep, All of 'Em); 28. Jesus Feeds a Crowd (Matthew 14:13–21; Mark 6:31–44; Luke 9:12–17; John 6:1–14); 29. Jesus Meets Zacchaeus (Luke 19:1–10).

Stories that show that God keeps God's promises: 4. Waiting for Baby Isaac (Genesis 17; 18; 21:1–7); 7. God Splits the Red Sea (Exodus 5–15); 16. Elijah, the Widow, and the Last Cup of Flour (1 Kings 17); 20. The Prophets (Yep, All of 'Em); 21. An Angel Visits Mary (Luke 1:26–56); 23. Jesus Is Born! (Matthew 1:18–25; Luke 2:1–7); 25. Wise Men Visit Jesus (Matthew 2); 43. The Holy Spirit Comes at Pentecost (Acts 2); 44. Peter Heals, Then Preaches, Then Gets in Trouble (Acts 3–4); 40. The Women Visit Jesus' Tomb (Matthew 28:1–10; Mark 16:1–8; Luke 24:1–12); 41. Breakfast on the Beach (John 21); 42. Emmaus (Luke 24:13–35); 52. Revelation (Revelation).

Stories that show that God is with us: 1. Creation (Genesis 1); 2. The Dream Is Disrupted (Genesis 3); 4. Waiting for Baby Isaac (Genesis 17; 18; 21:1–7); 5. Joseph (Genesis 37–45); 6. A Conversation with a Burning Bush (Exodus 3); 7. God Splits the Red Sea (Exodus 5–15); 8. God Provides Manna and Water in the Wilderness (Exodus 16); 12. The No-Fight Battle (Judges 6); 13. God Speaks to Young Samuel (1 Samuel 3); 17. God's Still, Small Voice (1 Kings 19); 19. Daniel and the Veggies (Daniel 1); 21. An Angel Visits Mary (Luke 1:26–56); 23. Jesus Is Born! (Matthew 1:18–25; Luke 2:1–7); 24. Angels and Shepherds (Luke 2:8–20); 25. Wise Men Visit Jesus (Matthew 2); 31. Jesus Welcomes the Children (Matthew 19:13–15; Mark 10:13–16; Luke 18:15–17); 40. The Women Visit Jesus' Tomb (Matthew 28:1–10; Mark 16:1–8; Luke 24:1–12); 41. Breakfast on the Beach (John 21); 42. Emmaus (Luke 24:13–35); 43. The Holy Spirit Comes at Pentecost (Acts 2); 45. Persecution Comes (Acts 6–12); 46. Philip and the Ethiopian Eunuch (Acts 8:26–40).

Stories that show that God is powerful: 1. Creation (Genesis 1); 3. Babel (Genesis 11); 4. Waiting for Baby Isaac (Genesis 17; 18; 21:1–7); 6. A Conversation with a Burning Bush (Exodus 3); 7. God Splits the Red Sea (Exodus 5–15); 8. God Provides Manna and Water in the Wilderness (Exodus 16); 11. Rahab (Joshua 2); 12. The No-Fight Battle (Judges 6); 17. God's Still, Small Voice (1 Kings 19); 16. Elijah, the Widow, and the Last Cup of Flour (1 Kings 17); 19. Daniel and the Veggies (Daniel 1); 21. An Angel Visits Mary (Luke 1:26–56); 25. Wise Men Visit Jesus (Matthew 2); 26. Jesus Extends a Wedding Party (John 2:1–12); 28. Jesus Feeds a Crowd (Matthew 14:13–21; Mark 6:31–44; Luke 9:12–17; John 6:1–14),; 30. Jesus Walks on Water (Matthew 14:23–33;

Mark 6:45–51; John 6:16–21); 32. Four Friends Bring a Fifth Friend Through a Roof (Mark 2:1–12; Luke 5:17–26); 33. Jesus Raises Lazarus (John 11:1–46); 34. Jesus Heals a Woman and a Girl (Mark 5:21–43; Luke 8:40–56); 40. The Women Visit Jesus' Tomb (Matthew 28:1–10; Mark 16:1–8; Luke 24:1–12); 41. Breakfast on the Beach (John 21); 42. Emmaus (Luke 24:13–35); 43. The Holy Spirit Comes at Pentecost (Acts 2); 47. Paul Meets Jesus (Acts 9:1–19); 52. Revelation (Revelation).

Stories that show that God helps us: 2. The Dream Is Disrupted (Genesis 3); 5. Joseph (Genesis 37–45); 6. A Conversation with a Burning Bush (Exodus 3); 7. God Splits the Red Sea (Exodus 5–15); 8. God Provides Manna and Water in the Wilderness (Exodus 16); 12. The No-Fight Battle (Judges 6); 17. God's Still, Small Voice (1 Kings 19); 19. Daniel and the Veggies (Daniel 1); 22. An Angel Visits Joseph (Matthew 1:18–25); 29. Jesus Meets Zacchaeus (Luke 19:1–10); 32. Four Friends Bring a Fifth Friend Through a Roof (Mark 2:1–12; Luke 5:17–26); 34. Jesus Heals a Woman and a Girl (Mark 5:21–43; Luke 8:40–56); 45. Persecution Comes (Acts 6–12).

Stories that show that God cares for us: 2. The Dream Is Disrupted (Genesis 3); 4. Waiting for Baby Isaac (Genesis 17; 18; 21:1–7); 5. Joseph (Genesis 37–45); 8. God Provides Manna and Water in the Wilderness (Exodus 16); 9. The Law—Love God; Love Thy Neighbor (Deuteronomy 6:5); 10. The Law—Festivals and Jubilee (Exodus 20; 23; 31; Leviticus 23); 16. Elijah, the Widow, and the Last Cup of Flour (1 Kings 17); 23. Jesus Is Born! (Matthew 1:18–25; Luke 2:1–7); 28. Jesus Feeds a Crowd (Matthew 14:13–21; Mark 6:31–44; Luke 9:12–17; John 6:1–14); 29. Jesus Meets Zacchaeus (Luke 19:1–10); 31. Jesus Welcomes the Children (Matthew 19:13–15; Mark 10:13–16; Luke 18:15–17); 32. Four Friends Bring a Fifth Friend Through a Roof (Mark 2:1–12; Luke 5:17–26); 34. Jesus Heals a Woman and a Girl (Mark 5:21–43; Luke 8:40–56); 41. Breakfast on the Beach (John 21); 52. Revelation (Revelation).

Stories that show that God frees us: 6. A Conversation with a Burning Bush (Exodus 3); 7. God Splits the Red Sea (Exodus 5–15); 10. The Law—Festivals and Jubilee (Exodus 20; 23; 31; Leviticus 23); 29. Jesus Meets Zaccheus (Luke 19:1–10); 32. Four Friends Bring a Fifth Friend Through a Roof (Mark 2:1–12; Luke 5:17–26); 34. Jesus Heals a Woman and a Girl (Mark 5:21–43; Luke 8:40–56); 50. Communion Gone Wrong (1 Corinthians 11:17–34).

Stories that show that God loves us: 9. The Law—Love God; Love Thy Neighbor (Deuteronomy 6:5); 20. The Prophets (Yep, All of 'Em); 23. Jesus Is Born! (Matthew 1:18–25; Luke 2:1–7); 29. Jesus Meets Zacchaeus (Luke 19:1–10); 31. Jesus Welcomes the Children (Matthew 19:13–15; Mark 10:13–16; Luke 18:15–17); 33. Jesus Raises

Lazarus (John 11:1–46); 38. Jesus Washes the Disciples' Feet (John 13:1–20); 40. The Women Visit Jesus' Tomb (Matthew 28:1–10; Mark 16:1–8; Luke 24:1–12); 41. Breakfast on the Beach (John 21).

Stories that show that God invites everyone: 1. Creation (Genesis 1); 3. Babel (Genesis 11); 7. God Splits the Red Sea (Exodus 5–15); 9. The Law—Love God; Love Thy Neighbor (Deuteronomy 6:5) 11. Rahab (Joshua 2); 18. Josiah and the Law (2 Kings 22–23); 24. Angels and Shepherds (Luke 2:8–20); 25. Wise Men Visit Jesus (Matthew 2); 27. Jesus Calls the Twelve (Matthew 4:18–25; Mark 1:16–20; Luke 5:27–30; John 1:35–51); 29. Jesus Meets Zacchaeus (Luke 19:1–10); 31. Jesus Welcomes the Children (Matthew 19:13–15; Mark 10:13–16; Luke 18:15–17); 35. The Samaritan Woman at the Well (John 4:1–42); 43. The Holy Spirit Comes at Pentecost (Acts 2); 44. Peter Heals, Then Preaches, Then Gets in Trouble (Acts 34); 46. Philip and the Ethiopian Eunuch (Acts 8:26–40); 48. Peter's Vision and Cornelius's Invitation (Acts 10); 49. Paul Knows the Unknown God (Acts 17:16–34); 50. Communion Gone Wrong (1 Corinthians 11:17–34).

Stories that show that God listens to us: 14. The People Want a King (1 Samuel 8–13); 17. God's Still, Small Voice (1 Kings 19); 34. Jesus Heals a Woman and a Girl (Mark 5:21–43; Luke 8:40–56); 35. The Samaritan Woman at the Well (John 4:1–42).

Stories that show that God speaks to us: 2. The Dream Is Disrupted (Genesis 3); 4. Waiting for Baby Isaac (Genesis 17; 18; 21:1–7); 6. A Conversation with a Burning Bush (Exodus 3); 9. The Law—Love God; Love Thy Neighbor (Deuteronomy 6:5); 10. The Law—Festivals and Jubilee (Exodus 20; 23; 31; Leviticus 23); 12. The No-Fight Battle (Judges 6); 13. God Speaks to Young Samuel (1 Samuel 3); 16. Elijah, the Widow, and the Last Cup of Flour (1 Kings 17); 17. God's Still, Small Voice (1 Kings 19); 18. Josiah and the Law (2 Kings 22–23); 20. The Prophets (Yep, All of 'Em); 21. An Angel Visits Mary (Luke 1:26–56); 22. An Angel Visits Joseph (Matthew 1:18–25); 24. Angels and Shepherds (Luke 2:8–20); 27. Jesus Calls the Twelve (Matthew 4:18–25; Mark 1:16–20; Luke 5:27–30; John 1:35–51); 29. Jesus Meets Zacchaeus (Luke 19:1–10); 40. The Women Visit Jesus' Tomb (Matthew 28:1–10; Mark 16:1–8; Luke 24:1–12); 42. Emmaus (Luke 24:13–35); 43. The Holy Spirit Comes at Pentecost (Acts 2); 46. Philip and the Ethiopian Eunuch (Acts 8:26–40); 47. Paul Meets Jesus (Acts 9:1–19); 48. Peter's Vision and Cornelius's Invitation (Acts 10); 49. Paul Knows the Unknown God (Acts 17:16–34).

Stories that show that God picks unlikely people: 6. A Conversation with a Burning Bush (Exodus 3); 11. Rahab (Joshua 2); 12. The No-Fight Battle (Judges 6);

13. God Speaks to Young Samuel (1 Samuel 3); 15. Anointing David to Be King (1 Samuel 16); 21. An Angel Visits Mary (Luke 1:26–56); 24. Angels and Shepherds (Luke 2:8–20); 25. Wise Men Visit Jesus (Matthew 2); 27. Jesus Calls the Twelve (Matthew 4:18–25; Mark 1:16–20; Luke 5:27–30; John 1:35–51); 29. Jesus Meets Zacchaeus (Luke 19:1–10); 31. Jesus Welcomes the Children (Matthew 19:13–15; Mark 10:13–16; Luke 18:15–17); 34. Jesus Heals a Woman and a Girl (Mark 5:21–43; Luke 8:40–56); 35. The Samaritan Woman at the Well (John 4:1–42); 40. The Women Visit Jesus' Tomb (Matthew 28:1–10; Mark 16:1–8; Luke 24:1–12); 46. Philip and the Ethiopian Eunuch (Acts 8:26–40); 47. Paul Meets Jesus (Acts 9:1–19).

Stories that show that God guides us: 5. Joseph (Genesis 37–45); 6. A Conversation with a Burning Bush (Exodus 3); 7. God Splits the Red Sea (Exodus 5–15); 9. The Law—Love God; Love Thy Neighbor (Deuteronomy 6:5); 10. The Law—Festivals and Jubilee (Exodus 20; 23; 31; Leviticus 23); 12. The No-Fight Battle (Judges 6); 13. God Speaks to Young Samuel (1 Samuel 3); 15. Anointing David to Become King (1 Samuel 16); 16. Elijah, the Widow, and the Last Cup of Flour (1 Kings 17); 18. Josiah and the Law (2 Kings 22–23); 22. An Angel Visits Joseph (Matthew 1:18–25); 24. Angels and Shepherds (Luke 2:8–20); 25. Wise Men Visit Jesus (Matthew 2); 42. Emmaus (Luke 24:13–35); 43. The Holy Spirit Comes at Pentecost (Acts 2); 48. Peter's Vision and Cornelius's Invitation (Acts 10).

Stories that show that God is joyful: 1. Creation (Genesis 1); 4. Waiting for Baby Isaac (Genesis 17; 18; 21:1–7); 10. The Law—Festivals and Jubilee (Exodus 20; 23; 31; Leviticus 23); 23. Jesus Is Born! (Matthew 1:18-25; Luke 2:1–7); 24. Angels and Shepherds (Luke 2:8–20); 26. Jesus Extends a Wedding Party (John 2:1–12); 31. Jesus Welcomes the Children (Matthew 19:13–15; Mark 10:13–16; Luke 18:15–17).

Stories that show that God is mysterious: 6. A Conversation with a Burning Bush (Exodus 3); 13. God Speaks to Young Samuel (1 Samuel 3); 16. Elijah, the Widow, and the Last Cup of Flour (1 Kings 17); 21. An Angel Visits Mary (Luke 1:26–56); 30. Jesus Walks on Water (Matthew 14:23–33; Mark 6:45–51; John 6:16–21); 40. The Women Visit Jesus' Tomb (Matthew 28:1–10; Mark 16:1–8; Luke 24:1–12); 42. Emmaus (Luke 24:13–35); 43. The Holy Spirit Comes at Pentecost (Acts 2); 49. Paul Knows the Unknown God (Acts 17:16–34); 52. Revelation (Revelation).

Stories that show that God is knowable: 1. Creation (Genesis 1); 4. Waiting for Baby Isaac (Genesis 17; 18; 21:1–7); 5. Joseph (Genesis 37–45); 13. God Speaks to Young Samuel (1 Samuel 3); 18. Josiah and the Law (2 Kings 22–23); 21. An Angel Visits Mary

(Luke 1:26–56); 23. Jesus Is Born! (Matthew 1:18–25; Luke 2:1–7); 31. Jesus Welcomes the Children (Matthew 19:13–15; Mark 10:13–16: Luke 18:15–17); 49. Paul Knows the Unknown God (Acts 17:16–34).

Stories that show that God is just: 6. A Conversation with a Burning Bush (Exodus 3); 9. The Law—Love God; Love Thy Neighbor (Deuteronomy 6:5); 29. Jesus Meets Zacchaeus (Luke 19:1–10); 50. Communion Gone Wrong (1 Corinthians 11:17–34); 51. Philemon (Philemon); 52. Revelation (Revelation).

ACKNOWLEDGMENTS

This is my favorite part—the chance to thank the many wonderful people who made this book real.

First, to the members of the Kids + Faith Community: Thank you for bringing the Great Big Bible Story Walkthrough into your homes. *Wonder* would not exist without the years we did a Bible story a week on the GBBW. And thank you for sharing your stories with me. I admire how you are weaving your unique, wonderful lives following Jesus and inviting your kids along.

Pomona Valley Church: I love following Jesus into the world with you. Thank you for wanting to help families everywhere and making it possible for me to do this work alongside my role as your pastor. And a special thank-you to the kids in our church. You all are brilliant, delightful, and just plain fun.

To my editor, Beth Adams: You are delightful to work with and your understanding and support for this book meant the world.

To my agents for this book, Andrea Heineke and Alex Field: Thanks for the many ways you helped me navigate the process.

To the team at Hachette, for the creativity and expertise only you can give, my thanks.

The Works Consulted section holds the names of scholars to whom I am indebted, whether I've taken their class or just read their work. I have a greater love for the Bible and the God whose story is told there because of their contributions. Their work hasn't just shaped my work, it has shaped my faith, and I'm grateful.

Curtis, this book would never have happened without you. Your help with biblical research was incalculable, to say nothing of the myriad ways you have supported me.

Mom and Dad, love you GABAMTTWWW.

Riley and Peyton, you ask the best questions about the Bible and remind me this matters just by being you.

ABOUT THE AUTHOR

Meredith Miller is a pastor and parent whose unique combination of seminary training, twenty-plus years of experience in family ministry, and research expertise make her especially equipped to help families get to know Jesus. Her ideas, scripts, and tips for talking about God and the Bible are practical and fun, making her a trusted voice for families who want to help their kids grow in faith in fresh, healthy ways.

Meredith is the lead pastor of Pomona Valley Church. Previously, she's been curriculum director for megachurches and a research assistant and consultant for the Fuller Youth Institute. Meredith holds a master's degreen in Divinity from Fuller Theological Seminary, as well as a BA in Religious Studies and Spanish Language & Literature from Westmont College.

RAISING READERS
Books Build Bright Futures

Thank you for reading this book and for being a reader of books in general. We are so grateful to share being part of a community of readers with you, and we hope you will join us in passing our love of books on to the next generation of readers.

Did you know that reading for enjoyment is the single biggest predictor of a child's future happiness and success?

More than family circumstances, parents' educational background, or income, reading impacts a child's future academic performance, emotional well-being, communication skills, economic security, ambition, and happiness.

Studies show that kids reading for enjoyment in the US is in rapid decline:

- In 2012, 53% of 9-year-olds read almost every day. Just 10 years later, in 2022, the number had fallen to 39%.
- In 2012, 27% of 13-year-olds read for fun daily. By 2023, that number was just 14%.

Together, we can commit to **Raising Readers** and change this trend. How?

- Read to children in your life daily.
- Model reading as a fun activity.
- Reduce screen time.
- Start a family, school, or community book club.
- Visit bookstores and libraries regularly.
- Listen to audiobooks.
- Read the book before you see the movie.
- Encourage your child to read aloud to a pet or stuffed animal.
- Give books as gifts.
- Donate books to families and communities in need.

Books build bright futures, and **Raising Readers** is our shared responsibility.

For more information, visit **JoinRaisingReaders.com**

Sources: National Endowment for the Arts, National Assessment of Educational Progress, WorldBookDay.com, Nielsen BookData's 2023 "Understanding the Children's Book Consumer"